A

HEDGE

AWAY

DANIEL LOMBARDO

A
HEDGE
AWAY

The *Other* Side of
Emily Dickinson's Amherst

Daily Hampshire Gazette • Northampton Massachusetts

Emily Dickinson
Wood Engraving by Barry Moser

Table of Contents

Acknowledgements

Thanks to Nick Grabbe who published much of this material in earlier incarnations in the Amherst Bulletin; to Peter DeRose, publisher of the Daily Hampshire Gazette, Northampton; to Pip Stromgren for editing, advice, and myriad hours of work; to Florence DeRose for her splendid design and layout; to the Jones Library, Inc., Amherst, in whose *Tales of Amherst: A Look Back* (The Jones Library, 1986) earlier versions of "The Death of Edward Dickinson," "The Loss of Gib," and "Edwin Marsh and the Funeral of Emily Dickinson" appeared. The photograph of Count Alexander Bianchi appears courtesy of the Martha Dickinson Bianchi Trust, Amherst, Massachusetts; all other photos are courtesy of the Jones Library, Inc., Amherst, Massachusetts. Thanks to Barry Moser and R. Michelson Galleries for use of the portrait of Emily Dickinson, and thanks to Polly Longsworth for her preface, her valuable comments on the text, and her unfailing kindness and generosity. Special thanks, beyond words, to Karen Banta.

Preface

Dan Lombardo writes in the tradition of Jay Leyda, the scholar who said of Emily Dickinson, "Only the closest juxtaposition of her poems with a complete chronology of her life and times . . . would reveal how much a part of her world she was."

Leyda's theory that there was an "omitted center" around which the riddle-loving poet spun her art is here joined by Lombardo's gift for storytelling, for resurrecting lost-to-memory incidents and personalities of nineteenth century Amherst that bring her world alive.

Lombardo has been curator of the town's special collections at the Jones Library for fifteen years, and nearly that long has written a weekly "Amherst Bulletin" column on town history. His talent and delight lie in reactivating, with ironic wit and an historian's eye, the exploits, celebrations, horrors, and dramas that were commonplace fare of a smaller, harsher, but no less human Amherst. Lombardo weaves a rich tapestry, revealing issues we still grapple with — health care, poverty, racial and sexual discrimination, the criminals and misfits among us. But it's the restored personalities of local merchants, ministers, professors, housewives, visitors, crackpots and rakes, engaging in an array of human predicaments, through whom Lombardo educates us to the past century and this very special two-college village.

The lives of Emily Dickinson and her family dominate, filter, and to a degree warp most literary views of nineteenth-century Amherst. While respecting the tendency, even catering to it, Lombardo rights our vision, supplying the "stuff of life" from which the reclusive but cannily aware poet daily spun straw into gold.

Polly Longsworth
Dickinson biographer, author of *Austin and Mabel: The Amherst Affair and Love Letters of Austin Dickinson and Mabel Loomis Todd* and *The World of Emily Dickinson.*

Introduction

What is — "Paradise" —
Who live there —
Are they "Farmers" —
Do they "hoe" —
Do they know that this is "Amherst" —
And that I — am coming — too —

Do they wear "new shoes" — in "Eden" —
Is it always pleasant — there —
Won't they scold us — when we're homesick —
Or tell God — how cross we are —

You are sure there's such a person
As "a Father" — in the sky —
So if I get lost — there — ever —
Or do what the Nurse calls "die" —
I shan't walk the "Jasper" — barefoot —
Ransomed folks — won't laugh at me —
Maybe — "Eden" a'n't so lonesome
As New England used to be!

Emily Dickinson

Poem #215

*The top of Emily Dickinson's glass
conservatory can be seen behind the Dickinson hedge.*

It is said that humans moved into what we call the Connecticut River Valley nearly 10,000 years ago. We don't know what they thought of it, but since then everyone from Henry James to the creators of Mutant Ninja Turtles seems to have an opinion. The great 19th century singer Jenny Lind thought she saw paradise along the river. Garrison Keillor described the Valley as a place of visionaries and idealists. It has always had, he said, "people who did not see the world as it is but as it should be, and therefore ran into trees often times."

Several millennia of human habitation have had the effect of making the Connecticut Valley a wonderfully human place to be. As Emily Dickinson said of her town in the Valley's center, "The Amherst Heart is plain and whole and permanent and warm."

We know of only 10 poems and one letter that Emily Dickinson had published before her death in 1886. After burning most of the letters Emily had received, her sister Lavinia sought fervently to publish her nearly 2,000 poems. It wasn't until four years later, on November 12, 1890, that a volume called *Poems of Emily Dickinson* was made public.

The Victorian era had no preparation for Emily's rare, imaginative style. Her poems were fragmented, rhymes inexact, and the lines appeared odd on the page, with their scatterings of dashes and capital letters. One English critic proclaimed that Dickinson might have become a fifth-rate poet "if she had only mastered the rudiments of grammar and gone into metrical training for about fifteen years."

A reviewer in the Atlantic Monthly didn't think that "an eccentric, dreamy, half-educated recluse in an out-of-the-way New England village can ... with impunity set at defiance the laws of gravitation and grammar. ... oblivion lingers in the immediate neighborhood."

Ironically, such reactions were to poems that Emily's editors had taken great pains to alter to fit the tastes of the period. Of the 116 in the first book, over 50 had been changed by Mabel Loomis Todd and Thomas Wentworth Higginson. Words were added or deleted, rhymes were changed, grammar and punctuation regularized, and the poems were given titles Dickinson hadn't intended. Nevertheless the poems were still considered by many to be "so rough, so rude, that art seems to have faltered."

Some did immediately recognize the genius of the poetry. William Dean Howells considered the poems among the best of world literature, but an English reviewer immediately questioned whether Howells was serious. He himself called the poetry a "farrago of illiterate and uneducated sentiment."

So many were intrigued by Dickinson's poetry and her mythic life, however, that the first book went through 11 printings in two years. Many other volumes of poems and letters followed. Meanwhile, Mabel Loomis Todd acted as publicist, lecturing and reading Dickinson poems. In talks delivered from Amherst to Hawaii, Todd pointed out that Emily had not always been a recluse, and had traveled to Washington, Philadelphia and Boston. At the same time Todd, a good spin doctor, was careful to sustain Emily's image as the mysterious bird-like poet of Amherst.

Dickinson continues to be unfairly stereotyped as the Queen Recluse, separated physically and psychologically from her surroundings. When referring in an early poem to her sister Lavinia, and her sister-in-law Sue, who lived next door, she wrote,

One Sister have I in our house,
And one, a hedge away ...

(Poem #14)

For Emily being "a hedge away" eventually did become an immeasurable emotional distance. Yet the poet remained all too aware of the physical world beyond the hedge, one that was rich with gritty, morally compromised, sometimes violent, and often funny real life.

We know she read the great literary magazines of the day, like Harper's and The Atlantic Monthly, that she loved Shakespeare and the Brontes. But what did she, like most of us, read daily? The local newspapers. She was an eager consumer of The Springfield Republican, The Hampshire and Franklin Express, and The Amherst Record. And we know Emily read them for more than serious news and editorial commentary. In a letter to Josiah Holland (an editor of the Republican) and his wife, Emily asked,

"Who writes those funny accidents, where railroads meet each other unexpectedly, and gentlemen in factories get their heads cut off quite informally? The author, too, relates them in such a sprightly way, that they are quite attractive. Vinnie was quite disappointed to-night, that there were not more accidents — I read the news aloud, while Vinnie was sewing. The Republican seems to us like a letter from you, and we break the seal and read it eagerly."

(Letter #133)

When Emily Dickinson died, the world hardly knew what to make of her. Suddenly, all eyes turned toward the town of Amherst and blinked at this strange creature. Now, more than 100 years later, interest in all things Dickinson has exploded. Yet romance and myth obscure the poet and the life going on just the other side of the hedge. How close did problems of opium and prostitution come to the solid brick Dickinson Homestead on Main Street? Why did Emily's niece marry the mysterious Count Bianchi? And in Amherst, the literary, academic town, what was Poco selling to college students besides old clothes?

In the collection of short pieces that follow, we see Emily's part of the Connecticut River Valley from a perspective not normally seen. It's a view that can tell us a lot about the Emily Dickinson we thought we knew. And, in its strange parallels to our world today, a lot about ourselves.

The Dickinson Family Tree

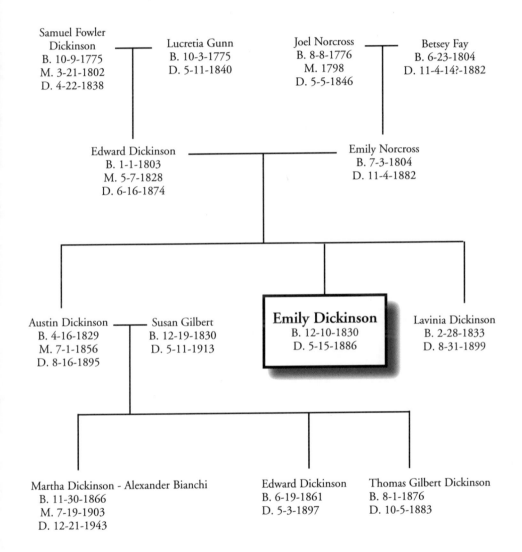

Samuel Fowler
Dickinson
B. 10-9-1775
M. 3-21-1802
D. 4-22-1838

Lucretia Gunn
B. 10-3-1775
D. 5-11-1840

Joel Norcross
B. 8-8-1776
M. 1798
D. 5-5-1846

Betsey Fay
B. 6-23-1804
D. 11-4-14?-1882

Edward Dickinson
B. 1-1-1803
M. 5-7-1828
D. 6-16-1874

Emily Norcross
B. 7-3-1804
D. 11-4-1882

Austin Dickinson
B. 4-16-1829
M. 7-1-1856
D. 8-16-1895

Susan Gilbert
B. 12-19-1830
D. 5-11-1913

Emily Dickinson
B. 12-10-1830
D. 5-15-1886

Lavinia Dickinson
B. 2-28-1833
D. 8-31-1899

Martha Dickinson - Alexander Bianchi
B. 11-30-1866
M. 7-19-1903
D. 12-21-1943

Edward Dickinson
B. 6-19-1861
D. 5-3-1897

Thomas Gilbert Dickinson
B. 8-1-1876
D. 10-5-1883

Chapter One

THE DICKINSONS AND
THEIR FRACTURED CIRCLE

Phoenix Row, Amherst, Massachusetts

Of the Heart that goes in, and closes the Door
Shall the Playfellow Heart complain
Though the Ring is unwhole, and the Company broke
Can never be fitted again?
  #1098

Warm and Wild Maggie Maher and One-Armed Tom

In the summer of 1868, Maggie Maher suffered two tragedies. She nursed her father through the illness that killed him, and wrote "My Joy is turned to griefe." Within weeks her sister's husband, Thomas, lay near death after falling 30 feet from a building. Born in Ireland, both Maggie and Thomas were servants in Emily Dickinson's household. They were part of the "downstairs" circle of people who maintained the Dickinsons' complicated lives.

Over the years the Dickinsons employed several Irish immigrants to work in their houses, barns, and gardens. Margaret Maher, though, became more than a cook and maid to Emily and Lavinia Dickinson. One Dickinson scholar said, "she was a protective bulwark — keeping intrusion from the poet. ... Her healthy presence made her as vital to the skeptic poet as any member of 'the peculiar race' of Dickinsons."

With her sisters and brothers, Maggie came from Tipperary in the 1850s. Her parents' later arrival completed the family's arduous journey to Amherst. Maggie never married, but her older sister Mary wed an earlier Irish arrival, Thomas Kelley.

Maggie's first job here was working for the Boltwoods in their pillared house by the Amherst Common. Her letters written to the family in later years reveal rich details of immigrant life in Amherst, and of the comfortable lives of the Dickinsons.

Maggie nearly left Amherst for good when she moved with the younger Boltwoods to Hartford. But double tragedies in 1868 brought her back. In a letter to Clarinda Boltwood shortly after her father died, she wrote, "This is a World of trouble our trouble was Never so much as it is at present. My dear Brother Thomas was almost killed last saterday at 4 o clock he still lives But we dont know how long he may My dear sister what will she do the father of seven children the lord may comfort her. ... he fell 30 feet from a building. ... we cant tell how (his arm) is going to be yet all say that it got to be cut off. ... the dath of dear father lies in a cloud of sadness on me and I can't get over it he died in my armes and I never can forget it."

Two of the Dickinsons' Irish servants: Tom Kelley, center, with glasses, and Maggie Maher, top, center, in white. Seen at Tom and Mary Kelley's 50th wedding anniversary, 1903.

Maggie began working for the Dickinsons in March of 1869. She was, at first, unhappy and wanted to somehow return to the Boltwoods. "I am lonsom in Amherst," she wrote, "there is one grate trouble that I have not half enough of work so that I must play with the cats to Plase Miss Vinny you know how I love cats." But the Dickinsons grew very attached to Maggie and would have no other in her place.

Tom Kelley, though he did indeed lose his arm, worked for both Dickinson households on Main Street. It was to him that Emily ran in 1882 when Otis Lord, the last man she loved, was ill: "Tom had come," Emily wrote, "and I ran to his Blue Jacket and let my Heart break there."

Of Maggie, Emily wrote she was "warm and wild and mighty ... the North Wind of the Family, but Sweets without a Salt would at last cloy." When Maggie was ill, Emily missed her and claimed the household would fall apart:

"All are very naughty, and I am naughtiest of all.
The pussies dine on sherry now, and humming-bird cutlets. ...
What shall I send my weary Maggie? Pillows or fresh brooks?
Her grieved Mistress"

Maggie long outlived the Dickinsons, dying in 1924 at the age of 85. Tom, with his one strong arm, was one of six Irish workmen who carried Emily's coffin to the grave, at her request. In 1903, he and Mary Kelly celebrated their golden wedding anniversary and were featured in the Springfield Union as a prospering family. As opposed to other immigrants of whom it presumably didn't approve, the paper described them as the "Type of Immigrants America Welcomes."

The Dickinson Family Robbed During Hard Times

The home of Emily's brother, Austin Dickinson, was robbed in 1885, when work was hard to come by.

"The prospects for a general revival of business during the coming year is more promising than it has been for half a dozen seasons." These hopeful words of 1885 were from the owners of the paper mills near the home of Emily Dickinson. A family of lawyers, it would seem hard times would barely touch the Dickinsons, and Emily would be in no danger of running out of paper.

The grim truth of how fragile life outside the Dickinson Homestead was, could be seen in the number of reports of homelessness, theft, and of women resorting to prostitution. With the robbery of Emily Dickinson's family it became evident that hard times trickled up to even the most prosperous households.

Amherst had genuine sympathy for residents who suffered from hard times, but not much for those from elsewhere who came to town looking for work. The Amherst Record called the homeless "tramps" and clearly approved of the harsh treatment they were given in the winter of 1885: "Policeman (Sylvanus) Moody accompanied two more tramps to Northampton in an easy carriage on Tuesday, making nine from this town this fall, and all of them have been provided for this winter, either by the county or at the state's expense. Three were sent to Bridgewater for nine months each, and Hampshire county takes care of the others.

"Tuesday's guests were sent up for six months at Northampton jail. ... They struck Amherst Sunday night, having been on the march three days in pursuit of work, and finding none were discouraged and refused to beg or tramp any farther. Dennis Hagerty, 35 years old, hailed from Swate, Ireland and James Ryne, 21 years old, from New Foundland.

"Judge Strickland's sentence of six months brought them to their senses and they were all broke up, meditating upon the sweet perfumes, the bright skies and still brighter prospects of work next May and June, when they would be detained in their winter quarters, privileged only to gaze on stone and mortar, and sniff the odors of the prison, and grubbing still at the county's expense, earning the county eight cents a day at bottoming chairs."

Weeks later, when the temperature of January 1886 went below zero, the paper told of another "tramp" who rattled the door of Blodgett's hat shop on the common. He asked the watchman to direct him to the police station where he might find a bed for the night after having walked to Amherst from Ware.

While some men roamed from town to town, hard times forced some women into prostitution. Arrests for prostitution in and around Amherst hit their peak in the late 1890s, after Emily Dickinson's death. But reports of the problem elsewhere in New England appeared often enough in her lifetime. For example, the story of a woman's descent "from Wellesley to ruin" was printed in the Amherst Record in 1886: "Miss Kate Doughan, 22 years old and one of the most beautiful and most disreputable of women in New Haven, was arrested for improper conduct on the streets and lodged in the lock-up, where she tried to hang herself."

Meanwhile in Western Massachusetts, a gang of thieves had been systematically looting several towns. According to the Amherst Record, "The craftsmen seem inclined to rise in their profession and it has become the fashion with them to enter the second story of the houses they plunder, which are those of the first residents in town, and they also keep pretty seasonable hours."

In early November 1885, the gang struck Amherst, ransacking the homes of the Hills family (hat factory owners), the Gaylord family of South Amherst, and Austin Dickinson's house. Emily, Austin's sister, was next door at the family homestead when his house, the Evergreens, was robbed. According to the paper, "Jewelry to the value of perhaps $100 dollars, besides a small sum of money in Ned's (the son's) pocket-book in a bureau, was taken, and the things in the rooms in the second story were a good deal disturbed.

"The robbery was thought to have been committed while the family were at their dinner, or between six and seven o'clock, and the robbers entered through a window near the piazza."

Emily sent a brief message next door to her nephew Ned: "Burglaries have become so frequent, is it quite safe to leave the Golden Rule out over night?"

Burglaries and hard times quickly faded from the concerns of the Dickinsons, for in that same month Emily took to her bed. Six months later the poet died.

Emily's Doctor
Searches the Brain for
the Seat of the Soul

In the 1890s, Dr. Orvis Bigelow stood before the Amherst Club and gave a talk that could be seen as a symbol for the times. It was, oddly enough, a graphic description of what science knew of the human brain. Bigelow, the last doctor to care for Emily Dickinson, wondered where the intellect was located, and where in the brain the soul was centered. These were apt questions in a college town dedicated to developing the intellect. And his talk came just as Dickinson's books were establishing Amherst as a center for the soul.

Bigelow spoke before the assembled professors, clergy, businessmen and lawyers of the Amherst Club. The club began in 1891 as an all-male social group that sponsored speakers, had a reading room, and played a lot of billiards. Membership was by invitation only, and it had its rooms on South Pleasant Street, at the Amherst Common.

Dr. Bigelow came to Amherst from Vermont in 1865. Though a rural doctor, Bigelow was highly regarded and had a remarkable grasp of the latest research on the brain. Like others, Bigelow had given up the old idea that the functions of the brain were reflected in bumps on the head. Bumps around the ears, for example, had meant one was combative and devoted to food.

Bigelow, however, was well aware of what the Civil War taught us about the brain. Soldiers with ghastly head injuries helped identify brain functions in specific locations. Later scientists probed the brains of animals with electricity, to discover sensory responses and levels of consciousness.

When Dr. Bigelow gave his lecture to the Amherst Club, he walked to the common from his house on North Pleasant Street, the same house Emily Dickinson had lived in between the ages of 10 and 25. He began his talk by noting studies that showed the size and weight of the male brain was consistently larger than that of the female. From this he drew no conclusion.

The audience may have been appalled when Bigelow turned to the effects of death by hanging on the brain, or when he claimed sunstroke could lead to suicide or homicide. Then the doctor told the following sad story as an example of how science advanced in the 19th century: "A boy aged 5 years who was a great chatterbox fell out of the window and injured the left frontal bone which was found depressed. There was no paralysis but the boy had entirely lost his language. The wound healed in 25 days but the child although intelligent remained dumb.

Dr. Orvis Bigelow (seated right and surrounded by his family), cared for Emily Dickinson in her final illness.

"A year afterwards he was accidently drowned — and at the autopsy it was found that the third left frontal convolution had been destroyed by the injury he had received."

It is fitting that it was Dr. Bigelow who attended Emily Dickinson in her last days and pronounced her dead on May 15,

1886. Each in their own way was fascinated by the brain and the soul. The words "soul" and "brain" appear in many dozens of Dickinson's poems. And no one can forget her question, "Dare you see a Soul at the White Heat?"

Bigelow identified the gray portions of the hemispheres as the seat of the soul and the frontal lobe as the seat of intellect. The doctor correctly predicted that the world stood at the threshold of a revolution in psychology. He ended his talk with the following: "What is the mind; how is it connected with the body? Are the mind and soul identical? I will leave these questions to be answered by the theologians, lawyers, judges, and professors of our club."

Mabel's Secret Diaries

The brilliant and controversial Mabel Loomis Todd, editor of Emily Dickinson and paramour of Austin Dickinson

Some 19th century diaries are tantalizingly vague, others pack more life onto a page than any Victorian potboiler. In the 1890s, for example, Mary Broad Brown wrote, "I went over to Dr. McCook's church to a Women's Christian Temperance Union meeting all alone. It was real good." On the other hand, Mabel Loomis Todd's diaries tell us of a terrible drought in Amherst, the annual return of students to town, about editing Emily Dickinson's letters, troubles with servants, and the illness of her not-so-secret lover — all within the space of a few pages.

Mabel Todd, writer, lecturer, editor of Emily Dickinson, lived in Amherst for 35 years. Her husband was David Todd, the Amherst College astronomer known for his study of eclipses and his search for Martians. (Hoping to get his radio equipment closer to Mars, he attempted several balloon ascensions. On one expedition a confused farmer shot his balloon down over his field, on another he was blown off course into Quebec. Amherst College nudged Todd into early retirement, and he ended his days in an institution, devising a plan to acquire eternal life.) Mabel was a hyperactive participant in dozens of town and college activities, which we can see in detail by picking any month in her life.

In September of 1894, Amherst was in the midst of the worst drought in nearly 60 years. Reservoirs and wells gave out, a team of horses could be driven across the low Connecticut River, and crops failed. Todd's entry for September 2nd reflects the fear that was beginning to set in: "I felt really ill, and lay down and rested all day... . Went to bed at seven. At six it was as thick & strangely yellow as the famous 6th of September in 1881. We could not see over a few hundred feet all day. Gas and lamps looked white. It is smoke from burning forests, and dust. It grew thicker all day, & finally became positively weird."

On September 14 she notes the arrival of Amherst College students: "In the Evening we went to the President's annual opening reception. Very pleasant time, though depressingly hot, and a good many really interesting freshmen. The old students all seemed very happy to be back."

Todd is credited as a founder of the Mary Mattoon Chapter of the D.A.R., the Amherst Historical Society, and the Amherst Women's Club. The two latter connections are touched upon in this same month. Mabel had two meetings to write and revise the Women's Club constitution, a process she described in a rather odd way: "After dinner walked up to Mrs. Maynard's and had another seance over the Constitution." At the end of the month she recorded visiting "old Mrs. Emerson and her family," whom Mabel later convinced to donate her house to the Historical Society.

In the 19th century, many Amherst families employed servants. In the beginning of September, Mabel hired a man named William to help care for The Dell, the house she and David Todd lived in on Spring Street. On September 30, she wrote, "William left this morning, and I am relieved. He had become very disagreeable."

In one way or another, Emily, Austin, and Vinnie Dickinson also played a part in Mabel's September diary. She referred more than once to her work on the publication of Emily's letters: "Pages upon pages of proof, and the preface. I sent down Chapter X. Everything now in the printer's hands except Index, and Contents." Misunderstandings with Vinnie over royalties led to this comment: "More disgusting treachery from Vinnie — after having arranged the whole matter of my having half the proceeds of the 'Letters' with Austin ... ."

At this time, Mabel and Austin's now-famous relationship was at a critical point. They enjoyed carriage rides together, which Mabel described with passion: "... we had one of the most delicious drives in our experience; to Sunderland Park — how beautiful it was! The brooks rustling down like spring, fringed gentians in blossom, the air like wine. We went out to the old fence of blessed memory." But things didn't look good for Austin.

Throughout September 1894, Austin had severe respiratory problems. On the 23rd Mabel noted, "Dear Austin has at last seen Dr. Seelye about his little irritating cough." And the next day, "I saw dear Austin for a little while. He is coughing a great deal — has been more or less all summer, but today he really feels sick. It worries me greatly." On the last day of the month he was worse yet: "Dear Austin has a scary bronchial cold, and seems white and dragged." Austin Dickinson, the center of many Amherst lives, died the following August.

Just Who Was Count Bianchi?

Growing up in the shadow of Emily Dickinson would have been tough for anyone. But for Emily's niece, Martha, life was especially bitter-sweet. Few took Martha's career as a poet seriously; her parents, Austin and Susan (Emily's brother and sister-in-law), had a marriage scarred by infidelity and probably alcohol. Then Martha married the mysterious Count Alexander Bianchi.

Count Bianchi has been purposely buried in history, leaving few clues as to who he was. After Madame Bianchi, as Martha was known, died at the end of 1943, a commemorative booklet was published, yet none of the essays mentions her husband. Frank Prentice Rand, who lived in Amherst in Bianchi's day, later wrote that after spending some time abroad, Martha "became attached and in some way detached from some-sort-of-titled husband. At least she returned to Amherst as 'Madam.'" Rebecca Patterson's book about Emily Dickinson calls Martha's marriage "a belated, foolish, and unhappy" one. The relationship soured within three years, the Count was sued by a Miss Terry, and was thrown in a New York jail.

It began in 1902, when Martha and her mother Susan Dickinson went to Europe for a year. Martha's friends read in the newspapers that on July 26, 1903, while in Dresden, she had married a captain of the Russian Imperial Horse Guards stationed in St. Petersburg. (The couple had actually married in Carlsbad, Bohemia, on July 19.) "Count" Alexander Bianchi, nearly eight years younger than Martha, had been born in Odessa in 1873. He was transferred to Boston in 1903, and the couple planned to arrive in Amherst that fall. When the Count was introduced to Amherst at a party, he supposedly grew bored and dropped out of the receiving line.

Later Amherst Town Directories list Alexander and Martha Bianchi as living in The Evergreens on Main Street, but the Count is never listed a resident taxpayer. He became the source of much local speculation, some of it spurious. According to a contemporary, Smith College English Professor Mary Jordan, Bianchi posed as a Russian, but was in reality an Austro-Italian. Madame Bianchi supposedly boasted of the Count's ancestral jewels, but Jordan contended Madame bought the jewels herself. Bianchi allegedly used up all of Madame Bianchi's money before drifting off. Alexander Bianchi did, in fact, spend time in a New York jail on fraud charges in 1907.

In 1904, the Count was introduced to Martha's friend

Alexander Bianchi, the "some-sort-of-titled"
Ukrainian who married Emily's niece, Martha Dickinson

Charlotte Terry of New York. In June of 1905, the Count borrowed $3,500 from Terry. His repayment check to her for 11,500 francs, drawn on a Paris bank, bounced. In February of 1907, the Count borrowed another $600 from the unfortunate Miss Terry. A New York gossip paper, Town Topics, claimed he borrowed the money "from a maiden of seed-time years, a Miss Terry, on the pretense of going on a honeymoon, although he has been married for years." A more reliable report says Bianchi claimed he needed the money to pay custom duties on a car he was importing to sell to a James Allison of Philadelphia. When Allison denied this, Charlotte Terry sued Count Bianchi.

The Count was arrested and placed in the Ludlow Street jail in New York. Somehow he was later released with Charlotte Terry's consent. He abandoned his marriage to Martha on June 20, 1908, according to court documents. Martha filed for divorce on April 14, 1919, and the divorce became final on March 2, 1920.

Madame Bianchi went on, like her Aunt Emily, to write poetry. She spent winters in New York or abroad, and summers alone in Amherst. Unlike her aunt, she took an active role in the outside world, doing heroic work for the Red Cross during World War I. The Count seemed to disappear, and was dead before 1943. The fact that the couple had no children resulted in the end of the Edward Dickinson line and, for reasons best known to herself, Madame Bianchi asked in her will that her famous house, The Evergreens, be burned to the ground. This final tragedy has been sidestepped only by complex legal maneuvering.

Chapter Two

WRITERS, REBELS, AND FOOLS: FAMOUS VISITORS

Amherst House, Amherst, Massachusetts

The Road was lit with Moon and star -
The Trees were bright and still -
Descried I - by the distant Light
A Traveller on a Hill -
#1450

Harriet Beecher Stowe's Daughter Plagued by Morphine

Harriet Beecher Stowe, author of Uncle Tom's Cabin, *visited her daughter in Amherst, and found her addicted to morphine.*

By the summer of 1872, when Harriet Beecher Stowe arrived in Amherst to stay with her daughter, Georgina, Emily had become a recluse. She never met Stowe, but knew of the famous writer and her startling work, and was probably aware that she was in town. When Stowe came to Amherst, however, she had little time to mix with the locals. Harriet Beecher Stowe found her daughter living in a large white house on Lincoln Avenue, suffering from a severe addiction to morphine that would eventually kill her.

Georgina's addiction was to remain a family secret for years. Meanwhile, Stowe, the celebrated author of *Uncle Tom's Cabin* had to prepare for her first lecture tour, about to begin in September of that year.

In 1864, Harriet Beecher Stowe and her husband Calvin had moved to their Hartford mansion called Oakholm. That same year, their daughter Georgina met a handsome, well-to-do minister, Henry F. Allen. An Episcopalian rector in Stockbridge, Massachusetts, Allen made frequent trips to Hartford to court Georgina. Stowe and her daughters stayed in Northampton in the summer of 1864, where Georgina was able to see more of Allen. They married in June, 1865. On April 17, 1872, Henry F. Allen became the third rector of Grace Episcopal Church in Amherst, and he and Georgina moved into their large Lincoln Avenue home.

Several months before the move to Amherst, in the winter of 1871, Georgina had fallen ill with severe depression and insomnia. A physician administered morphine, and the result was a common one for the times: Georgina arrived in Amherst with an addiction to the drug that would last the rest of her life.

By 1871, Harriet Beecher Stowe was gray haired and 60 years old. She had had great success as an author of novels and stories, and was convinced by the American Literary Bureau of Boston to undertake an arduous reading tour throughout New England. The thought of this terrified her, but the money was tempting.

Stowe made her speaking debut in Springfield, Massachusetts, on September 13, 1872. From there she went to Lynn and Salem, but each time she felt she had failed. Stowe was resigned to "simply speak my piece and take my money," which was usually a minimum of $250. In Boston she felt the added pressure of the biting accusations that her famous brother, preacher Henry Ward Beecher, was guilty of adultery. This scandal was to follow her throughout the tour. Meanwhile, her hypochondriac husband, Calvin, was barely able to care for himself and was in constant fear for Harriet, certain that she would die on the trains.

By the time Stowe spoke in Amherst, her tour had become a major event. Tickets for the October 7th engagement were in such high demand that a limit was placed on the number each person could buy. People came from several area towns to fill College Hall, and an extra train had to be scheduled from Belchertown. Stowe read from *Uncle Tom's Cabin, The Pearl of Orris Island,* and *Oldtown,* to rounds of laughter and applause.

The tour continued to be trying, however. The food and trains were wretched, and hotel rooms were lonely. Northern New England was in the grip of an epidemic among horses, and a quarantine in many towns kept people from travelling. The tour was profitable for the author, though, and with the proceeds she bought her famous Nook Farm in Hartford, next to Mark Twain's house.

Harriet Beecher Stowe signed for another speaking tour the following year. Georgina and her husband left Amherst in 1877, and 10 years later Georgina was finally killed by morphine.

When the Second Joan of Arc Came to Amherst

When Anna E. Dickinson lectured at the First Congregational Church of Amherst in 1865, she was so wildly popular that the mere mention of her name assured a large crowd. Unrelated to Emily, and little known today, she was recognized across the country then as an ardent fighter for women's rights and an enemy of slavery. When Thomas Wentworth Higginson published his book, *Eminent Women of the Age*, in 1868, he included Anna Dickinson.

Higginson was a confidant of Emily Dickinson, and the poet sent him her work for comment. The 1860s were Emily's most prolific period, but she was of course far from eminent. Higginson's book covered such well-known contemporaries of Emily as Florence Nightingale, Elizabeth Barrett Browning, and Jenny Lind. The chapter devoted to Anna E. Dickinson was written by the great reformer and feminist Elizabeth Cady Stanton. She refers more than once to Anna as a modern Joan of Arc.

Anna Dickinson was born in Philadelphia in 1842, and as a child was described as being "cross, sleepless, restless, and crying continually with a loud voice, thus preparing her lungs for future action." After her abolitionist father died, she was educated in Quaker schools. At the age of 13 she stopped in a law office and offered to do copy work for money to buy books. Her interest in human rights was awakened by the great orators of the day who spoke in Philadelphia, in fact she once scrubbed a sidewalk for a quarter so she could hear Wendell Phillips speak. Ironically, later in 1868 it was reported in the Springfield Republican that after hearing Phillips lecture in New York, "Miss Dickinson took the platform and sailed into him for deserting women."

When Dickinson applied for her first job teaching, she was told that her predecessor, a man, was paid $28 per month, but she would be paid $16. Her reply as she left was, "Sir, are you a fool, or do you take me for one?" After joining the Association of Progressive Friends in 1860, Dickinson herself began lecturing and surprised everyone with her passion and eloquence. She moved to William Lloyd Garrison's house in Boston, and helped several anti-slavery candidates win elections in New England. Crowds and controversy followed her everywhere. One commentator wrote, "There never was such a furor about an orator in this country. The period of her advent (the Civil War), the excited condition of the people, her youth, beauty, and remarkable voice, all heightened the effect of her genius ... . Her name was on every lip. Ministers preached about her, prayed for her as a second Joan of Arc, raised up by God to save ... the nation to freedom and humanity."

In early 1864, Anna Dickinson was invited to speak before both houses of Congress, foreign diplomats, and the President. The following day she met with Lincoln in the White House.

Dickinson spoke in Amherst on May 31, 1865, and again the

First Congregational Church, now College Hall of Amherst College, where activist Anna Dickinson spoke in 1865

following October 13. To its credit, the town welcomed her with great enthusiasm. Of her May lecture, the Amherst Record reported, "The talented lady delivered her inimitable lecture 'A Plea for Labor,' at First Congregational last Monday evening. The audience was large, and the stillness that prevailed evinced the deep interest felt at the recital of the wrongs endured by — God's injured ones, — working women. The lecture was a pattern of sound logic and good delivery. We cannot but hope, we cannot but believe, that Miss Dickinson is doing a great and good work, in using her influence in behalf of women who labor. Success be in her noble work say we."

Lotta Crabtree,
Victorian Superstar

Most of the buildings erected on the campuses in Amherst were named after great educators, wealthy donors, or poets. Names like Butterfield, Williston, Frost, and Dickinson appear on dormitories, classroom buildings, and libraries. The Crabtree House on the University of Massachusetts campus, however, was named after a rather racy 19th century actress whose tempestuous life became legendary.

Lotta Crabtree was born in New York City in 1847. She began performing on stage in the goldmining towns of California at the age of eight, working with her mother. Lotta's career eventually burgeoned into superstardom, and her name became a household word. She toured the country as an actress/comedian in the era of Sarah Bernhardt and Lillie Langtry, making enormous sums of money. Crabtree eventually bought the Park Theatre and the Brewster Hotel in Boston, and a racetrack in Attleboro, Massachusetts.

Though John Barrymore had called her "the Queen of the American stage," she was more of a pop star than a serious actress. Many of her plays were written for her, and demanded little or no intellectual effort on the part of the audience. In reviewing her play "Musette" in April, 1881, the New York Herald remarked that Lotta's role "had no more to do with unfolding the story than it has with solving a problem in Euclid." Playwrights created characters based on Lotta's eccentricities, and wrote patchwork plots that invariably ended happily.

Lotta's connection with UMass (then the Massachusetts Agricultural College), came toward the end of her life when she began writing her will. The actress had amassed a fortune of $4,000,000 and she wanted much of it to go to help animals and the poor. While leaving relatively little to her relations, she set up the Dumb Animal Fund to provide drinking fountains for dogs, cats, and horses all over the country. There was enough, it was said, to "slake the thirst of the animal population of every city and most ... towns in the U.S.!" Her concern for animals also led her to create the Lotta Agricultural Fund — $1,250,000 for interest free loans to graduates of the Massachusetts Agricultural College. Lotta died in the Boston's Brewster Hotel in 1924.

Her will was bitterly contested, with 101 people stepping forward to claim her as a relative. The entire country watched as 34 Boston law firms fought to settle the will and determine whether

Lotta was competent when she wrote it.

The trustees of Lotta's estate later determined the Dumb Animal Fund for drinking fountains to be impractical, and added the money to the fund for the Massachusetts Agricultural College. Thus, in Emily Dickinson's Amherst, the University of Massachusetts has the Crabtree House, in honor of a remarkable benefactor, the Victorian superstar Lotta Crabtree.

A Shocking Speech by the Fighting Parson

Amherst College President William A. Stearns, who welcomed the shocking Rev. Brownlow to town.

In the midst of the Civil War, on June 7, 1862, Amherst was visited by the famous Fighting Parson, William G. Brownlow. Brownlow was from Tennessee, yet he passionately supported the North, and thus suffered imprisonment and was later forced to leave the state. The Hampshire and Franklin Express described his visit as a "great day in Amherst — a day to be long remembered by her citizens."

Rev. Brownlow was invited to speak by the students of Amherst College, who sympathized with the persecuted Unionists of Eastern Tennessee, of whom Brownlow was a leader. Their invitation to him emphasized the "noble stand which you, though menaced and exiled by traitors, have maintained against the Rebellion." The town was in for quite a shock, however.

When the Fighting Parson arrived on the special Amherst, Belchertown, and Palmer train, the streets were lined with students and citizens, and the sounds of the Belchertown Cornet Band echoed in the streets. At 2 p.m., the Village Church was filled and Amherst College President Stearns opened the program with a "fervent and impressive prayer."

Brownlow began by referring to his "diseased throat" and how as an itinerant Methodist minister he had been forced to preach in a low voice. But, he reported, when he recently turned his efforts to denouncing "this cursed rebellion, my voice came to me, and I verily believe that I could have been heard half a mile." He called the rebellion "the most wicked vile and devilish the world ever saw ... instituted by men who are low and vile ... the dregs of the streets and gutters."

In a speech that was enthusiastically received with bursts of applause, Brownlow turned his wrath to certain Southern leaders. He called Senator Mason of Virginia "a miserable, corrupt, whiskey-rotted, brandy-bloated, beef-headed scavenger ... a miserable lying, pompous dog." In a rather shocking opinion for a man of the cloth, Rev. Brownlow proclaimed that Mason "ought to have had a grind-stone tied about his neck, and sunk in the waters of Boston Harbor, as Adams and his comrades served the British Tea."

Mason left for Europe with John Slidell, whom Brownlow described as "a hideous Orang Outang." For all senators who joined the rebel congress, Brownlow recommended that their "lying tongues ought to be plucked out of their mouths, and fed to mean dogs, and their bodies suspended by grass ropes to trees."

It is evidence of the extremes of human emotions, and the breakdown of morality during war, that Amherst so warmly responded to a man who shouted, in a foreshadowing of Naziism, "I am an advocate of extermination! and wiping off from the face of the earth the whole infernal race of traitors and peopling the country with a better race of men, if the rebellion continues."

William Brownlow went on to become the governor of Tennessee in 1865, and a U.S. Senator in 1869.

P.T. Barnum
Humbugs the Connecticut Valley

The Great Phineas T. Barnum was scheduled to lecture in Belchertown on December 4, 1854. His topic was "The Philosophy of Humbug," and his intent was to unfold the laws of the art of humbugging honest people, an art which had made him rich. Ironically, Barnum failed to show up, which left the ticket holders feeling as though they had indeed been duped by the master of humbug.

Barnum had been born in Bethel, Connecticut, in 1810. His first great triumph came in 1835 when he bought the rights to exhibit Joice Heth — a woman purported to be the 161-year-old former nurse of George Washington. For $1,000 Barnum got her and a bill dated 1727, which stated she had been sold as a slave of the Washington family. Heth told stories about "dear little George" and sang hymns. Barnum advertised her as "the most astonishing and interesting curiosity in the world," the first person to "put clothes on George Washington."

Barnum's genius for fraud surfaced early. When attendance during a New England tour of Joice Heth fell off, Barnum himself sent a letter to a Boston newspaper suggesting Heth was a fraud, "made up of whalebone, india-rubber, and numberless springs." This sparked a controversy which brought the public back in droves.

After a turn at selling Bibles in the 1840s, Barnum opened his American Museum in New York. It was the kind of institution described by Henry Tappan as a place "for the exhibition of monsters, and for vulgar dramatic performances," and was the most popular museum of its kind in the country.

Barnum's most famous put-on was the "Fejee Mermaid," which consisted of a body of a fish and the head and hands of a monkey. Showing it almost tripled the receipts of his American Museum. The exhibit was backed by an extensive media campaign and "scientific" lectures by a "Dr. Griffin." Again, this created much controversy, and a debate over biblical interpretation and evolution. All of it helped fill Barnum's pockets.

Barnum went on to conquer Europe with Tom Thumb, then he brought back Jenny Lind, the Swedish Nightingale, who became a superstar and made a fortune for Barnum. But by 1854, Barnum described himself as "weary, fagged, tired, and almost sick." Speculation in real estate and business caused Barnum's bankruptcy. It was at this time that Barnum was scheduled to lecture on "The Philosophy of Humbug" in Belchertown. Of this non-event it was said that Barnum "gave a demonstration of his topic by not appearing."

On December 18, 1854, Barnum did lecture in the Connecticut Valley. First in South Hadley, then Belchertown and Northampton. An extra train was scheduled to carry those from Amherst to Belchertown to hear the lecture there. His Northampton lecture was heard by one of the largest audiences ever gathered in town hall. The Hampshire Gazette noted, "P.T. Barnum, the Prince of Humbugs, lectured on humbuggery to an audience of 1100-1200! Vive le Humbug!" By some accounts, though, Barnum's lectures there were "decidedly stale and unprofitable."

The climax of Barnum's career was his circus, "The Greatest Show On Earth," which he began in the 1870s. When he died in 1891, the New York Times said, "Since the beginnings of history there has been no showman to be compared with him." Seven weeks after his death an attempt was made to steal Barnum's body and hold it for ransom.

Belle Boyd,
Rebel Spy

Thirty-two years after the Civil War, Amherst welcomed the notorious rebel spy Belle Boyd. Boyd had become legendary as a daring spy who risked gunfire to get messages to the rebel general Stonewall Jackson. On May 13, 1892, Belle Boyd spoke to a packed house in Amherst's Town Hall, to benefit Amherst war veterans.

Belle Boyd came from Martinsburg, Virginia, where she was born in 1844. At the start of the Civil War she and her mother held off Union soldiers who wanted to raise a flag over their house. When one of the soldiers tried to force his way in, the young Belle shot him dead. She was tried and was acquitted on the grounds of justifiable homicide.

While Boyd was staying at her aunt's house, part of it was occupied by Union officers under General James Shields. Boyd overheard their plans to destroy the town's bridges as they retreated, and she undertook a hazardous journey through the lines to inform Stonewall Jackson. At 18 years old she dodged gunfire and artillery shells to get her message through. Boyd went on to spy openly for the Confederates and to serve as a courier and scout for J.S. Mosby's guerrillas. She was arrested and imprisoned twice, but managed to be released.

In 1864, Belle Boyd sailed on a blockade runner to England bearing letters from Confederate president Jefferson Davis. The ship was intercepted by a Union vessel, but Boyd used all her skill to distract Union Lt. Sam Hardinge. He allowed the Confederate captain of the ship to escape, for which he was later court-martialed. In August 1864, Hardinge married Boyd in England.

After the war, Belle Boyd went on to debut on the English stage, and in 1865, she published her book, *Belle Boyd In Camp and Prison*. Her American stage debut came in 1868. The later years were spent on the lecture circuit where, as the Amherst Record put it, she had "an attractive presence, a handsome countenance, shapely form and pleasing voice."

Amherst forgave Boyd for working for the enemy in the Civil War and welcomed her eagerly. It was in fact the local Civil War veterans group that invited her and received the profits of her "thrilling narrative."

Francis Burnett: A Fair Barbarian

One of the best sellers of the 19th century was the children's book *Little Lord Fauntleroy*. With that book its author, Frances Hodgson Burnett, achieved enormous popularity and wealth. Burnett created a sensation wherever she went, and when she lunched at Austin and Susan Dickinson's house in 1880, even Emily Dickinson paid her respects — in her own way.

Francis Burnett was born in England in 1849, and she moved with her family to Tennessee when she was 15. Three years later her phenomenal writing career began with her first publication, in Godey's Ladies Book. Among her more than 50 novels are some of the most successful children's books of all time, including *The Secret Garden* and *A Little Princess*.

Burnett travelled extensively, moving easily between the States and Europe. April of 1880 found her in Canada; then in May, Burnett visited Amherst while on her way to Harriet Beecher Stowe's Nook Farm in Hartford. Burnett later recalled her visit to Austin Dickinson's house: "Indeed I remember well the wonderful Spring day — half a lifetime ago it seems when I was driven through just awakening New England country from Springfield to Mr. Dickinson's house where we lunched & in the midst of luncheon there was brought to me from Miss Emily Dickinson a strange wonderful little poem lying on a bed of exquisite heartsease in a bowl."

The Burnett book about to make the rounds at that time was called *A Fair Barbarian*, about a young American returning to the England of her ancestors. In March of 1881, Emily Dickinson wrote, "The neighborhood are much amused by A Fair Barbarian."

The book's main character, Octavia, is described as "careless of the conventions" and "forward," as she upsets the stiff English town she visits. It was almost inevitable that when a theatrical version of the story was done in Amherst in 1883, the controversial Mabel Loomis Todd (about to become mistress of Emily Dickinson's brother Austin), would play Octavia.

One popular form of entertainment in Amherst before the electronic age was the "private theatrical." Amateurs performed plays in each other's homes, with cambric curtains, stamping heroes and tinsel-clad heroines. On November 23, 1883, "A Fair Barbarian" was performed in the library of Amherst College Professor of Greek Richard Mather. Wives and daughters of faculty members performed, as well as both Mabel and David Todd.

The Amherst Record was very impressed, reporting that "the art of the players was so perfect that the scenes introduced seemed most realistic." Mabel Todd was singled out for lavish praise, with such phrases as "characteristic grace ... a rare union of startling piquancy and unexpected tenderness." The reviewer claimed Amherst had finally mastered the art of theatre.

The cast of "A Fair Barbarian," with David and Mabel Todd seated center, 1883.

Matthew Arnold and Our Hairy Ancestors With Pointed Ears

When Matthew Arnold spoke in Amherst in 1883, Amherst was not impressed. The great Victorian poet, and literary and social critic, was invited to speak at Amherst College as part of his American lecture tour toward the end of his life. But Arnold had little but disdain for American culture, and Amherst made it clear that Arnold's barbs stung.

Matthew Arnold had achieved fame for his attacks on English society, which he divided into the Barbarians, the Philistines, and the Populace. His central work, *Culture and Anarchy*, proclaimed his mission to educate and humanize the Philistines. The book has been labelled a masterpiece of ridicule.

If English society didn't measure up to Arnold's expectations, the tastes and manners of America hardly impressed the man at all. Particularly galling to Americans was the way Arnold dismissed our great literary figure, Ralph Waldo Emerson. The Amherst Record didn't even wait for Arnold to arrive in Amherst before it displayed its feelings. It coldly reported, "Matthew Arnold seems to be making quite a stir among the critics in cities where he has given his 'new' lecture, which someone has discovered was published in the Popular Science monthly a year ago."

Arnold stayed with Mark Twain while lecturing in Hartford. The Amherst Record delighted in quoting the mediocre reviews, which called his talk a disappointment and "an old lecture."

Arnold spoke to a large audience at College Hall at Amherst on December 7. His lecture on literature and science pitted the two against each other, and declared literature infinitely superior, while admitting he actually knew little about science. The Amherst Record thought he knew little about lecturing, too, and advised him to cut his talk down from 65 minutes to 30. It sardonically suggested that "Mr. Arnold might learn something from Ralph Waldo Emerson, whom he calls no great poet, nor man of letters, nor philosopher."

Arnold's statement of his case against science was considered extremely unfair, especially his disparaging remarks about "our hairy ancestor, with pointed ears, arboreal in his habits."

There were two people in the audience that night whose views would be very interesting. Emily Dickinson's brother Austin and his son Ned were there, according to Austin's diary. But both were still in a state of near-shock, having lost Austin's eight-year-old son Gilbert to typhoid fever only two months before.

John Burroughs
in the Connecticut Valley

The great naturalist John Burroughs visited the Connecticut Valley in Massachusetts more than once in his long life. The first time was in 1886 when he took Smith College students on nature walks and then visited Amherst. Another visit, however, was uncharacteristically in a Rolls Royce, with three other famous men.

Burroughs was born in 1837 on a farm in the Catskill Mountains. His mentor was Ralph Waldo Emerson, whom he met at the West Point Library while teaching nearby. In 1863, Burroughs went to Washington, D.C. There he met Walt Whitman who became his close friend and advisor.

After Burroughs left Washington in 1873, he settled on a small fruit farm in West Park, New York. He planned and helped build the stone house overlooking the Hudson River. There at Riverby

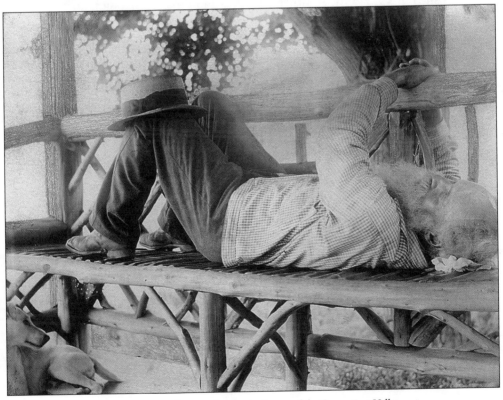

The naturalist John Burroughs was taken by the beauty of the Connecticut Valley, which he visited for the first time in 1886.

and nearby at Slabsides, Burroughs wrote many of his 25 books. Slabsides was a rustic retreat built about two miles from Riverby, and among the early visitors there were John Muir and Theodore Roosevelt. Slabsides is still maintained by the Burroughs Society.

On April 27, 1886, John Burroughs made the following entry in his journal, describing Northampton and Amherst: "Reach Northampton at 2 pm. Beautiful country; the heart of New England, a ripe mellow country. The meadows a great feature. So many colleges all about seem to give an air of culture which our state lacks.

"Great enthusism among the college girls. I led great packs of them to fields and woods and helped them identify the birds by their calls and songs. Two or three times a day we go forth, once to the top of Mt. Tom. On Wednesday the President drives me to Amherst, a beautiful place, a sort of high island in a great rolling plain."

The Hadley writer and photographer Clifton Johnson became a close friend of Burroughs while writing *John Burroughs Talks*, published in 1922. One summer a most extraordinary procession arrived at the Johnson farm at the foot of Mount Holyoke. John Burroughs, Henry Ford, Thomas Alva Edison, and the tire maker Harvey Firestone, drove up the dirt road. The Johnson boys were called in from hoeing corn to meet the famous visitors, and Irving Johnson remembered eagerly looking to see the car Henry Ford drove. The group, out on one of their auto-camping trips, had arrived, not in a Ford, but in a Rolls Royce. They were, however, followed by a Ford which had been relegated to carrying their luggage.

Bronson Alcott, the Crooked Stick

When Bronson Alcott, the eccentric dreamer and Transcendentalist, came to Amherst, the town was so taken by him that most were reluctant to see him leave. The father of Louisa May Alcott arrived here on December 6, 1878, to lecture on "Concord Authors." Though Emerson had spoken in Amherst many times, this was the first time that one of the great Transcendentalist group visited to speak about the group itself, and the town eagerly awaited Alcott. The newspapers referred to the "unsurpassed conversational powers of this venerable associate of Emerson and Hawthorne."

The "venerable" Bronson Alcott has sometimes been regarded more as a Don Quixote who is both laughed at and loved. Born in Connecticut in 1799, he had little formal education, but went from being a peddler to a pioneer in teaching reform and organic gardening. In 1842, he established the communal farm, Fruitlands, in Harvard, Massachusetts. Based on religious love and vegetarianism, the commune failed, partly because the members were reluctant to use animal labor to till the rocky soil.

The generous Emerson found a way to help the impecunious Alcott by hiring him to build a summerhouse on his land in Concord. With the visionary Alcott as architect and the practical Henry Thoreau as carpenter, it became a comedy of errors. Thoreau had to jump madly as Alcott felled trees without looking. Alcott's design called for nine corner posts to honor the nine muses, and an infinite number of gnarled and knotted branches to honor his whim for gingerbread. As Thoreau said, "Ah he is a crooked stick himself." Emerson thought he would call the structure "Tumble-down Hall," but his mother's appellation, "The Ruin," is what stuck. Emerson never used the summerhouse, but 15 years later he was still hiring Alcott to make repairs on it.

Alcott's most stunning gift was his speaking ability, which he could never quite transmit to paper. When Alcott spoke at Amherst's College Hall, he dazzled his audience with stories of Emerson, Hawthorne, Fuller, Thoreau, and his own family. The newspaper reported, "We have been led by the magic of these gray hairs and this child-heart to a truer appreciation of the scenes amid which, as the head whitened, the heart has grown more and more childlike. ...The magician brought upon the stage the weird figure of Hawthorne... the gifted Margaret Fuller... the intensely individual Thoreau."

People were especially touched by episodes from Alcott's life, such as his stint as a Boston school teacher, "receiving to his school a poor, ignorant black girl, and, when patrons threatened, firmly refusing to turn her away."

Alcott was induced to stay in Amherst longer, and he gave one of his famous "conversations" on Saturday night at President Julius Seelye's house. On Sunday evening he visited the senior class prayer meeting, which had to be moved to larger quarters. Some students had wanted to hear Alcott at College Church that morning, but Alcott was not invited because the faculty didn't consider him sufficiently orthodox.

The visit had been an overwhelming success, though, and the community was pleased to hear Alcott say "I am for Amherst" as he left.

Home of the "crooked stick," Bronson Alcott, in Concord, Massachusetts.

Chapter Three

POETRY WAS IN THE AIR, RABID DOGS AND TYPHOID IN THE STREET

Pleasant Street, Amherst, Mass.

Pleasant Street, Amherst, Massachusetts

'Tis so appalling - it exhilarates -
So over Horror, it half Captivates -
The Soul stares after it, secure -
To know the worst, leaves no dread more -
#281

Debating the Image of a New England Town in the 1890's

Booming development in 20th century Amherst has forced the town to reevaluate its image of itself. The disappearance of farms, and the town's attitude toward business and profit fuel many an argument. Back in the 1890s when Amherst was genuinely a village rather than a small city, similar debates raged as the town approached the 20th century.

In 1892, an anonymous "Old Citizen" described Amherst as "almost the most beautiful place in the world" in the Amherst Record newspaper. He lauded the beautiful country setting, the literary culture, the excellent markets, good schools and factories. By the 1890s, the village contained about 4,500 people in 874 houses. Overall, there existed 18 acres of land in Amherst for every house then in existence.

The writer argued for retaining Amherst as a village, and keeping it from expanding to the size of a town. The village had come a long way since the days when the common was a muddy morass, trampled by cows. The common had been redesigned and replanted with the advice of Frederick Law Olmsted, and Village Improvement Societies had been active in various parts of town since 1857. But the writer was distressed by the amount of noise and garbage that increased as Amherst grew. Factories shattered peaceful mornings at 6 a.m. with "a steam gong fit only for an Inferno." Garbage from grocery stores was swept into streets that were littered with handbills for quack physicians, tin cans and broken bottles. The sidewalk before the post office on South Pleasant Street was decorated with "rubbish, the decaying fruits of summer, old shoes, hat brims, papers, tin-ware, too much to name." Another nuisance was the "naughty, quarrelsome, and often lisping courseness and profanity" of children loitering on street corners.

The writer hoped that a renewed effort at cleanliness, flower-planting, and a new public library would help create an ideal Amherst Village.

The other side of the debate called for a growing "real" Amherst rather than a nostalgic "ideal" one. By the 1890s, Amherst had running water piped in from nearby Pelham, electric street lights, and railroad connections to Boston, New York, and Washington. By 1900, an extensive trolley system crisscrossed the entire valley. Some felt Amherst should capitalize on this progress and advertise aggressively in newspapers and pamphlets. But first, according to one writer, the hotels and boarding houses had to be

Stray dogs on Main Street, in front of Phoenix Row.

cleaned up. To the great annoyance of visitors, hotels in town served bad food, service was careless and the locals were known for their raucous banquets.

Describing the "real" Amherst, one writer saw a town divided by religious factions and social snobbery. He blamed the social stratification on professional men's wives, who formed exclusive circles. The other major Amherst problem was an anti-business spirit. Some wanted to "suppress all sights, sounds and smells that have the least hint of a business nature in them, and to reduce the town to a state that might be termed one unending literary Sunday." In this atmosphere the newly formed Board of Trade would have a hard time attracting any businesses, unless they brought no "sound of whirring wheels or rattling gears" and their employees wore "carpet slippers or moccasins."

Then, as now, these issues spurred a good deal of angry argument as a traditional village way of life confronted a booming new era.

Behold What a Stench
a Fish Scale Causeth

The smell of dead fish emanating from Henry E. Paige's Fish and Oyster Market caused sufficient excitement in Amherst to inspire a first-rate protest. It was the spring of 1873 when the fish became so ripe that Paige was the object of a series of newspaper articles. These were written in the form of biblical parodies, which tended to obscure the facts behind this mysterious story.

What seemed to irk Amherst was the fact that Paige was an out-of-towner, having come from "the east country and intermarried among Amherstites." Now these Amherstites were "known far and near as a tribe having much brains, and as great consumers of brain food, which is Fish."

Paige established his fish market in about 1875 in the basement of Gunn's Hotel, at the northwest corner of the common. "Year after year he trafficked with the Amherstites, giving them shad, cod, whale, herring and other brain food in exchange for shekels." Two merchants in the same building, however, complained to William Gunn (the building's owner), that Paige had "held the nuisance of fish-scales under our nostrils until we are pickled and saturated." Their identities are hidden behind biblical terms, but they were certainly Julius Hall, insurance agent, and Horace Ward, dealer in wool, meat, hides, and fertilizer. The two gave Gunn an ultimatum: Either the fish market would go or they would. Paige was told to depart and "take your brain food and your brain smell with you."

"Then it came to pass that when Paige heard the Gunn shoot off, he took himself to Johnny the carpenter, and said, build me a tabernacle wherein I may exchange fish for shekels." Carpenter John Beston built a new fish market, but an unnamed wool merchant nearby complained. He and others in the area sent letters to the landowner who lived in "Gotham," apparently Northampton.

The landowner told Paige to "Get thee gone, pull up stakes ... and get thee hence before the dawn of all fools' day." Paige sent around a petition asking for support among his customers "who didn't smell fish so strong." Two unnamed town leaders signed it, implying that "they didn't believe an occasional sniff of a dead fish ever killed anybody." Hall and Ward feared the fish market would remain in the basement of Gunn's Hotel. They made it clear to Gunn that they were through wasting gallons of cologne "as a counter irritant to the unholy odor of fish."

It became clear to Paige that "the Amherstites preferred to have their fishmongering done on some other planet than the one on

Gunn's Hotel, with the odorous fish market on far right, corner of North Pleasant and Amity.

which they dwelt." Paige packed his things and like (F)Ishmael wandered. He moved his business north into the country and sent fish into town for his customers.

By 1886, Henry Paige was out of the fish business for good, and had become foreman of Paige Brothers Livery Stable on Amity Street. By 1892, he was a veterinarian, living on South Prospect Street until his death in about 1923.

Here endeth the chronicle of the great fish stench.

The Lock-Up By the Wallowing Hogs

Throughout most of its history, the Amherst Police Department has had to contend with facilities that ranged from merely bad to appalling. Descriptions of what used to be called the "lock-up" are enough to churn one's stomach: In 1882, the lock-up cells were said to be "not fit for a dog to be locked up in." The Amherst Record indignantly stated that "certainly the town should be as humane to prisoners as most men are to their brutes."

In 1873, the Massachusetts General Court passed a law requiring towns over a certain size to provide jail cells and a jail keeper. In that year Amherst built its first jail. It was built onto the rear of the firehouse, which was just south of today's Fire Department on North Pleasant Street.

The jail was a two-story brick building, 22 feet by 30 feet. It had four cells and a room for the "keeper" on the first floor, with each cell containing two iron beds. The second story consisted of one large meeting room, used for caucuses, courts, and public meetings, in the days before Amherst had a town hall. Within 10 years, however, the selectmen complained that this arrangement was inadequate for such town functions, and recommended something less primitive. Town Hall wasn't built, however, until 1889.

While the selectmen described the surroundings for prisoners as "unpleasant," the Amherst Record minced no words. On the south side of the jail was "a stinking cess-pool" and a pig pen. The paper reported that "nobody who has been about these premises, especially in the warm season, will forget the fact that the stench has been enough sometimes to sicken the hogs wallowing in the mire close underneath the eaves of the lock-up."

To the north of the jail was Lewis Spear's blacksmith shop, on the east the firehouse, and beyond the cesspool on the south was Gunn's Hotel and Restaurant. All of these blocked any light that might have raised the atmosphere above that of a dungeon.

Amherst's first policeman was Fiske A. Thayer, appointed in 1872. He worked only at night, from 9 p.m. to 6 a.m., and his duties included that of lamplighter for the town's kerosene lamps. He was paid $2.00 per night, 351 nights per year. Amherst had only one policeman, plus volunteers, until a second was hired in 1893. By 1936 there were four paid policemen stationed in the basement of Town Hall.

The old lock-up was taken down in October 1930. In the 1930s the three cells in the Town Hall basement were described as

The North Pleasant Street firehouse, behind which was the dark, cramped lock-up.

having bare wooden bunks with no mattresses. In 1953 while work-ing out of the basement, the police had a phone booth on the com-mon, and the use of a radio in the fire station. With the crime rate rising, this system was completely outdated. The station itself was improperly heated and the prisoners' toilets consisted of a galva-nized bucket in each cell. This changed with a remodeling in 1955.

Committees and consultants made reports on the inadequate facilities in the 1970s and early 1980s. When the recent move for a new station began in 1983, officials described the police station in the same terms used during Emily Dickinson's day: They said it resembled a dungeon.

Wading Through Ashes
in a Litter-ary Town

How did tons of dirty coal ash inspire an Amherst poet to pen a clever 33-line verse?

In the winters of the 1870s and 1880s people used colossal amounts of coal in their stoves and furnaces. Shops around the Amherst Common dumped their ashes out into the street all winter until, by spring, enough had piled up to build a "bastioned fort," as the newspaper complained.

The selectmen of Amherst refused to clean up after the shops. They did offer to empty ash receptacles if shop owners could be persuaded to supply them and use them. As the newspaper described the situation, "Ashes are disagreeable in every respect, dirty to look upon, dirty to tread upon, and worse than bare ground for sleighs to run upon ... . A few ashes thrown into the street now and then are scarcely noticeable; but when everybody is permitted to use the highway for a dumping ground the quantity will be sufficient to build a bastioned fort in front of Merchant and Phoenix rows."

During this period Amherst had Village Improvement Societies for the center of town, East Street, North and South Amherst, and Cushman village. Their main purpose was to landscape the public areas of town, but orange peels and dead cats also became their concern.

In 1877, the Amherst Village Improvement Society sponsored the town's Fourth of July Celebration as a fundraiser. On that day a broadside of a poem was distributed among the crowds. Called "Give, Oh! Give" and subtitled "There is nothing that lasts but trouble and dirt," the anonymous poem was fearless in describing Amherst's problem:

> *Pity, kind gentle folk, friends of humanity,*
> *Only a moment we'll tax your urbanity,*
> *Only a moment we ask for your ears,*
> *Only a cent or two we beg with tears;*
> *Give for the looks of our beautiful town,*
> *Three cents, or four cents, and then we'll be gone,*
> *Give but a penny for cleanliness' sake,*
> *To invest in broom and shovel and rake,*
> *To clean off the streets and gutters around,*
> *The crossings and walks of our litter-ary town;*
> *The crossings, we fain would make see the light*
> *So long safely buried from every one's sight*

In dust — a plan worthy of greater renown,
Long followed in our economical town,
To sweep, too, the walks which the churches near by
Have taken the contract, they say, to supply
Every year with ashes and half burnt coals,
Perchance their one way of reaching men's soles.
Give, Oh! give nobly to help sweep the town,
Five cents, or six cents, and then we'll be gone,
To pull up the burdocks, grown up thro' the street,
To remove orange peel, traps for unwary feet,
To summon a squad of strong-bodied Pats,
To gently but firmly remove dead cats,
The mountains of ashes built up thro' the town,
Though we reverence their age, we fain would see down,
And perchance, when we've accomplished these feats
We would buy some water to sprinkle our streets.
Pity, kind gentle folk, friends of humanity,
Only a moment, we'd tax your urbanity,
Only a penny, we've begged it since dawn,
Eight cents, or ten cents, and then we'll be gone.

It would be decades before the era of oil heat, and meanwhile the ashes piled ever higher.

Packs of Snarling Curs

In the 1980s, the pit bull terrier became the bane of many New England towns. The controversy serves as a reminder of earlier canine problems in and around Emily's Amherst. In 1861, dogs killed 25 sheep in Amherst in one night. After another 30 years of ineffectual laws, the death of Addison Carpenter from a rabid dog further irritated an already angry town.

In colonial days a dog that bit or killed sheep was punished by hanging. Many places in New England where these executions took place still bear names like Hang Dog Swamp or Hang Dog Lane. By the 1860s, Amherst was attempting to control the dog population by licensing, but dog owners were reluctant. The town often had to remind owners to license their dogs by publishing threats in the papers.

On October 8, 1861, dogs viciously killed 25 sheep in South Amherst, in what the newspaper called a "Great Slaughter in One Night." Farmers Randolph and Thayer lost 16 sheep, Luther Nash six, and three were killed on the Town Farm (for the poor).

By the time Addison Carpenter was bitten, calls for dog control had become overwhelming. Carpenter had been born in Nassau, New York, in 1818, but he lived most of his life in South Amherst. There, he had raised a puppy that in April of 1891 bit his hand while Carpenter played with him.

The dog was "acting queerly" and was killed the next day. Carpenter ignored the bite until mid-May when he began showing symptoms of rabies. His friends insisted he go to Massachusetts General Hospital, where his sudden death greatly saddened the Amherst community.

It was thought that the dog may have bitten other dogs before it was killed. The Amherst Record lashed out at farmers who kept dogs, describing Amherst's situation as one where "a pack of snarling curs may roam the streets, singing loud-voiced solos to the moon at all hours of the night, frightening horses so that they run away and smash carriages and likely enough their occupants, scaring women and children out of their wits and occasionally sampling a human leg or arm when they feel the need of a change of diet, killing poultry and utterly destroying flocks of sheep."

The newspaper suggested that since the liquor evil had been controlled by high license fees, the dog license fee should be raised from $2.00 to $10.00 or more. "We don't believe there are a dozen dogs in town that are worth $10.00, even to their owners, and such action would certainly tend to promote the survival of the fittest."

A letter to the editor the following week described several dog attacks on the streets of Amherst and suggested an anarchic solution: Townspeople were urged to carry firearms in the streets and use them to "suppress this abominable dog nuisance."

Should the Poor Be Sent to Alaska?

Should the poor and the homeless be sent to the Amherst Town Farm, the Northampton Insane Asylum, or to Alaska? In the spring of 1878, America debated such issues at a time when the country was coming out of a deep recession and there seemed to be more homeless than ever. Today, Congress wants to shift responsibility from the Federal to the local level. Ironically, in 1878, local governments could hardly cope, and were looking for answers on a national level. One such debate played itself out on the Amherst Common where a minister and a selectman nearly came to blows.

In the 1800s, the running of a poor farm or "alms house" was one of a town's major activities. In 1836, Amherst purchased Medad Vinton's farm on the South Amherst Common and hired a warden, a doctor and a minister to watch over the town's poor. A number of Amherst residents were sheltered in other towns, for which Amherst was billed. The report of the Pauper Account in the Annual Report of the Selectmen and Overseers of the Poor for 1878 was discouraging: "This account makes us the most trouble of any of the town matters, and we cannot better express our convictions than to quote part of last year's report: 'Our outside poor are a great expense to the town and trouble to the overseers. In most cases they

The poor farm in South Amherst, burned down by an inmate in 1882.

are in cities or other towns away from here. In case of sickness with these persons who are living away from the Alms House, the expense is likely to be great. ...There seems to be no diminution on the poor account, and the amount of money required for their care during the year no one can tell."

Among the "inmates," as they were called, were a number of Dickinsons, Kelloggs, Hawleys, and other well known local names. One interesting case involved Anna Lothrop who was cared for at the Northampton Insane Asylum. Her bill for a year there was $47 and the selectmen wanted to be reimbursed by Anna's father, Charles.

Charles Lothrop was a retired minister who lived in a reasonably good house in the center of Amherst. Lothrop refused to pay the bill and accosted Dwight Palmer, Chair of the Selectboard, on the matter. It was on a Friday night in front of the Post Office that Palmer was stopped by Lothrop. According to the newspaper, Rev. Lothrop gave him "an exhibition of his conversational abilities and his saintly temper." Quite a crowd gathered, and few seemed to have much sympathy for the retired minister. As the Amherst Record reported, "There are some people who would be ashamed to have their children supported as town paupers while living in elegant style, with money enough apparently for all their needs. But this is a queer world, and tastes differ."

Like today, the national debate was at times bitter. One journal called for a new humaneness. Thousands had recently become poor while others scrambled for wealth. The nation should be one of "truth, honesty, and piety," the true wealth of the people. Meanwhile, a Professor Butler of Madison, Wisconsin, proposed that all "tramps" should be drafted into the army and sent west to rid the nation of "Indians."

Amherst's John E. Williams wrote a response to this in the best satiric tradition of Jonathan Swift: "We have repeatedly urged the advisability of transporting tramps to Alaska. An eastern savant now declares that if the warm stream of the Pacific had access to the Arctic Ocean it would render habitable an immense area now covered with snow and ice. It would lower the temperature of the tropics, and raise it in the temperate zone on this continent so as to add vastly to the habitable area and give to the whole of North America a climate similar to that of western Europe.

"Happy thought. Let us dig a ditch a hundred miles wide and say five hundred feet deep through the peninsula of Alaska, and let us send our tramps to do the digging. That will give them something to do, and more than double the habitable area of North America. This is the better way. There could be none better. It should be at once put into operation. It would force the tramps to work or to starve and would cure the evil that now threatens society."

Amherst's Poor Farm was burned down by one of its residents in 1882. It was rebuilt, then closed and sold in 1914.

The Manifest Insanity
of the Hat Factory Feud

Competition among rival fire companies, sports teams, and businesses was very lively in the 19th century. By the 1890s, for example, a feud developed between the two rival Amherst hat factories. The hat making industry in Amherst was justly famous as being the largest of its kind in the country. Fame and success aside, at certain times of the year the hat factory feud manifested itself "by certain exhibitions of insanity."

As Emily Dickinson grew, so did the town's factories. Hatmaking went from a small shop operation to a major industry with national distribution. Two large factories, the Leonard M. Hills Company and the Henry D. Fearing Company, were within

Hills Hat Factory workers with giant hat.

sight of the Dickinson house. In 1892, George B. Burnett & Son of New York bought out the Fearing Company, and went head-to-head with the Hills Company.

Employees of both companies were fiercely loyal, and with 150-200 people at each factory, a feud grew into quite a wild affair. In February of 1897, the Burnett Company arranged to hold a banquet at the Massasoit House in Springfield. The company hired a special train to take employees there by way of Northampton, but the Hills Company had other ideas. The Hills people grabbed the train for themselves, forcing the Burnett employees to take another train, which went by way of Palmer.

With the Burnetts finally seated in the dining room of the Massasoit, the Hills people forced their way into the hotel, overpowered the police and tried to break through the doors to the banquet. Failing that, they instead stole the ice cream meant for dessert, broke at least one window to the dining room, and tossed in a "stinck-pot." The latter caused "an intolerable stench in the room," as one can well imagine.

According to the Amherst Record, the men fired revolvers, broke furniture, and terrified hotel guests sufficiently to require that the civil authorities intervene.

The feud continued into the next morning, back in Amherst. Employees of both factories marched through the streets singing songs "more noisy than polite."

The Amherst Record was so shocked by all this that the paper sarcastically referred to the factory owners as "sane and self-respecting citizens." The newspaper made it clear that this was not a "harmless ebullition of animal spirits, showing a commendable shop spirit." On the contrary, such outrages should have resulted in arrests and fines, but didn't.

Both factories went out of business in the mid-1930s, after tastes in hats changed and competition from imported Italian hats altered the industry.

Chapter Four

BIRTH AND DEATH:
FROM ONE DOLLAR DELIVERIES
TO THE CITY OF THE DEAD

Main Street, Amherst, Massachusetts

Drab Habitation of Whom?
Tabernacle or Tomb -
Or Dome of Worm -
Or Porch of Gnome -
Or some Elf's Catacomb?
#893

Rejoicing With Trembling
in the 19th Century

Giving birth in the early 19th century was often an event filled with mixed emotions. Mortality rates were high for both mother and child, and even a successful birth could be an ordeal. Doctor Isaac G. Cutler was the most popular Amherst doctor of the time, and his birth records are a fascinating chronicle of life and death. Ironically, no mother's name appears in his accounts; for each birth Cutler recorded only the father's name.

Isaac G. Cutler was born in Pelham in 1782, the son of Dr. Robert Cutler, and Esther Garnsey of Amherst. The family moved to Amherst in 1787, where Isaac went to school before studying at Williams College. He married Nancy Hastings on December 24, 1807, and practiced medicine in the Amherst area until his death on November 29, 1834. Cutler's accounts list over 1,300 births between 1805 and 1833.

Among several babies Cutler delivered who were later to become prominent, the most famous was Emily Dickinson. The entry for December 10, 1830, reads simply as follows: "Edward Dickinson Esq. 10 g." Emily's mother, Emily N. Dickinson, is not mentioned, the "10" is the day of the month, and "g" is for girl. When Emily was born, Edward's concern about the responsibility and expense of raising a family became apparent. He bought Emily's mother a copy of Lydia Maria Child's *The Frugal Housewife*, "dedicated to those who are not ashamed of economy."

Cutler delivered all of Edward Dickinson's children, and some of Emily's aunts and uncles as well. Other typical entries include "Chauncey Hamilton (father)   7 (of February) Dead," with no name or sex of the child. Twins were listed as "Martin Baker March 3 (1811) twins g," for girl twins, or "Moses Nash 29 (November) twins b & g," for a mixed set. It is said, by the way, that for normal births Dr. Cutler charged one dollar for each baby, and 50 cents each for two deliveries in the same neighborhood.

On the same page that Emily Dickinson's birth appears, is the birth of another outstanding Amherst author, Helen Fiske (later Helen Hunt Jackson). The line for her birth states "Profess. N.W. Fisk (Oct.) 14 (1830) g." Nathan Fiske was a professor of Latin and Greek at Amherst College. He and his wife had lost their three month old son, David, a year earlier.

Upon Helen's birth, her father wrote to Mrs. Martha Vinal of Boston, "You will perhaps be agreeably surprised to hear that Mrs. F. has a little daughter, whose voice was heard first last evening about half past eleven ... . Dr. Cutler and Mrs. Hitchcock were at hand in good season. Every thing now appears flattering, but we have been taught by severe experience to rejoice with trembling."

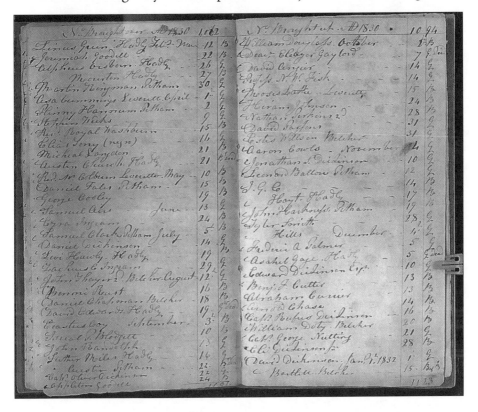

From Dr. Isaac Cutler's account book. Entry marked on right is for the birth of Emily Dickinson, December 10, 1830. Her father's name, rather than her's, appears with the day of the month and "g" for girl.

A Deadly
Town Meeting

In the spring of 1888, a special session of Amherst Town Meeting became so divided and bitter that one commentator said, "No history of Amherst will be quite complete without the record of yesterday's special town meeting." What was it that caused the legendary Dickinson, Hills, Parmenter, Seelye, and Hitchcock families to duck from invectives flung at Town Meeting? It was the age-old problem of where to bury the dead and whether taxpayers should pay the bill.

West Cemetery, Amherst's oldest, had been set out in 1730. It was expanded by two acres (described as "bleak, barren, and untill-able hence suitable for this purpose") in 1818. Fifteen years later the town bought land for the North and South Amherst cemeteries.

West Cemetery reached its capacity in about 1873. The select-men announced that only three plots were left where it could "be stated with certainty that no one was buried." It wasn't until 1887, however, that the town voted to search for a new burial site.

Simultaneously, a private group was organized in April of that year as the Amherst Cemetery Association. In July this group, made up of Henry F. Hills (hat manufacturer), Julius W. Seelye (President of Amherst College), Austin Dickinson (Emily's brother), O.D. Hunt (fire insurance agent), and George Cutler (dry goods dealer), purchased land on Strong Street for a private cemetery.

In March of 1888, the town voted to purchase the land (which had been the Joseph Dickinson farm), from the Amherst Cemetery Association, though it wasn't for sale. The association sold it to the town, however, at a more than 40 percent profit.

Within a week, the Blizzard of 1888 struck. During the fierce storm, Palmer's Block, where town meetings were held, caught fire. The blizzard kept fire fighters from the building and it was lost. The town decided it would need a new town hall instead of a cemetery, and decided to sell the cemetery land back to the Amherst Cemetery Association — at a considerable loss. Only one month later, on May 19, the town appeared to change its mind again, and created a committee to look for another cemetery site.

In the midst of all this, the infamous April 17 Special Town Meeting occurred. Nearly everyone in Amherst turned out, for, as the Amherst Record reported, "no business, whether it be spring work on the farm or work in a shop, was too important to detain them at home." The editors sarcastically described the day as one filled with "bright speeches and witty remarks," where "gems of elo-quence were dropped from the lips of natural born orators in (their)

When West Cemetery reached capacity one of Amherst's most bitter town meetings followed. (Photo by Anthony Martin.)

naturalness and simplicity." The reality was quite different.

Austin Dickinson was chosen moderator for the event, the business of which was mainly cost-cutting. Funds for a town library were dropped, then an argument over the costs of street lighting broke out ("The first gun was fired by that earnest, veteran farmer, Aaron Ingram"). But the real so-called "tug of war" began when Charles Parmenter stood to speak. Parmenter, a sewing machine dealer who lived in Pelham but worked in Amherst, questioned the town having bought the Joseph Dickinson farm from the Amherst Cemetery Association.

Parmenter implied that the selectmen had rigged the petition which initially called for the purchase, then rammed the vote through at a town meeting. Of his remarks, the newspaper said, "Mr. Parmenter did not openly accuse any one of fraud and duplicity ... (but he) blindly insulted by insinuation and otherwise the gentlemen who have served the town year after year."

Speaking for the Cemetery Association, Austin Dickinson and President Seelye were thoroughly annoyed that the town bought the farm for a cemetery and would sell it to build a town hall instead. Perry Irish, representing the average person, told a touching story of having no place in town to bury his son. He had to borrow a plot for temporary interment until a new cemetery could be established.

Another faction claimed the Cemetery Association had shrewdly trapped the town into buying a worthless piece of land. When Austin Dickinson tried to sort this out and take votes on the multiple amendments that were proposed, the meeting nearly fell apart. His call, at one point, for a standing vote caused so much confusion that the vote had to be cancelled and taken again.

Ultimately, Town Meeting decided to auction the farm which, as stated above, was bought back by the Cemetery Association at a loss to the town. At the next town meeting in June, the town's new cemetery search committee made the extravagant proposal to buy the William S. Clark Estate, at a cost triple what was previously paid for the bought-and-sold Dickinson farm.

With the leadership of Austin Dickinson and the landscape advice of the Olmsted Brothers, the extraordinary Wildwood Cemetery was eventually created, independent of the town's fruitless arguments.

After the town voted to contribute to the upkeep of Wildwood, all that was left were the recriminations. The Amherst Record blamed Charles Parmenter for one of the worst series of town meetings in history: "It demonstrates the shortsightedness of the individual who daily drives in from Pelham to look after the affairs of Amherst, who on the pleas of unfairness and intrigue, tried to defeat every project looking to the improvement and welfare of the town."

The Terror
of 1827

When Susan Worcester opened her door one summer night in 1827, something frightened her so badly that she passed out. By the next morning she suffered the miscarriage of twins. Rumors circulated of a strange creature haunting the center of Amherst, but it wasn't until 45 years later that someone came forward to resolve the mystery.

Samuel Worcester was one of the earliest instructors at Amherst College. After studying for the ministry he began teaching at Amherst in September 1823. A year later he was appointed a teacher of languages and librarian of the college. College President Hitchcock hinted at the misery of Worcester's life when he wrote, "he has experienced severe domestic afflictions, such as a miracle alone can remove."

Worcester married Susan Dix of Salem in 1825. Ten years later they left Amherst when Worcester became minister of the Tabernacle Church in Salem. The Worcesters were long gone from Amherst before the terror of 1827 was explained. It was in 1867 that a letter by a Noah Yale appeared in the Hampshire Express, a letter that "unravels what at the time was a profound mystery."

Noah Yale, born in Amherst, was a farmer and apothecary. Writing from Michigan, he unburdened himself in these words: "In the 1820s, being somewhat given to fun and frolic, I manufactured a sole-leather mask. It was a non-descript character of the human face divine. Having prepared a spongy piece of sole-leather and cut it to a length one third longer than the human face; Then a coarse wooden die made for the purpose, provided an enormous nose and having provided eyeholes, made the eyebrows of pieces of sheepskin with white, short wool, I then proceeded to make a mouth of yawning dimensions, in the corners of which goose-quills were inserted to represent teeth, and shoe pegs filled up the space between. To provide the beard, several cows' tails were made to be minus the long hair. A cap for the head, made of sheep-skin with the wool on, being attached to the sole leather completed the caricature.

"Thus provided I amused myself, as most boys would, in my own neighborhood, and among my associates, until it had become an old story, and the mask was laid aside. I will state that the mask had so frightful an appearance that my young associates would scringe and shrink back when I approached them with it on, notwithstanding that they saw me put it on. Some months after the mask had ceased to amuse, and had been laid aside, a young friend of mine, when at my house saw the mask and borrowed it, since which time I have never seen it. But from time to time, after lending it, I heard of strange frightful objects being seen in the vicinity of the College, and about the middle of town ... .

"On a dark night there was a rapping at the door, and the wife of the said professor went to answer the call. She shrieked and was found insensible by the family. Medical aid was immediately summoned, but sad to relate, two dead babes were found in the house the next morning."

Yale's letter was written only a few months after Rev. Worcester's death in 1866. Yale's story, however, has a few loose ends. In Dr. Isaac Cutler's account book there is an account of Susan Worcester delivering one stillborn, not two. Yale said their house was on the west side of the Common, but evidence places it a mile north. Yale "unravelled a profound mystery," but as in all versions of history, memory and imagination cover reality with a mist.

The Cost of Shaving
a Dead Man

Why was it that in the Amherst of 1878 it cost at least $2.50 to shave a dead man, and only 10 cents for a live one? Long before Jessica Mitford's *The American Way of Death* questioned the costs of funerals in 1963, one man in Amherst protested funeral practices. He lambasted funeral directors for exorbitant fees that caused one's

Emily Dickinson's footstone, now gone (center), in West Cemetery.

heirs to "go to the poor house straight from the graveyard."

Writing in the May 1878 issue of the Amherst Record, a man identified only as "Smith" claimed that a service rendered when one was alive suddenly cost 10 to 30 times as much when one was dead. While Amherst paid only $3.00 for a man and a pair of horses to work a whole day on the roads, it cost $6.00 to $8.00 for the same man and horses to pull the town hearse for one hour. A coffin would cost from $10.00 to $40.00 to build, but the charge was usually double. Unlike today, with our recent reforms, mourners had no idea what the costs would be until they received the bill. Smith concluded, as modern sociologists have, that people's grief was taken advantage of, as was their desire not to appear stingy when a loved one died.

The history of funeral customs is an astonishing one. Egyptians abandoned the embalming of the dead after large parts of the population converted to Christianity. Embalming continued to be used in the case of monarchs, though, since it was necessary to show that the monarch was actually dead before a new one took over. One exception was Queen Elizabeth I of England, who asked not to be embalmed. Thus, a lady-in-waiting reported that while lying in her coffin for 34 days in Whitehall, the Queen's body "burst with such a crack that it splitted the wood ... whereupon next day she was fain to be new trimmed up."

In America, the funeral was a family's responsibility until the late 19th century. The family washed and laid out the body, draped it in a winding sheet, ordered a coffin from a local carpenter, and carried it to the church and graveyard. Between the death and funeral, the body lay in the family parlor where mourners took turns watching over it — mainly to be sure there were no signs of revival.

The first undertakers came from the professions of livery stable keepers, carpenters, cabinetmakers, or church sextons. In cities some midwives and nurses laid out the dead. Bodies were usually kept from immediate decay with ice until Thomas Holmes came along. During the Civil War, Holmes rushed to the front and offered to embalm the dead for $100 each. He returned to Brooklyn a rich man, but embalming did not become common until after 1900. Only since Victorian times have we beautified the body, housed it in a luxurious coffin, surrounded it with flowers (against the initial opposition of the church), and hired someone to direct the proceedings as a theatre piece.

In 1878, Smith complained that "while it costs to live, it is more expensive not to." He recommended the British system, which advertised the complete costs of funerals in newspapers. These advertisements gave prices for every level from a first-class hearse and coach with lots of velvet, to children's funerals, and one-horse carriage funerals, down to "Walking funerals at extremely low prices." Smith surmised that in the latter case, "it is probable that only the animated portion of the funeral is expected to walk."

"We All Liked Him
Too Well to Kill Him"

Ed and Norman Smith had been away from Amherst for nearly 40 years when they revealed two things: They were bad but sincere poets, and they at one time attempted to kill Uncle Appleton King.

The boys had grown up in the 1850s and 60s on a farm just north of the center of the Amherst village of Cushman. This small community of mills clustered around a river was known at that time as "The City." The family left town in 1868 and it wasn't until 1905 that Ed and Norman returned for a look at their radically changed home town.

In a letter from Pittsburgh, his new home, Norman later recalled their reactions: "The first thing that struck my brother and knocked him silly, was the exceeding smallness of the hills as compared with the lofty mountains he had carried in his memory so long. When we were boys and lived on the farm on the hill just above the 'city' we were occasionally allowed to go with grandfather a mile or so to the grist mill at Still Corner, and we used to think it was about eighteen million miles ... . The road is almost disused now, and grass has grown up between the wheel tracks. It skirts along the base of Brushy mountain, densely wooded, and famous in my boyhood for its huckleberries; it passes by the site of the old Allen place which of

The Cushman section of Amherst, where the Smith boys considered killing Uncle Appleton King.

yore was the abode of Abby and Sukey Allen ... ."

"The old mill at Still Corner has sadly changed in forty years; a little more rickety, and almost ready to collapse; we climbed the bank behind it, and had a glimpse of the old pond, and it seemed but yesterday that I fell into its waters and was pulled out and laid upon a pile of shavings to dry.

"We took a cut across the fields to see Sears trout brook once more. It runs through what used to be Sears sugar orchard, empties into Mill river at the extreme corner of our old farm. But we found the sugar trees all cut down, the old saphouse an undistinguishable heap of ruins, and all covered with a heavy growth of underbrush ... . Everything was changed, and for the worse."

Norman's memories sometimes overflowed into verse, as in his ode to "The Old Brick School-House," written in 1902:

Back again to dear old Amherst, to the hamlet in the hills,
To the village still and peaceful, save the music of the mills,
Save the low and muffled roaring of the dam at Cushman's pond,
And the distant hum of grinding at the paper mill beyond.

Here, I learned my early lessons, hither came through sun and snow.
And but yesterday it seemeth though 'twas forty years ago;
Came from Maple Hill each morning, came with Frank, and Will, and Lu,
Through the shady country roadway, decked with posies fresh with dew.

But Norman Smith didn't fail to remember the less poetic parts of his boyhood, including what he called the "attempt on the life" of Appleton King: "It was in Sears sugar orchard that we boys used to come and help the Sears boys boil sap all night long, whiling away the time by dipping into such classics as 'Squint Eyed Bob,' 'Snaky Snodgrass' and other standard works; varying the monotony by occasional games of high, low, jack, and eating a peck or two of apples ... . I remember one day, we boys, having become filled with strange ideas of robbery and murder (due doubtless to the classical reading herein before mentioned) went up the road past Kellogg's woods, and piled up a lot of stones in one of the wheel tracks, reasoning thereby that the first unfortunate vehicle that came that way would be upset, the occupants killed and then we young ruffians could appear when all was over and get the wallets of the dead.

"After placing the stones, we ran down the hill, and taking refuge in our 'robbers' cave,' waited developments. Shortly, we heard the rattle of an approaching wagon, and from our lurking place we saw the genial face of Uncle Appleton King jogging along in his old buggy. We looked at each other in dismay; how did he escape destruction, why wasn't he killed?

"We rushed back to our pile of stones, and found that the good old man had got out of his buggy and tossed them against the fence. So much for our blood-thirsty attempt at highway robbery."

Forty years later, as F. Norman Smith and his brother Ed walked the old roads of Cushman filled with memories and regrets, Norman had one more thing to say about the Appleton King escapade: "We agreed among ourselves that we were glad Uncle Appleton escaped unhurt, for we all liked him too well to kill him."

The Cold and Lonely
Death of a Cobbler

On January 15, 1878, an old man died alone in a second floor room above Main Street in Amherst. For 10 months, William Newell had both lived and worked as a cobbler above Deuel's Drugstore, a half mile from the Dickinson Homestead. He was found on the floor of his room, weak and nearly starved, and he died a few days later. Newell's is an unusual story, for he wasn't just another transient, poverty case on the edge of society.

William Newell was born on May 19, 1802, in Pelham. When he was 16 years old his father apprenticed him to a shoemaker in Hadley for three years. At 19 he set out on foot as a journeyman shoemaker, travelling for four or five years throughout New England, New York, New Jersey, and Pennsylvania. He returned to Pelham to work and to marry Chloe Myrick.

In 1849, Newell discovered the high mineral content in springs near Amethyst Brook, on his land. The springs began to attract local people, then invalids came to drink and stay nearby. The increasing popularity of Orient Springs led Newell to build a small house there and to obtain an innkeeper's license. Later a bowling alley and other attractions were added.

Unfortunately, business transactions with a man named Ballou, who bought Orient Springs in 1858, ruined Newell financially. To support himself and his wife, Newell worked in Amherst, first for Samuel Carter, then on his own as a cobbler. For nearly 20 years he worked in the small room on Main Street, walking there from Pelham six days each week. What little money he made he brought home to his wife.

Chloe paid off the mortgage on their homestead, but the title somehow was made out only in her name. In the spring of 1877, Chloe Newell asked her husband to leave their house. The community seemed to side unanimously with Mr. Newell. The Daily Hampshire Gazette called it a "most outrageous injustice," and "a sample of what a woman, destitute of any trace of womanly feeling, hard-hearted, and cruel beyond the power to describe, can do." The newspaper apparently didn't bother to ask Mrs. Newell for her side of the story.

Newell moved into his cobbler shop where he slept amid his tools, a desk, a few books, a stove, and his mineral collection. He eked out a scanty living fixing shoes and selling minerals to Amherst College geologists and students. Local people sometimes gave him food to help him get by, but by January, 1878, he was so weak from hunger and illness that he could barely move about the room.

On Thursday, January 10, Charles Adams brought Newell some food, but found him on the floor in a corner. Word was sent to the Pelham Selectmen, who provided a nurse to stay with Newell. Dr. C.F. Sterling did what he could, but malnutrition and pneumonia killed Newell on the following Tuesday.

The Amherst Record said he died in the place he loved, where he could study and handle his minerals, and where "the thorn in his flesh — his wife — could not annoy him."

Amherst's
"City of the Dead"

In the mid-1800s, when Amherst was a small village, everyone knew when a neighbor was ill and near death. It was the custom for the church bell to toll at the hour of death. The bell tolled the age, one time for each year, of the deceased, and thus, without words, the village knew. By the time Emily Dickinson died, on May 15, 1886, bells were instead rung during funerals. The church bell would mark a stately, slow cadence of perhaps six strikes per minute.

In the 1870s, Oliver M. Clapp was the stone carver responsible for most of the grave markers in West Cemetery. It was said that his granite monuments — some 10 to 12 feet tall — were as fine as could be found anywhere. In 1877, he was hired to restore many old stones that had weathered beyond recognition, and to build new monuments where others had crumbled. The rough paths were graded and the grounds landscaped.

An anonymous description of the cemetery paints a very Victorian picture of the scene: "Riding in our Cemetery a few days since, after an absence of five years, I noticed what changes were there ... . How many are there congregated and what a lapse of years, since the green earth first welcomed them.

"The visit was full of sad enjoyment, so many family (plots) were beautiful, so many ancient monuments renovated, and erected as new. In one corner, as you enter on the north entrance, stands an old stone erected in 1819, of a young girl, an orphan, carefully reared and educated by an indulgent guardian, eloped with an unknown lover, reared to adorn society, to be an ornament to a home, her life eventful. Death occurred in less than one short year. A young man, perhaps a descendant, was leaning upon the stone with a note book. Carefully he brushed aside the grass to read what the hand of affection had dictated.

"At another — a young girl sitting on a mother's grave; how that sorrow had blighted that young mourner's life. At another, a father cut off suddenly, the home made desolate. Another, the beautiful babe — bright anticipations there nipped in the bud; still another that interested me greatly — a handsome shaft, erected by Perez Dickinson to replace old stones made illegible by time and neglect.

"Improvements have made a great change to those who once frequented it, before the pleasant drives, the grading and apparent arrangement out of confusion. The fragrant flowers seemed to give a cheerful good morning. We feel tenderly toward those that are laid there, to walk softly; to speak low, that we disturb not the sleeping echoes."

During the year that followed the cemetery's renovation, the curmudgeonly writer known only as "Smith" began writing lengthy essays in the Amherst Record. One such questioned "Why a service for a dead man should cost ten, twenty, or thirty times as much as a similar service rendered a living man." Smith saved his most caustic remarks for the custom of wearing black: "Mourning millinery is another item of expense, and of large profit to those who furnish it ... . What sense there is in jumping into a mass of crape when a friend dies we are unable to see, and then the awkward manner of getting out of it, after the sharp edge of their sorrow is worn off, and the person who has lived in a wilderness of crape wishes to haul in the advertisement of their bereavement, is often times ridiculous in the extreme.

"The first thing noticed in a woman desiring to shake off crape, is the adoption of mitigated mourning; that is, dress goods with a narrow line of white in a mass of black, then some rather hasty marriage contract is entered into and they blossom out all of a sudden like a peony."

Smith opposed all such Victorian sentiment and decorum and concluded, "In view of this subject we are much impressed with the importance of holding on to life as long as possible, to economize and accumulate, to have every moment industriously employed so that one's estate may pan out enough to at least settle the funeral expenses when the shuffling off the coil can be postponed no longer; even if one's heirs go to the poor house straight from the graveyard."

Chapter Five

EDUCATION: DICKENSIAN, DEFIANT, AND BRILLIANT

The Common, Amherst, Massachusetts

A precious - mouldering pleasure - tis -
To meet an Antique Book -
In just the Dress his Century wore -
A privilege - I think -
        #371

Flogging &
Feruling in 1820

The primary school Emily Dickinson attended, on North Pleasant Street.

Our image of early 19th century schoolhouses is often a blurred one, colored by what Hadley writer Clifton Johnson called the "charm of the old school days." Emily Dickinson and her siblings, entered a primitive Amherst public school system, like most children in town. Some left first-hand accounts that shatter the image of the "charming" one-room schoolhouse.

When Charles Blair recalled what school was like in Amherst in 1820, his most vivid memory was of being lifted out of his seat by his ears. Blair's teacher was John Parmenter, considered one of the best in Amherst at that time, notwithstanding his "flogging and feruling" of students. For some now forgotten infraction, Parmenter lifted Blair by his ears three times and set him down with such force that he split the seat board.

Charles Blair was born in Amherst in 1812, and after schooling he became a machinist, married Eunice Blodget in 1833 and moved to Canton, Connecticut, six years later. When he reminisced about his youth, he recalled that West Street was called Mount Zion, and East Street, where his school was, was referred to as Sodom.

The school Blair attended was one of the old district schools, built in about 1804. It was a one-story building, 60 feet by 20 feet, and low enough for the taller boys to reach the eaves. The unpainted wooden schoolhouse had a chimney at each end and a door in the northeast corner. Boys hung their hats in the entrance, and the girls placed their hoods and other garments in a cupboard next to one of the fireplaces. This cupboard also held the schoolmaster's supply of rods for enforcing the rules. Plain wooden seats were arranged on three sides of the room. Two students sat in each of the seats, which were arranged one above another in three tiers. The girls sat on the west side of the building and the boys on the east. Younger students sat in the first row, with the older ones behind them.

This kind of seating arrangement helped keep order in a school where the age range was from five to 21. There were as many as 80 students, but the school term was only three months long. Boys would attend when the farm schedule allowed, and usually only until they were of age. Girls might attend until they were old enough to marry. Parents were requested to send wood to heat the schoolhouse, but occasionally the short winter term ended early when the wood ran out.

The school day started with a Bible reading, then a reading from Caleb Bingham's *The American Preceptor*. Next, the students did writing exercises while the teacher made or mended their goose quill pens. Girls studied grammar, which was thought unnecessary for boys. While Blair was there, no one was formally instructed in math, which they were expected to learn on their own.

While Charles Blair's strongest memory of his Amherst schooling was the day his teacher pulled his ears and cracked his seat, he grudgingly accepted this as the custom. Schoolmasters, according to Blair, seemed to think there was "no other way of keeping such a lot of wild boys under subjection except through fear."

A Complete and
Finished Nincompoop

Among the letters of Ira Chaffee Goodell is a remarkably frank portrayal of the 12 schoolmasters who taught him in Belchertown between 1807 and 1819. Whether a good master or "an ignoramous of a jackass," none of Goodell's early teachers escapes his biting wit.

Ira Chaffee Goodell was born in 1800 in Belchertown, a farming town bordering Amherst, from which he escaped to become an itinerant portrait painter. After 1824, he travelled to Pittsfield, Chester, Westfield, and North Adams. In 1829, he painted portraits in upstate New York, later settling in New York City. His accounts reveal his expensive tastes in wine, silk cravats, and Swiss watches. Expenses for his children's mahogany coffins, leeching, and art supplies reveal daily needs and daily troubles.

By 1836, Goodell had painted nearly 1,500 portraits at about eight dollars each. Hoping to increase his wealth, Ira invested in Belchertown property. He then eagerly joined the mulberry tree craze (in hopes of producing valuable silk), which cost him dearly.

On April 22, 1838, shortly after the death of his son, Angelo Byron, Ira wrote at length from New York to his brother Newton, about his early schooling at the Log Town school, in what is now the Dwight section of Belchertown. Ira characterized the old schoolhouse as having been in such bad condition that "a master of any gumption" would not consent to teach there.

Of the "Twelve Caesars" who taught Goodell over the years, he allowed that only a few were at all worthy — a Mr. Lee, Charles Haskell, and Reuben Cook, among them. Sam Shumway was "a poor critter in every particular," Jesse Peck of Pelham "was tolerable good in licking and that was about all." Martin Thayer, "The Lord God Almighty Thayer," was a "contemptible strut of a dandy, and an ignoramous of a jackass ... . The Apostle Mr. Titus Smith of Granby could do nothing; he had so much of God and religion in his soul, praying was about all he did."

Goodell described the Rev. Sebastian Columbus Cabot as a "Philosopher and Gentleman ... . His Literary and Scientific attainments were greater than any that ever taught in the Old Logtown Shell. The Scholars loved the Old Gentleman." David Rogers, on the other hand, was a "Snarley yow of a teacher," and the scholars "put the veto upon him and destroyed his usefulness." Luther Hunt of Shutesbury was "as savage as a Hyena, but he did not kill any of his pupils, although they came near killing him. He was a complete and finished nincompoop."

Ira Goodell's disappointment with his old schoolhouse was so complete that he suggested the faculty of Amherst College (many of whom were ministers), should pronounce a funeral oration over "the old crazy worn out house." Myrrh, aloes, and frankincense should be sprinkled over that place of "so many hard scenes." Better that a torch be put to it, and its ashes placed in an urn as a monument to suffering and distress.

Emily was a student at Amherst Academy on Amity Street, from 1840 to 1847.

Ink Blots and Grease Spots
– Early Library Societies

We sometimes take for granted the great wealth that our local libraries offer. The fact that virtually everyone, whether they pay taxes or not, can use a library without putting down a dime is considered only right and natural. But in the early Connecticut River Valley, books were relatively rare and expensive, and the library societies that grew there had stiff membership fees, restrictive rules and severe fines. The records of one such society, begun in the southwest corner of Amherst in 1842, reveal the consequences of everything from torn pages to grease spots on borrowed books.

By 1840, Amherst had been divided into school districts, with each district responsible for building its own schools. Several of them went further and established a kind of adult education in the form of library societies. On December 26, 1842, voters within school district #6 met in their school house to organize a library.

District #6 was along West Street as far north as about Potwine Lane. On January 2, 1843, the society voted Captain Oliver Dickinson (a distant relation of Emily) moderator, and selected Stephen Puffer as the society's first librarian.

While societies like this gathered at schoolhouses, the books were actually kept at the home of the librarian. Their collections were usually less than 100 volumes, often all purchased with uniform bindings from Harper & Brothers, New York. For variety, district libraries sometimes exchanged books.

Amherst district libraries seemed to grow out of the town's first social library, held in about 1793 in the South East Schoolhouse. To join, each person paid $2.00, plus 18 pence per year for three years. The group met every two months, and each member could borrow no more than two books.

The District #6 library association was similar. It met to borrow books once every other month; the librarian kept the books in his house; and no more than two books could be borrowed at a time. While the first article of the bylaws stipulated that males above 21 years of age were entitled to one share in the library, it wasn't until the 13th article that women, almost as an afterthought, were recognized as having rights to join the group.

Unlike today when anything on library shelves can be easily seen, the borrowers first had to choose lots before choosing books. Like choosing sides in sandlot baseball, each person chose one book, according to the lots they picked. They then went around again and again until everyone made their selections.

Article 11 spelled out penalties for damages to books: "Every proprietor taking out books shall be subject to the following fine for injuries done the same: For every leaf torn out, not less than four nor over twelve cents; for every leaf torn not gone, not less than two cents, not over six cents; for grease spot or writing with a pen or pencil, blot or stain with dirty hands or otherwise, not less than two cents, not over eight; for injuries done the bindings of the books, in proportion to the damages done the book." Ironically, the very pages these rules appeared on were marred by several large blue inkblots.

I shall now risk a breach of library ethics and reveal the names of several men fined for not returning books in the 1840s: Spencer Smith, Ebenezer Williams, Jason Thayer, David Bartlett, and the estimable Captain Oliver Dickinson. Each was fined a minimum of 10 cents, in the days when an average worker's wage was about a dollar a day.

The Disastrous
Rebellion of 1837

Mrs. Howland's School on North Prospect St.
Emily Dickinson's nephew, Gilbert, second row center, with white collar.

In the long history of student activism at Amherst College, one event stands out as an example of a protest gone too far. It began in 1834 and Moses Kimball Cross, one of the participants, described it as, "one of the most extensive and disastrous rebellions that any college ever experienced."

In the 1830s, the college was in the midst of several very passionate religious revivals. Concurrently, Amherst was also struggling with the issue of slavery. At that time the college had an unusually high number of southern students, who supported slavery, and a large number of students very committed against it. In 1833, both a Colonization Society and an Anti-Slavery Society were formed on the campus. Students divided into two hostile camps, and the administration attempted to suppress both groups. But in the following year it was neither slavery nor religion that caused the greatest rebellion on campus. It was the relatively innocuous issue of student recitations.

In 19th century colleges great honor was attached to being chosen to speak at commencement exercises, at recitations of literary societies, and at other formal events. In 1834, Amherst College students became incensed at the manner in which such students were chosen, and at the fact that students were not allowed to decline such honors. Amherst students consisted mainly of men preparing for the clergy, and the junior class was considered the most pious to have ever entered the college. Yet it was the junior class that rebelled nearly to the point of self-destruction. They petitioned the college trustees in 1834 and in 1836 to abolish the system of choosing students for recitations and suggested an egalitarian system in which all students could take part.

The trustees refused, which created a sudden rash of students refusing to accept the honor of reciting. This snowballed until 1837 when William Gorham of Enfield refused to speak and was brought before President Heman Humphrey. Humphrey dealt with Gorham severely, and Gorham boasted to his friends that he was "abusive" toward the president.

The faculty required Gorham to sign an apology or face expulsion. Gorham rewrote the apology and signed it, but it wasn't acceptable in that form. Nearly the entire junior class rallied in Gorham's support, and scrawled their support on the wall of the College Chapel. Everyone in the class was then required to sign a "confession" or be expelled from the college.

One by one students began to sign, and as one of them said, "like a flock of sheep when one or two leap over a wall, the whole company followed in a brief space of time, and law and order were triumphant."

Thirty-six years later, Professor Tyler pointed out that enrollment declined after the rebellion and that in 1873 the effects were still being felt.

The Night the Cannons
Roared in Amherst

It was only seven days after the death of Emily Dickinson that Amherst erupted in a wild celebration, the likes of which hadn't been witnessed in years. No Presidential election, nor even the surrender of Lee's army had caused so much riotous joy as the Amherst College victory over Yale at a famous baseball game held on May 22, 1886.

For Amherst College, baseball, then called "ball nine," had been a depressing game. Their team had been performing badly, it hadn't beaten Yale in seven years, and few people, even in Amherst, bet on it to win. The grandstands were overflowing with fans at the now long gone Blake Field. Every livery team in Northampton was engaged to go to Amherst, and hundreds arrived from surrounding towns.

Excitement grew, inning by inning, as the over-confident Yalies began to lose their early lead. The close game ended, very unexpectedly, with an Amherst win of 5 to 4. Students, professors, and citizens went mad with joy. One professor pulled the college chimes, another rang the college bell. Students rushed to their rooms to gather horns and noisemakers. The Amherst Record reported that "the tall man embraced the short man, the lean man the fat ... and all tried to waltz to the fish horn racket. The fat man was hardly a thing of beauty with his hat stove in, the torrents of perspiration streaming down his inflamed visage."

The celebration went far into the night, getting even louder when the boys brought a Massachusetts Agricultural College (now UMass) cannon to the Town Common. Amherst got the permission of President Greenough of Mass Aggie to fire the cannon, but some of the rival Aggie students relieved the cannon of its critical parts. President Greenough became so wrapped up in the celebration that he took his lantern in hand and brought spare parts for the cannon. Even he seemed eager to blast the village. "Seldom," the newspaper reported, "does a dignified president of a great college become so interested in another institution." While he was busy hunting up spare parts, the stolen parts were supposedly in the pockets of the Aggies who stood around watching and laughing at the president's predicament.

Round after round of blanks were fired from the cannon, as a huge bonfire lit the center of town. Students dragged a float draped in the college colors along Pleasant Street, containing the victorious team. Fireworks added to the "indescribably hideous" racket.

An anonymous citizen wrote a letter to the editor of the Record that dampened the joy of the event. The bonfire and horns were acceptable, but he drew the line at the cannon firing. "We were compelled to have our nerves torn to pieces by the senseless whim of a few boys" who sought to "torture those hopeless citizens who happen to live near the village common." He compared the boys to savages, and quoted President Lincoln, who he claimed said, "For those that like that sort of thing, that is about the sort of thing they like."

The Threat of
Gunshots and Arson

The one-room district school on East Street.

In 1987, a riotous University of Massachusetts graduation cele-bration closed down the center of Amherst. Such behavior appalled townspeople, yet it was only an echo of the 1890s. Just prior to the Amherst College commencement of 1892, a polite social order broke down after — once again — a baseball game. The situation quickly turned ugly. Students stormed the sheriff's house, someone fired a shot, vandals struck, and later arson was threatened.

Tension had been building for weeks as the townspeople grew impatient with the general rowdiness of students. The students themselves were feeling frustrated as rain postponed two baseball games against Williams College. On Wednesday June 1, 1892, Amherst finally played Williams on Pratt Field. Pent up frustration and the normal end-of-school excitement exploded when Amherst beat Williams, 19 to 8.

As usual on such occasions, the Amherst students built a bonfire. The Amherst Record, however, described their means of gathering material as "characteristic of Sherman's foragers." A barrel of lemonade appeared, and the rumor was that it was spiked with something considerably stronger.

There had apparently been continual friction between the town's sheriff, William W. Smith, and the students. Between 10 and 11 o'clock, a group of revelers visited the sheriff's house on South Pleasant Street and "indulged in a noisy serenade." This serenading mob began to throw stones at the house and to hurl insults at the sheriff's wife and daughters. The latter act pushed the sheriff's patience to the limit and he burst forth from the house armed with his revolver and fired a shot into the air.

The next morning it was discovered that the windows and sidewalk of William Hunt's stove shop on South Pleasant were smeared with red and green paint. The Amherst Record tried to calm the tension by encouraging mutual forbearance by everyone. Then the situation became even uglier after 14 Amherst College students were summoned before superior court in Northampton, on June 15, to answer the charges of disturbing the peace and assaulting Sheriff Smith. Later in the week Sheriff Smith received a threatening letter saying that unless he dropped the case, his house would be burned down. According to the newspaper the letter was "couched in the most filthy and indecent language and was, of course, anonymous." The paper condemned the letter as cowardly and dared the writer to carry out the threat. He never did.

After eight of the students pleaded guilty to the charges, anger dissipated. Both the town and Amherst College went on to enjoy the speeches and concerts of that year's commencement.

A Seance and a Town Meeting
Decided the Fate of Mount Toby

When the Amherst College Class of 1849 decided to change the name of Mount Toby in Sunderland, it stirred up more trouble than had been bargained for. After pioneering the recreational and scientific use of the mountain, the students felt entitled to rechristen it with a more appropriate name. The result was a run-in with Sunderland Town Meeting, and an imaginary seance in the tower of Amherst College.

Amherst College students were steeped in the geology of the Connecticut River Valley. Their reverence of the local landscape went beyond science to a poetic, almost religious devotion. It had become something close to a tradition for the college to improve on "common or vulgar" local names by replacing them with "splendid ... classical and euphonical" ones. Amherst students had already successfully named Mount Norwottuck and Turner's Falls.

The senior class of 1849 discovered that Mount Toby, one of the higher hills in the area, was inaccessible. They approached Moses Hubbard, the major landowner of the hill, who gave his permission to cut a trail to the top and clear the trees to open the impressive view. Feeling they had conquered a neglected peak, they were inspired to rename it, for "no poet would dare to write a poem, if he must introduce into it the name of Toby. It would kill the finest epic in the world."

On June 8, 1849, the senior class announced that they would soon rechristen the mountain. Their choice was the name of the Indian sachem who deeded it to the whites for 80 fathoms of wampum. They claimed that Mettawompe had "the best claim to have his name attached to the mountain; especially as one of the last of an abused race, to whom such a tribute is due." But Sunderland planned to protest the deposing of their hero Elnathan Toby, after whom they had named the mountain.

On June 14, the boys held a ceremony on top of the mountain, surrounded by a view described as "strikingly grand." The young men, including Edward Hitchcock Jr. (son of the eminent geologist), made passionate speeches. Instead of champagne, the mountain was rechristened with a bottle supposedly filled with water from "the Caspian Sea, Lake Ooroomiah in Persia, the river Euphrates, the river Jordan, and the river Connecticut." Then they ran a flag marked "Mettawompe" up a pole. More grand speeches on history and geology were given, and a call was made for the junior class to rename nearby Mount Tom "when they should have arrived to the dignity of seniors."

The ceremony closed with a surprise return from the grave of the deposed Elnathan Toby, played by William Palmer. Waving a rusty musket he demanded his right to the mountain. Also making a return appearance from the grave was Mettawompe, played by George Ferguson. He argued with Toby that the mountain was the throne of his ancestors and they should be duly honored. The crowd cried "Mettatwompe forever!" except for several Sunderland protesters who sided with Toby.

Sunderland was sufficiently annoyed by this to bring the issue before Town Meeting the following November. They voted overwhelmingly to reject the new name. They considered Toby a heroic pioneer, the first white man to climb the mountain, and a man who lived "In times which tried men's souls."

By this time the Class of 1849 had graduated and only a few members were still in the area. They therefore "summoned a mesmeric meeting of its members upon the top of the College Tower." With only a few students there in body and the rest in spirit, they countered Sunderland's objections. The students accused Sunderland of neglecting the mountain and the memory of its heroic Toby. Names were not property, they claimed, and since they had made the noblest use of the mountain the students had a right to name it. The class called on their successors to continue the renaming of the landscape "until the beautiful natural scenery of this region shall have such names attached to it that we shall not be ashamed to inform literary and scientific gentlemen from abroad, what those names are."

Ultimately, the students failed, for Mount Toby remains Mount Toby, and Mounts Tom and Holyoke have resisted their hopes for more melodious names.

Expelled for
Grinding Professors

In the late 1980s, editors of the Dartmouth Review clashed with the college administration and the result was an embarrassing controversy. The Dartmouth Review claimed freedom of the press when it published its inflammatory views of faculty. The college claimed the faculty had their rights abused when the Review staff disrupted classes in their quest for a story. Some students were expelled and national newscasters and columnists had a field day. In a parallel incident from the last century, an 1878 Amherst student publication was found to be so outrageous that the entire seven-member editorial staff was expelled.

Amherst College students enjoyed printing caricatures of their professors, but sometimes went too far.

The Olio was an annual guide to Amherst College written by each year's junior class. This guide to buildings and organizations seems really to have been a vehicle for humor and what were called "grinds." Grinds were satiric jests at the expense of the usually honored faculty and administration. The Olio of 1878, however, went a bit too far and the consequences were felt for years. The editors seemed to anticipate what would happen and printed the following disclaimer in the Olio's introduction: "Our aim has been to instruct and entertain our fellow students, while furnishing the outside world a real glimpse of college life. Whatever is written, is written for your good. Not in wrath but in mercy, with more in sorrow than in anger ... ."

The volume was filled with thinly disguised jibes and parodies written ostensibly to educate the "unendurable" freshmen and to lay bare the frailties of the "obnoxious" professors. Unfortunately, much of it was rather crude and sarcastic, especially the cartoons. Benjamin Emerson, Professor of Geology and Zoology, was pictured as a nearly toothless and bald organ grinder, charming an audience of animals. Another professor was shown wildly hopping and waving in front of a class, with one bare foot and a crazed look in his eyes. The faculty was enraged. One college newspaper said the cartoons were "too much like the school boy trick of drawing pictures of the teacher on a slate." The seven editors of the Olio were indefinitely suspended from Amherst College.

Just as in the Dartmouth Review case, the incident brought passionate debate. The Amherst Record came out in defense of the students, stating that the Olio "might have been irreverent, but was neither malicious in itself nor subversive of college discipline." The Record admitted that "the standard of veneration is fearfully low among the rising generation," but faulted College President Seelye for a lack of diplomacy.

Amherst students were sufficiently chastened. The Olio lost its bite the following year though it did keep some of its sense of humor. It was subtitled the "Expurgated Edition" and most cartoons were replaced by pleasant photographs of the campus. One of the few cartoons showed a broken grindstone and a crying student. The caption read, "Notice! No More Grinds Here!" The 1880 edition apologized for its mild contents by pleading "fear of premature graduation."

As for the seven suspended students, most returned to Amherst College. One went on to become an editor of the Springfield Republican (Edward Hill), two became lawyers (Henry Goodrich and Charles Libbey), two became school superintendents (Joseph Banta and Frank Richardson), and two became ministers (Edmund Alden and Henry Field).

The Johnson Chapel Controversy

Johnson Chapel, built in 1826, with Amherst center in the distance.

A notorious 1986 lawsuit that found the Bible Speaks Institute in Lenox, Massachusetts, guilty of fraudulently separating $6,000,000 from a follower, brings to mind an Amherst incident from the 1820s. In 1823, shortly after the founding of Amherst College, Emily Dickinson's grandfather, Samuel Fowler Dickinson, and Col. Rufus Graves were accused of improperly influencing Adam Johnson's will. The will left the bulk of Johnson's estate to Amherst College to build a chapel, Johnson Chapel. The lawsuit that followed stalled its construction and had to be settled by the State Supreme Court.

The cornerstone for the first building on the Amherst College campus, South College, was laid on August 9, 1820. Within two years that building had been outgrown, and the trustees decided to add a chapel, which would also include recitation rooms, a laboratory and a library. Meanwhile, Adam Johnson of neighboring Pelham was in declining health. Johnson had been born in 1753, the son of one of Pelham's original settlers. Lame and unable to do heavy work, he had sold the family farm in 1800. Having never married, Johnson had no descendants to inherit his considerable estate.

Samuel Fowler Dickinson made frequent visits to Johnson in Pelham in order to convince him to leave his property to Amherst College. As an inducement, he brought with him the promise that the new college chapel would bear Johnson's name. Dickinson, a lawyer, even offered to draw up Johnson's will. On February 26, 1823, he executed the will, which stated that out of an estate of $6,559.12, $4,000 would be donated to Amherst College. Johnson died the following August.

One week after Johnson's death, Ralph Waldo Emerson visited Amherst and described the young college as "an Infant Hercules." Emerson also noted in his journal that "A poor one-legged man died last week in Pelham, who was not known to have any property, & left them 4000 dollars to be appropriated to the building of a Chapel, over whose door is to be inscribed his name ... ."

Johnson's brother, Thomas, was understandably miffed to receive only 12 dollars out of the remainder of the estate. A poor man living in Greenfield, he contested it. The man claimed Samuel F. Dickinson, Rufus Graves, and the Trustees of Amherst College had taken advantage of his brother when he was in a weak state of mind. Later, William Tyler, Amherst professor and historian, suggested that Johnson was not in the same class as other founders of the college and that Dickinson and Graves preyed upon his desire to perpetuate his name.

The college began the erection of the chapel in 1826, when the State Supreme Court absolved Dickinson and Graves of all charges and the funds were released. The chapel was dedicated on February 28, 1827. Thomas Johnson angrily wrote his own will, in the form of a 24-page pamphlet. In it he bequeathed to Amherst College "nothing but woes and maledictions." He claimed that the "Amherst College Trustees were making merchandise of the poor, the widow and fatherless."

Adam Johnson's name was duly placed over the door of the chapel, but it was stolen as a student prank in 1829. It wasn't replaced until 1871.

The Cremation of Anna Lytt

When Anna Lytt died in 1882, a bizarre late night funeral was held, filling the streets with devils, ghosts, and rowdies. In reality, Anna Lytt was "analytical geometry," and the mourners were the members of the Amherst College class of 1885. They happily laid to rest the dreaded math course in the kind of mock funeral that had become a tradition at the school.

Mathematics had been burned and buried by Amherst College students since at least the 1860s, usually with good humor, music, and drink. Occasionally, as with the class of 1873, there was a little too much exuberance. The students "serenaded Dr. Hitchcock, Professor Mather, and Mr. Dickinson with horns, creating so much noise and terror in town that a child is said to have been born unexpectedly ... . During a reprimand of the class by Dr. Stearns, W.J. Swift giggled, and was expelled on the spot by Professor Harris."

A program in the shape of a 3-D coffin accompanied Anna Lytt's funeral. In addition, an eight-page booklet was printed, with orations, poems, and a cremation song for the occasion. The procession formed on November 15, 1882, near Zion Chapel on Woodside Avenue. There were four "arch-fiends" on horseback, followed by the North Amherst Cornet Band, "whose make-up," according to the Amherst Record, "suggests the thought that Amherst should have a society for the prevention of cruelty to children."

The class of 1885 followed, dressed in gym shirts and plug hats. A wooden statue of Anna (said to have been "a good deal board by the exercises"), was supported by two ghosts. The devil, with horns, hooves, and tail, led a wildly costumed contingent, looking like "Irish, French, Germans, Indians, and Shutesburyites." Horses pulled a hearse containing the shrouded coffin.

With torches blazing, and dirges playing, the funeral stopped to chant a song about geometry in front of President Seelye's house on College Street.

The climax of the funeral occurred on Blake Field, near today's Pratt Field. The coffin was placed on a great funeral pyre, a mock bishop gave an oration, and then Anna Lytt was cremated. The Amherst Record reported that "there was not a dry eye in the class, but that the throats of some were dry was evidenced when spiritual consolation was offered in the shape of two kegs of cider."

Hot Goo
in the 1890s

The use of slang can reflect the daily life of an era more realistically than standard, printed English. The informal language of Amherst College students in the 1890s, for example, was filled with color, music, and humor. Surprisingly some of that slang is still in use today.

In today's slang, one might call something good by calling it bad. In the 1890s something particularly good was either "dead smooth," or "just out of sight," a phrase that was again very popular in the 1960s. Other accolades included "hot stuff," "hot tomatoes," or "hot goo." "Goo," by the way, was an all-purpose word used for slushy sidewalks, muddy roads, or anything wet and unpleasant.

Slang at Amherst College was fairly typical for a New England college, but there were some differences. At Harvard a dull student would "grub" out his courses, at Wesleyan he would "grind" them out, at Cornell "bone" them out, at Princeton "pole" them out, and at Amherst College "plug" them out.

Some of the 1890s student terms still in use include "cramming, flunking, bluffing, and cribbing." But to fail an exam would mean to be "in the soup," to "get it in the neck," or "get it where the chicken got the ax." On the other hand, an easy exam was, like today, a "snap," or it could be "snapped." Even the poorest student could "rush the hide off it." It could also be described as "neat" or their "particular fruit." To live in a dorm would be to "hang out" there. A student might leave the dorm to go to a "hash house" where various "muckers" spread their bread with "grease" and flavor their coffee with "cow juice."

A lone student on an Amherst street was described as "swinging down the street, his hands seeking his knees through the path of his trousers' pockets." If he were with a young woman, someone might remark, "Binks thinks he cuts all sorts of social ice, don't he? She's a peach; I wouldn't mind myself if I could cut fog with such a girl." A young woman was also called a "fairy," "queen," or "cooler." About a particularly beautiful woman, one would have said, "She's a bird of the desert, ain't she?"

Something Amherst students had little of was money, but they seemed to make up for it with an abundance of words to describe it. One joke that went around had a sophomore asking a friend to lend him "a five dollar William." "What do you mean?" "Oh, I'm not familiar enough with the article to call it a bill." Some of the terms for money were "stuff," "tin," "chink," and "spon." Silver dollars had their own terms, illustrated by the following:

"Yesterday I had money to burn, but I had to pay out a lot of 'shekels' for laundry, five 'plugs' for shoes, fifteen 'doles' for clothes, and then I had to lend Shorty a few 'plunkers' to pay his Society dues. Fifty-five 'sinkers' for tuition, eight 'copeks' for lab fees, and four 'cartwheels' a week for board don't leave a man many 'stamps' for soda, I can tell you."

All of this makes it seem as though Amherst students in the 1890s had "more fun than a goat," as they would have said.

Though many slang words of the 1890s survived, one major trend has shifted. While our slang derives largely from television and computer technology, 19th century slang was derived from agriculture, making creative use of horses, cows, goats, and pigs.

The Golden Age
of New England Academies

On June 7, 1886, one of New England's venerable academies burned to the ground. Monson Academy had been attracting students from many parts of the world and was part of the "golden age" of New England academies. Yet the connection of the school with Amherst and the Dickinsons is little known.

Much is known about Emily Dickinson's paternal grandfather, Samuel Fowler Dickinson. In 1812, he, Noah Webster, and others launched a campaign to begin Amherst Academy. The success of the academy helped lead to the start of Amherst College, and again Samuel Fowler Dickinson was central in fighting for that institution. Dickinson's enthusiasm was unmatched by his business sense, and he quickly exhausted his own assets in the process. In 1833, he had to sell his home and accept a position in Cincinnati.

Emily Dickinson's other grandfather, Joel Norcross, has been largely ignored. Eight years before Samuel Fowler Dickinson helped found Amherst Academy, Joel Norcross did something similar. He became the largest contributor to Monson Academy, after inheriting much of the family estate in that town. For many years he was a trustee and the treasurer of the school. But while Samuel Fowler Dickinson's fortunes dwindled, Joel Norcross prospered, running a general store, and investing in real estate.

Monson Academy developed a national reputation within a few years and then began attracting students from England, Greece, Turkey, China and Japan. Its graduates helped open the West and to carry Christianity to the South Seas. The fates of both the Monson and Amherst academies seemed to cross continually. Monson's first headmaster, Simeon Colton, went on to become principal of Amherst Academy in 1830. One of Colton's earliest acts in Amherst was to send every tavern keeper a letter threatening to prosecute any who sold liquor to his students. One of Monson's graduates, Evangelinus Apostilides Sophocles, later taught Greek at Amherst Academy. Sophocles went on to become a notable professor at Harvard, as well.

Emily Dickinson's mother attended the academy in Monson that her father, Joel Norcross, had helped found. In 1863, when the academy needed funds for renovation, the Dickinsons sent $50.00.

As the century wore on, Amherst Academy suffered from the rival growth of free public high schools, and the building was taken down in 1868. Monson Academy continued to flourish, but when a fire broke out in 1886 in the lamp room and woodshed, the loss was nearly total. Yet within one year the school was rebuilt and ready to take on the 20th century.

The Burning
of Mount Holyoke College

Emily Dickinson entered Mount Holyoke Seminary in 1847. Cinders from this burning building fell on surrounding towns in 1896.

A shower of cinders and pieces of burning carpet fell on the South Amherst farm of Louise Merrick. It was Sunday afternoon, September 27, 1896, and in South Hadley the main building of Mount Holyoke College was burning to the ground.

The cornerstone for the college had been laid in 1836. Mary Lyon was the founder of the school, then known as Mount Holyoke Female Seminary, and it was the first institution designed exclusively for the higher education of women. By the time of the fire, the original building had been expanded into a quadrangle, including a gymnasium, piazzas, and an adjoining water tower, electric plant, and greenhouse.

In the previous century, the first private academy open to both boys and girls had been opened in South Byfield, Massachusetts, in 1761. As for public schools, girls weren't allowed to attend in this state until about 1790, and then only in the summer when boys weren't there.

When Emily Dickinson entered Mount Holyoke Seminary in September, 1847, she began two terms of a rigorous education and lifestyle. It was a school of intense missionary zeal and strict regimentation. In its one large building students lived, studied, and did domestic chores. Dickinson chafed somewhat under the pressures, complaining of having to give a daily account of all her actions. One had to confess the breaking of silent study hours, receiving company in one's room, and "ten thousand other things, which I will not take time ... to mention."

Fasting days seem particularly difficult to us today. One was expected to abstain from all worldly pleasures, "society, reading, study, walking, riding, writing letters, worldly musings," and to "afflict the soul by bringing painful subjects before the mind," according to Mary Lyon's writings.

Though Dickinson wouldn't devote her life to Christ, many Mount Holyoke women did, becoming missionaries in India, Turkey, and Japan. In 1888, the school became Mount Holyoke Seminary and College, and in 1893, it dropped "seminary" from its name. When the historic original seminary building burned in 1896, news spread to many parts of the world, to "wherever Holyoke women were holding up the ideals of the gospel," as the Boston Congregationalist reported.

The fire may have started in the laundry room. Fortunately, alarm boxes had been installed in nearly every corridor, and the women had been drilled in how to escape. Fire steamers came from Holyoke and Northampton, but arrived too late. The students and teachers were remarkably efficient in saving the library books and their belongings. Only a Miss Knapp was "overcome by the excitement" and had to be taken to the Holyoke hospital. A tramp attempted "to levy upon some of the goods" but was promptly arrested. The glow from the flames was visible from many surrounding towns, and hotels and lodging houses in the area were crowded with the displaced students. Local families generously opened their homes to the students in a spirit of hospitality.

*From Amherst
to Beirut*

*Emily Dickinson's close friend Abby Wood and her husband Daniel Bliss left Amherst for the
Middle East in 1856.*

The American University of Beirut was the focus of many acts of terrorism in the 1980s. In 1983, terrorists shot Acting President Malcolm Kerr twice in the head. While our attention was rightly on the large issues, few have been aware that a close friend of Emily Dickinson was involved in the founding of the university. In 1866, Abby Bliss went to Beirut with her husband Daniel, where he organized the American University, a unique 19th century school, and a 20th century political target.

Abby Maria Wood was born in 1830, the same year as Emily Dickinson, in Westminster, Massachusetts. After her father Joel Wood's death in 1833, she came to live in Amherst with her uncle Luke Sweetser, a neighbor of the Dickinsons. She and Emily became fast friends while attending Amherst Academy and, in fact, Abby became part of Emily's close circle called "the five." This included Abby Wood, Abiah Root, Harriet Merrill, Sarah Tracy, and Emily.

Abby was swept up by the fervent religious revivals of the time and officially joined the church in the summer of 1850. Emily never joined the church and their friendship drifted from this time. Of Abby, Emily wrote, "She is more of a woman than I am, for I so love to be a child — Abby is holier than me ... . She will be had in memorial when I am gone and forgotten."

Abby's change in direction partially accounted for her attraction to Rev. Daniel Bliss, born in Vermont in 1823, whom she married on November 23, 1855. Bliss received a B.A. in 1852, an M.A. in 1855, and a D.D. in 1864, all from Amherst College. Abby and Daniel Bliss went to the Middle East in 1856. By 1864, they were in London raising funds for the American University of Beirut, then called the Syrian Protestant College. The college had been incorporated in 1863, and its endowment was raised in England and America.

When Daniel Bliss, the school's first president, laid the cornerstone, he spoke in highly idealistic terms: "The College is for all conditions and classes of men without regard to colour, nationality, race or religion. A man white, black or yellow; Christian, Jew, Mohammedan or heathen, may enter and enjoy all the advantages of this institution for 3, 4, or 8 years; and go out believing in one God, in many Gods, or in no God. But it would be impossible for any one to continue with us long without knowing what we believe to be the truth and our reason for that belief."

When classes began in the fall of 1866, the college's stated aim was to use Christian learning to help carry the Gospel to "unenlightened" lands. Eventually, however, the religious aspects were made secondary to education. From the start efforts were made to respect the students' culture. Classes were taught in Arabic for several years, until it became too difficult to find qualified teachers and up-to-date texts.

The American University of Beirut is a direct outgrowth of the kind of education the Dickinsons helped establish in Amherst. To its credit, the university has been called the most influential American institution of learning outside the U.S. It helped mold the idealogy and supply the leaders of the Arab national movement in the East. Virtually every government in the Arab world today contains at least one Cabinet member who graduated from the university.

Daniel was president of the American University of Beirut until 1902, and continued to live there until his death in 1916. Abby Bliss had visited Amherst in the summer of 1873. Emily was by then living as a recluse, yet Abby was able to see her, face-to-face, as few did in those years. Abby Wood Bliss died in 1915.

Was It Murder
at Amherst College?

*President Hitchcock couldn't forgive the
brutal assault on Jonathan Torrence.*

Amherst College students have a long history of creative and
sometimes outrageous pranks. Whether it was the stealing of the
statue of Sabrina or the hiding of a cow in South College, Amherst
has reacted with amusement and exasperation. But in 1847, when
a freshman died after a practical joke, college president Edward
Hitchcock considered it a crime of murder.

When Jonathan Torrence came from Enfield to enter Amherst
College in the fall of 1847, he had every intention of becoming a
minister. His brother William had graduated from Amherst in
1844, and was described as having an excellent character as a scholar
and a Christian.

It had been a tradition at Amherst for the upper-classmen to
assault the freshmen in various ways for the first few weeks of the

autumn semester. According to President Hitchcock, "But even when fun and sport are the professed object, such recklessness and abuse are often witnessed to result in lasting, and sometimes fatal effects."

One chilly night in the fall of 1847, Jonathan Torrence lay sleeping in his bed. Suddenly his door burst open and someone drenched him with buckets of water. Having just arrived from the country, and being unsure of what to do, he did nothing. He shortly withdrew from Amherst because of illness.

Hitchcock had become president of the college in 1845, at a time when his own health was very poor, and he didn't expect to remain in the position for more than a few years. Concerned for the health of Torrence, he stopped to see him several months after the incident. Hitchcock suspected the illness had originated with the treatment the boy received as a freshman, and upon seeing Torrence concluded it was true. He was dismayed to find the boy suffering the last stages of consumption.

"Do you now feel," Hitchcock asked, "as if you could forgive those who have murdered you?"

"Yes, I forgive them." Hitchcock could not forgive them though. Here was a boy on his death bed "solely as the result of the brutal assault of those who probably would prove only curses to the world." Torrence wouldn't, or perhaps couldn't, identify his assailants. When Hitchcock wrote his memoirs he concluded that Torrence was the "victim of a barbarous college custom. Whether his murderers still haunt the earth I know not, but I do know that they must meet him at the judgment seat."

Hitchcock felt that the professors' lectures against such pranks were "like feathers thrown against a hurricane," and that such problems made "a President's seat more often a cushion of briars and nettles than of roses and feathers."

Lest we be surprised at this "constant state of turbulence" at a college that trained men for the ministry, Hitchcock provides us with a possible reason. The Amherst president claimed that the more religious a college, the more certain would be the number of rowdy students, because parents sent unruly boys to such places for conversion.

The Starvation Stand-up
at Smith College

In the early 1890s, the social life of men at Amherst College was dry indeed. Tempted by two nearby female colleges, Amherst's young men went to great lengths to see women. But the restrictive visitation rules at Mount Holyoke made the school appear convent-like, and Smith's attempt at a social event with Amherst men was commonly dubbed "The Starvation Stand-up."

For Amherst men to reach Mount Holyoke or Smith in this period meant a trip by horse and buggy, or a ride on the infrequent trains to Northampton. Student Alfred Stearns claimed that in his four years, Mount Holyoke women played little if any part in the social life of Amherst College. Stearns felt that Smith's "Starvation Stand-up" or "Ten Mile Walk Around" was a poor attempt at

Smith College, on the other side of the Connecticut River from Amherst, where Amherst College men sought female companionship.

socializing and was a "gruesome affair." These parties were held in the evening at Smith and were crowded and stuffy. If floor space could be found there might be square dancing, but other dances were strictly forbidden. Refreshments were extremely meager and locating the serving tables a challenge.

The Amherst Student newspaper described such receptions as "a cross between a funeral and a kettle drum ... . We should call it a church sociable, but church sociables usually furnish something to gratify the inner man ... . We should call it the annual exhibition of the inmates of an orphan asylum, but the contribution box is not circulated."

Alfred Stearns and his friends decided to counter this with a dance of their own, which proved to be a local scandal. Five Amherst men and five Smith women planned to rent the gym at the Capon School in Northampton and hold a cotillion, without the knowledge of the college authorities. Since, because of curfews, an evening affair would have to end at 10 p.m., they decided to hold the dance at 10 a.m. Refreshments would be served at noon, and dancing would continue into the afternoon. To make it seem like a formal evening affair, shades would be drawn, lights turned up, and guests would come in full evening dress.

The date was set for Washington's birthday, and as the Amherst men left the train in Northampton the night before, they were met by a raging blizzard. They struggled to a hotel for the night and dressed in evening clothes the next morning. The Smith women were disappointed to learn that the men from Yale and Williams would probably not arrive because of the storm. Of course, the Amherst men were delighted to find that they would then be outnumbered by women.

The affair was a great success, but according to Alfred Stearns the "stiff-necked conservatives of Northampton" considered it a scandalous outrage.

Chapter Six

CRIME: CURSED, POISONED, SHOT, AND HANGED

Corner Please
Meadow St
North Amhers

The corner of Pleasant and Meadow Streets, North Amherst

The Whole of it came not at once -
'Twas Murder by degrees -
A Thrust - and then for Life a chance -
The Bliss to cauterize -
#762

The Curse of
Ebenezer Dickinson

Ebenezer Dickinson fled from his troubles in Amherst and reached Ohio by early 1816. With several friends and relatives suing him, and the authorities accusing him of theft, Dickinson had reason enough to leave. Not one to accept defeat easily, Dickinson hurled a curse upon the land that was at the center of his ill luck. His curse on Factory Hollow came back to haunt Amherst over the decades. For, coincidence or not, a series of fires destroyed the mills in the Hollow again and again.

Ebenezer Dickinson had been born in Amherst in 1779. He married Abigail Barrows, had five children, and joined the Pacific Lodge of Masons (only to be sued by its treasurer later). This well-to-do farmer then turned to a new enterprise. In about 1809, he built a three-story wooden cotton mill in Factory Hollow, North Amherst. With little experience, he set up machinery to spin yarn, but instead spun a tangled skein of bad debts and law suits.

In 1812, 10 men took over the cotton factory, and in 1814, Amherst Cotton Factory became the first legally chartered manufacturing corporation in Amherst. Among the 10 investors was Emily Dickinson's grandfather, Samuel Fowler Dickinson. The company made cotton yarn which it gave out to families to be woven into fabric on hand looms. Poor management, under a hired

This North Amherst mill, among others, burned after Ebenezer Dickinson left his curse on Factory Hollow.

English factory foreman, helped lead to the company's eventual collapse. This was just one of the investment blunders made by the well-meaning Samuel Fowler Dickinson. Unfortunately, this came at the same time (1813) that he needed cash for the building of his famous Homestead on Main Street.

Court records show Ebenezer Dickinson being called before the Supreme Judicial Court of 1815, held in Northampton. He had to answer suits being brought by Noah Mattoon, Lucius Field, the State of Massachusetts, and Abijah Dickinson, his own brother. The Court sent Sheriff Ebenezer Mattoon to fetch Dickinson, since he had already failed to appear for at least one other hearing. On May 1, 1815, Ebenezer Dickinson was ordered to make a complete list of his worldly possessions, under penalty of $100 if he refused.

At some point, Ebenezer broke into the cotton factory he once owned and stole a quantity of cotton yarn. The yarn was found by an officer in the garret of his house. Dickinson fled to Ohio and was not heard from until April, 1816. In a letter sent to his brother Abijah from Charlestown, Ohio, Ebenezer told of his arrival, of being sick for four weeks, and of purchasing a farm with 265 apple trees. Ebenezer asked his brother to sell some of his Amherst land, and added, "I shall make awl things Rite." But as for returning East to do so he could only say, "When I shall come to Amherst I Cannot tel."

Dickinson's parting curse on Factory Hollow seemed to be his lasting mark on the town. Cotton and woolen mills on the river at the bottom of the Hollow burned down in 1842, 1847, 1851, and 1857. Dickinson himself died poor and soon — within a year of his 1816 arrival in Ohio he was dead. Dickinson's wife and children bravely returned to Amherst.

A Twisted Tale of
Pursuit, Escape, and Death

Moses B. Dickinson was trusting, perhaps too trusting. Twice in his life he helped out men who were down on their luck, and both times he paid a price. The first time cost him the shame of being arrested; the second time cost him his life.

Moses was born in South Amherst in 1816. At age 15 he joined his father, Oliver Dickinson, in a successful business hauling freight between Amherst and Boston by horse and wagon. Moses and his brother, Waitstill, eventually bought the business, but the coming of the railroad in 1853 made their horse and wagon obsolete for long hauls.

Moses married Electa Dickinson in 1840, and the couple had seven children. After 1853, the family lived on a tobacco farm on the north side of Northampton Road. Moses had been a rugged, healthy man until illness struck and a physician prescribed morphine. According to one account, "The use of morphine at this time grew into a habit which he never resisted, and which made him irritable and cross in his family, — a habit much worse than liquor drinking ... . He was eccentric and his habit of using large quantities of opium increased this tendency to a marked degree. He did not believe in having his photograph taken, and the result is that no member of his family or brother or sister has his likeness in their possession." His entire family eventually left him to live the last days of his life alone.

In 1858, Charles Wiley stopped at Dickinson's farm and asked for a ride to Hadley. Dickinson offered to take Wiley in his wagon, not realizing he was aiding an escaped drunk in making a getaway. Wiley was a poor laborer, the son of Samuel Wiley and Sally Lombard. Constable Howe had arrested Wiley for drunkenness in Amherst on August 8th, but the man slipped out of jail.

Once in Hadley, Wiley convinced lawyer Robert Ingram to plead his case before the Amherst Selectmen. The unwitting Moses Dickinson agreed to drive Ingram to Amherst. There Ingram bargained that Wiley would stay away from Amherst during college commencement week if the Selectmen wouldn't prosecute him.

The Selectmen would only consent if Wiley would disclose how he had acquired the liquor — suspecting he had bought it from an unlicensed shop owner. Wiley refused. Dickinson and Ingram headed back to Hadley, apparently with Wiley hidden in the wagon. Constable Howe pursued them with a warrant for Wiley's arrest, but Wiley whipped the horses, jumped from

Dickinson's wagon, and ran off into the woods.

Moses Dickinson was arrested for his part in the escape, but was acquitted when it couldn't be proved that he knew Wiley was a fugitive when he got involved.

The second recorded time that Dickinson helped a desperate man was in 1875. In early November, Moses' wife left him. He then hired a homeless, probably insane man, Allen J. Adams, to help at the farm. On Thanksgiving evening, two of his sons found Dickinson's bloody body in his kitchen.

Ten years later, Allen Adams confessed to the ax murder of Moses Dickinson and was executed on the gallows of the Northampton jail.

An Old-Fashioned Hanging

Over 150 people gathered to watch as the sad life of Allen J. Adams ended on the gallows on April 16, 1886. Adams had slept fitfully the night before, complaining that his cell was too hot. At 6:30 in the morning he eagerly ate his last meal — eggs, doughnuts, crackers, and mince pie. He remarked to his jailor that he wanted a square meal to go on "as he was going on the Morning Glory." Adams added that he would not "blubber on the scaffold." Adams hoped it would "rain like hell" so no one would come out to see his execution, which was to take place in Northampton.

The father of Allen J. Adams owned a small farm in Amherst and was described as a "drunken, half imbecile." The Amherst Record said that "all accounts agree that the family were a good-for-nothing, shiftless set." Allen was said to be "low down on the scale of civilization, a coarse, ignorant, vain, conceited, ill-mannered brute."

Adams considered himself a tramp. After working on Moses Dickinson's farm for two or three weeks, he decided to murder the man, purely for the $150 Dickinson made from the sale of tobacco. "I wanted to kill him that day with a sled stake in the corner of the barn but didn't dare to because it was daylight." Instead, two days later, he murdered Dickinson with an ax while the man slept. Adams headed south, but he quickly was drugged and robbed of the money in New Haven.

Ten years later, Adams was living in Tennessee. He was overheard boasting of the murder, and it wasn't long before he found himself facing justice in Northampton. The gallows had been used only two times previously in Hampshire County in the 19th century. In 1806 and 1814, murderers had been hanged on Gallows Plain on Hospital Hill. Both times the event was accompanied by the town band, and it was claimed that thousands attended.

By the time of the Adams hanging in 1886, outdoor extravaganzas were considered too barbaric. Instead the gallows was set up inside the Northampton jail, more than 150 guests were invited, and the newspapers reported every grisly detail. Near the end, Adams was kept under constant watch, after he had slashed his legs with a knife. On the morning of the hanging Adams sneered and swore at every opportunity. He told Sheriff Clark to read the death warrant and be damned. When the sheriff read off Adams's name and his alias, Adams remarked, "Why the hell don't you take on a couple more names; who the devil are you going to hang anyway?"

Adams cursed Rev. A.M. Colton, who delivered the prayer, and the men who bound him and brought him to the gallows, calling them "damned cut throats and highway robbers." Sheriff Gallond placed the long black cap over Adams's head. As the noose was adjusted around his neck, Adams spoke his last words: "Don't choke me till the time comes."

The body fell at 10:37, and 18 1/2 minutes later "life was pronounced extinct." The Amherst Record listed the man's heart rate minute-by-minute as he died.

The hanging roused the changing feelings of people in the Valley. Seth Hunt wrote in the Springfield Republican that "capital punishment belongs to a dark heathenish age, when bloody sacrifices were deemed necessary to atone for sin and appease the wrath of the gods; but it is out of place here and now."

A Pelham
Murder Mystery

An abandoned barn in Pelham, the town that borders Amherst on the east.

What does one think when the dog brings home what appears to be a piece of human scalp? And what is to be made of the fresh blood found on the floor of an isolated, empty house? And the fact that in the basement of that house the dirt has been recently dug up? In Pelham, in August of 1876, all these clues came together and led to one conclusion: Murder.

King Street in Pelham no longer exists, having been discontinued in 1914. It ran off of South Valley Road and was the site of the old John Shaw farm. Dan Benjamin rented the Shaw place, but didn't live in it. Benjamin did plant a garden there, however, and in early August of 1876, his wife went to the empty farm alone to gather cucumbers. Upon stepping into the house she saw fresh blood on the floor. Mrs. Benjamin ran from the house and stopped Leonard Baker, who happened to be passing by with a cow. Baker told her he had heard noises coming from the house, further frightening the distraught woman.

Justin Canterbury was a Pelham blacksmith who had a shop in the southern part of town. At about the time of Mrs. Benjamin's gory discovery, Canterbury's Eskimo dog brought him what looked like a piece of human scalp covered with hair. This news reached Amherst along with the rumor that there was a freshly dug grave in the basement of the Benjamins' rented house. Amherst Sheriff George Gallond was called out to apply his Holmesian skills to this mystery.

Officer Gallond and several others went to Pelham on Saturday, August 19, 1876, and began to interview the townspeople. Justin Canterbury was of little help, having lost the piece of scalp. Yet he and his wife continued to insist that it was indeed human.

It was Leonard Baker who, after denying he knew anything, revealed the truth. Baker said that Dan Benjamin and Charles Kimball left the blood on the floor after trapping a woodchuck and skinning it there in the house. The grave in the cellar was actually the spot where a former tenant had buried a barrel of potatoes to keep them from freezing.

But what of the human scalp? Justin Canterbury's dog had dug up the shallow grave of an old horse that had belonged to Charles Kimball. The "scalp" was simply a piece of horsehide.

The Amherst Record commented that, "out of these things the suspicions and jealousies of the neighborhood and the excited imaginations have doubtless made up the story of murder."

The All-Night Stake-Out for Chicken Thieves

In 1876, Samuel Clemens' *Adventures of Tom Sawyer* was published, wherein Tom imagined himself unfurling a black flag with a skull and cross-bones on it. He saw himself as "Tom Sawyer the Pirate! — the Black Avenger of the Spanish Main," and decided to run away and begin his career as a buccaneer. Two years after the book was published, Amherst had its own Tom Sawyers and Huck Finns. Their romantic notions of striking out on their own led to a night in the lock-up, and to a trial that attracted throngs of excited onlookers.

A South Amherst farmer discovered stolen chickens in his field, left there by two would-be Tom Sawyers.

It was May of 1878, when a South Amherst farmer was out working in his fields east of the railroad crossing on South East Street. Though he was half a mile from any dwelling he heard roosters crowing. Following the sound, he located a box buried in the ground containing several chickens and roosters. The farmer notified Sheriff George Gallond, who considered the crime of the stolen fowl to be serious enough to set up an all-night stake-out at the scene.

Constable William Smith and his assistant Blanchard spent

Monday night, May 27th, waiting for the chicken thieves to return. Early the next morning several boys crept up and placed an assortment of groceries into another box hidden in the ground. The hidden box already contained tools and other survival supplies. The boys were promptly arrested and brought to the town jail on North Pleasant Street.

On Thursday, May 30th, the day of their trial, neighbors crowded the streets, eager to hear the details of the crime.

One at a time, the culprits told the same story before Justice Edward A. Thomas: Inspired by the enchanting stories of wild and adventurous buccaneers, the boys captured land in North Belchertown. There they planned to build a cabin and to go into the chicken business, using the fowl they had stolen. In their innocence they hadn't expected that their new lives would be discovered.

The boys plead guilty and, being minors, their names weren't published. Justice Thomas fined them from $3.00 to $20.00 each and gave them a stern lecture. The Amherst Record concluded that, "The advice of the officer will likely be heeded if chickens are in that way demanded again, and roosters that crow in the morning will be passed by as poor plunder."

Cattle Rustling
in The Valley

Every spring in the 1800s, farmers herded their cattle and sheep from Amherst up to the hill pastures of surrounding towns for the summer. Inevitably, when they brought the herds and flocks down again in the fall, they had fewer cattle than they started with. In 1876, for example, L.V.B. Cook of Belchertown noticed that a cow was missing from his herd. The subsequent search for a single bovine led to arrests, and bitter accusations of thievery, polygamy, and general low morals in the quiet town of Shutesbury.

Cook owned what was known as the Shores Farm on the North Belchertown road, which leads from Pratt's Corner to Shutesbury. He had hired Rector Pratt to look after his stock while in the pasture, but in October of 1876, Cook discovered that a young cow was gone. The hide of the heifer was later found half buried in the woods, and within a mile of it was a broken piece from the bottom of a buggy. The evidence was given to Sheriff George Gallond of Amherst to begin an investigation.

The next clue came while George LaPlatt was hunting in the area. LaPlatt came upon the spot where the cow had been hung up for butchering. The Amherst Record began pointing fingers at families in Pelham and Shutesbury, which had "long been notorious for being the harboring places of, and infested by a low-bred class of people called sneak thieves." Pelham and especially Shutesbury-bashing had become a custom in the Amherst newspaper by this time. The paper also accused certain families of polygamy and adultery, and particularly singled out the Shutesbury Pratt family for suspicion.

A break in the case came when Rufus Munsell, related to the Pratts by marriage, happened to stay at the Union Hotel on Main Street, Amherst. Sheriff Gallond noticed something peculiar about Munsell's buggy. Gallond found that the buggy piece found near the scene of the crime was a perfect fit for Munsell's buggy. This led to the arrest of Rufus Munsell and John Pratt (who was later released).

At Munsell's hearing in Shutesbury, Edward Webster was the prosecutor, and John Jameson the defending attorney. Testifying against Munsell was Ann Pratt, described as "a Spanish lady of some intelligence." She told of a night in October, during the Belchertown cattle show, when 13 Pratts stayed at the Munsell place on Belchertown's Great Hill. Mrs. Pratt recalled breakfasting on beefsteak and being shown the great store of meat laid in for winter use in the basement. When Ann commented, "Oh what a nice lot of meat you have got," the candle was at once extinguished.

It took nearly two years to bring Munsell and the Pratts to justice. Meanwhile, by the end of March, 1878, the Munsells and the Pratts were embroiled in accusations of polygamy and several were arrested. It was a complicated, sad case that is perhaps better left alone.

Shutesbury, where Amherst people thought cattle rustling and polygamy reigned.

Did Maria Wellman Poison Two Husbands?

When Alexis Smith married Maria Wellman in 1851, the couple left North Amherst to buy a farm in Vermont. A few years later Maria allegedly poisoned Alexis to death, and in 1878, she was accused of poisoning her second husband as well.

Alexis Smith was born in Bolton, New York, in 1809. For many years his family lived in Vermont, then in about 1838 his parents, Elijah and Rebecca, moved the Smith family to North Amherst.

Maria Wellman was born in Westminster, Vermont, in 1821. She received a reasonable education for the period and joined the church when she was young. While visiting relatives in North Amherst in about 1850, Maria met Alexis Smith.

The Boston Journal described Alexis as "a very quiet kind of man." His friends suggested that Maria must have done most of the courting. Reverend Rufus Smith married them in Brookline, Vermont, on May 28, 1851. The Boston Journal pointed out that the farm they moved to in Dummerston was bought in Maria's name.

Alexis died very suddenly one night in terrible spasms, though he had been in his usual good health that day. His mother and father were notified, and they immediately left Amherst for Dummerston, only to find that Alexis had been hastily buried. This led to a lot of speculation in Amherst about the nature of the death. Maria went on to marry Cyrus Hardy and to live with him and his son Frederick in Marlboro, New Hampshire. On April 1st, 1878, 19 year-old Frederick called a lawyer in Keene and asked that his step-mother be arrested for the murder of his father. Attorney General Mason Tappan interviewed Frederick and placed the case in the hands of Boston detective Moses Sargent.

An autopsy showed that Cyrus Hardy had been poisoned with strychnine. No one doubted that Maria had done it. She was arrested in Marlboro and taken to Keene by carriage, reciting Scripture and singing hymns all the way. As the carriage rolled down the main street of Keene she sang,

> Whate'er we do, where'er we roam,
> We're travelling to the grave.

At the Keene jail the sheriff's wife made her comfortable and gave her a Bible, from which she frequently read aloud.

The Boston Journal reported that insanity ran in Maria's family.

Her grandmother "died insane, her sister while insane cut her throat, and she now has an aunt who is insane."

It is quite certain that after poisoning two husbands, Maria Wellman spent the rest of her days under the primitive conditions of an asylum.

Killed by Poisoned Oysters

In the autumn of 1947, Professor Valentine made a macabre discovery in the basement of his home and called the state police. Valentine, a professor at Springfield College, had recently bought the old Burleigh farm in Palmer. In the dirt floor of his basement he had unearthed a gravestone that told the bizarre tale of a wife who killed her husband with poisoned oysters.

Valentine was afraid that beneath the gravestone would be found a body. When the state police arrived, one of them recognized the tombstone as the famous missing Gibbs stone from Pelham. The headstone, which was widely famed for its inscription, had disappeared from Knight's Cemetery in Pelham seven years before. Its startling inscription reads:

> *Warren Gibbs*
> *Died by arsenic poison*
> *March 23, 1860 Aged 36 years*
> *5 months and 23 days.*
> *Think my friends when this you see*
> *How my wife hath dealt by me*
> *She in some oysters did prepare*
> *Some poison for my lot and share*
> *Then of the same I did partake*
> *And nature yielded to its fate*
> *Before she my wife became*
> *Mary Felton was her name.*
> *Erected by his brother*
> *William Gibbs*

Warren Gibbs had been born in Prescott on September 30, 1833, one of eight children of Solomon and Olive Gibbs. Gibbs became a sawyer in Prescott, where he lived until at least 1850, and married Mary Felton. By 1860, Gibbs was apparently living in Pelham. Warren Gibbs did not live long enough to serve in the Civil War. During that war other members of the Gibbs family allegedly stole horses, painted them beyond recognition and sold them to the government.

When Warren Gibbs died in 1860, he was buried in Knight's Cemetery in Pelham. After his death nothing untoward was hinted at in the newspapers. No accusations of foul play, no arrests. It wasn't until 1884, after years of rumors, that Warren's brother

William erected the famous tombstone, etching in stone his damning verdict of Warren's wife Mary. The reaction to the epitaph was immediate: Mary's relatives demolished the stone.

Later, the tombstone was carved once again, and it was this stone that disappeared in 1940 and reappeared in Professor Valentine's basement in Palmer. Today the famous Poisoned Oysters Stone can be seen in the museum of the Pelham Historical Society.

The Alms House Poisoning in Hadley

Whether called alms houses, poor farms, or town farms, the 19th century institutions for care of the poor were often dismal settings for tragedy. The poor were housed together with the mentally ill, physically disabled, and the marginally criminal. Amherst's Town Farm, at the South Amherst Common, was burned to the ground by one of the residents in 1882. Hadley's Alms House was a similarly unfortunate place, where in 1886 Sarah Hunter attempted a mass poisoning.

Hadley bought a farm at the upper end of East Street in 1878 to run as a poor farm. Prior to that date the town paid individual families to board the poor. In addition, there seems to have been a separate "shanty" largely for poor blacks. The town expected a certain stigma to be attached to living on the poor farm, and thus limited the freedom of movement and other liberties of the "inmates."

On Saturday morning, October 30, 1886, Sarah Hunter, while living in the Hadley Alms House, poisoned all the food in the place. An article in the Amherst Record titled "Wholesale Poisoning at the Hadley Alms House," described Sarah as "not regarded as being very bright." She was the wife of Dexter Hunter, a Hadley farmer on Russell Road.

The matron of the Alms House, Mrs. Haskins, first detected a peculiar odor rising from some pumpkin that she was cooking for pies. She didn't think anything more about it until noon when she went to a jar to get some mixed pickles, what was then called "chow-chow," for the dinner table. The same smell, only stronger, was evident there.

Mrs. Haskins called her husband who recognized the smell as oil of cedar. He checked a bottle of it he had bought for killing fleas on a dog, and found it empty. The couple confronted Sarah Hunter, whom they suspected because they had earlier that day scolded her for punishing a small child who lived there. Sarah initially denied the charge, but later confessed, saying she meant to kill everyone in the house. Everything edible in the Alms House was thrown away before anyone was harmed, and Sarah Hunter was arrested.

In reporting news, the Amherst Record seldom made an attempt at objectivity. On December 29, 1886, the paper reported the outcome of the attempted poisoning. The grand jury had dismissed the case on the grounds that Sarah Hunter was "of weak mind and did not intend to do harm." The newspaper agreed that she was mentally unstable, but felt that, regardless of her mental abilities, she had attempted to poison many people and should have been given the maximum sentence allowed.

The Night Hoodlums Ruled Amherst

More than 100 Christmases ago, Amherst read the following disturbing headline: "Hoodlums Trying to Rule the Town — Three Shots Fired But Nobody Killed." It all began on Christmas Eve 1886 at a social dance put on by the employees of the Hills Hat Factory.

The Hills Factory Christmas Eve dance was held in Masonic Hall, which was on the third floor of Cook's Block on Main Street. Tom, Jack, and George White were the sons of "Irish John" White. Irish John was a farmer on East Pleasant Street, and his boys had a reputation for rowdiness. When the White boys appeared at Masonic Hall on Christmas Eve, the managers of the dance turned them away. They then went downstairs in the same building to Robert Kenfield's billiard hall, where they became so boisterous that Kenfield had to send for Night Policeman Tillson.

It was about 11:30 and Tillson had just completed his rounds near the railroad depot on Main Street. He walked through the rain back toward the center of town, stopping to turn out the gaslight in front of the Amherst Record office. Kenfield's urgent message reached Tillson as he was passing Kellogg's Block at the north end of the Common. The policeman ran up to the billiard room to find the White brothers brawling with each other. He got them out of the building and out on to the sidewalk, where Jack and Tom began to argue about where they would sleep that night.

Jack was described as being "insolent and ugly from the effects of liquor" when Tillson attempted to arrest him and take him to the town lock-up. At that point, according to the newspaper report, "a lively tussle took place, in which Tillson used his club to the best advantage he could." Several people gathered, but no one answered Tillson's call for help.

Jack's younger brother George joined the fray by breaking a bottle against Tillson's forehead, cutting him severely. Jack ran off while George went for Tillson again. Tillson pulled out his revolver, aimed at George and fired three shots, to unknown effect. Charles Osgood, a hat factory worker who had been at the dance, helped Tillson to Dr. Fish's office on Amity Street. The White brothers "took a sudden leave of absence" and Tillson pluckily continued his usual rounds until dawn, with his head in bandages.

Late in January, it was reported that George White had taken a livery team out of town, and then went by train to another state. The Amherst Record thought this a good time to establish a larger

Amherst police force, which at that time had only one night officer. As for George White, the paper suggested he would be better off if he returned to Amherst to "face the music, if any is to be made."

It's Hard to Ignore
a Shooting on Main Street

Main Street, Amherst, where an occasional murder could not be ignored.

Sometimes a newspaper says too much, sometimes too little. In the case of a shooting on Main Street in 1913, the Amherst Record reported only part of the story, in deference to an old Amherst family. After describing the arrest of Fred Brown for the attempted murder of Louis Dickinson, it promised to report later on the circumstances behind it. Instead, the newspaper backed away from the story. One has to either search the court records or the out-of-town newspapers to find the reason Brown shot Dickinson in the dining room of Sisson Hotel.

Louis H. Dickinson was a carriage painter whose shop was on Amherst's Main Street. He had been born in South Amherst in 1861, and he and his wife, Harriet Shaw of Belchertown, made their home on Main Street. Dickinson's path often crossed that of Frederick L. Brown, who also lived and worked on Main Street. Brown was 26 years-old, and he had worked for seven years delivering groceries for Shumway's Grocery Store.

Between 8:00 and 9:00 on Saturday night April 12, 1913, Louis Dickinson was playing cards in the office of the Sisson Hotel.

The hotel was a popular one, close by the Main Street railroad station. Fred Brown was delivering groceries to the hotel that night when he passed through the office. The two men saw each other, and shortly thereafter Dickinson had a bullet lodged near his spine. The Amherst Record would only say that "There had been bad blood between them for some time," and that the circumstances would not be described until after the court hearing.

A hearing was held in Northampton on April 19th, at which the recovering Louis Dickinson gave testimony. The final hearing before the Grand Jury was held on June 9th, with the attempted murder charge against Brown being dropped, and Brown being released.

The Amherst Record reported the bare facts, and omitted the sad reasons that drove the men to such violence. The Northampton Herald and the Hampshire Gazette, on the other hand, objectively filled in the missing facts, regardless of the potential embarrassment to those involved.

In court, Dickinson testified that Brown had been "intimate" with his wife for three years, frequently spending the evening with her, and occasionally walking the back streets with her. The Dickinsons separated in February and in March, Dickinson had grabbed Brown's collar and threatened to give him "a cuffing."

In the Sisson Hotel on April 12th, Dickinson spotted Brown and followed him into the dining room. He grabbed Brown, slapped him several times, then Brown pulled his revolver and shot Dickinson in the side. Sheriff David Tillson was called, and Dickinson was taken to the Amherst Cottage Hospital on Kellogg Avenue.

The trial was a revelation of human weaknesses gone awry. Accusations of drunkenness and infidelity were exposed, yet townspeople vouched for the character of both men. The court didn't find enough evidence to hold Brown and released him.

Frederick Brown left Amherst to work in Springfield. Louis Dickinson continued to live in Amherst with his wife and family until he died in 1936.

Poisoned in the Lost Town of Greenwich

Greenwich Church, lost along with the secrets of an arsenic poisoning when the town disappeared beneath the Quabbin Reservoir.

Many secrets died with the town of Greenwich when the waters of the Quabbin Reservoir washed over it. The town officially ended its existence in 1938, and among the questions left unanswered was the identity of Shubel Vaughn's killer. Did Vaughn's wife poison him, as most people seemed to think, or did someone, perhaps his own brother, give him the arsenic?

Jane Vaughn was born in Nova Scotia in 1870. In October of 1874, Jane advertised for a situation as a housekeeper, and was hired by J.F. Sampson of North Prescott.

Jane soon met Shubel Vaughn of Greenwich and married him two weeks later, on January 5, 1875. Their wedding day was only the second time the couple had set eyes on each other. Mrs. Vaughn testified later that the couple was relatively happy, but that "sometimes people do not always agree." The two had strong differences on the subject of religion.

Shubel Vaughn died on April 4, 1877. The local doctors, Lindsey and Orcutt, had been prescribing medicine for him up to within a week of his death, during which time Vaughn refused to take any medication from his wife. Vaughn said she was trying to poison him. As the man died, he complained of the soreness of his mouth and while his body was being prepared for burial one of his teeth fell out.

Within a short time, Shubel's 75 year-old brother Purrington Vaughn proposed to the widow, but he was turned down. Instead, Jane married Amos Doubleday the following October, a date thought by most to be too soon for a grieving widow. This apparently turned rumors and suspicion into action.

Shubel Vaughn's body was exhumed in December, 1877. Chemist William B. Hills of Boston dissected the body for analysis. All internal organs were examined and on January 5, 1878, tests on the liver revealed metallic arsenic.

In late May of 1878, Jane was accused of poisoning Shubel, and an inquest was held before Justice E.A. Thomas in Greenwich. Sixteen witnesses were questioned by District Attorney Bond of Northampton. Jane commented that she didn't know how Shubel had gotten the arsenic and she wished he were alive. Greenwich was said to be "thoroughly aroused" by the two-day investigation.

A week later the Amherst Record summed up the case with these words: "The whole testimony by no means proved her innocence, but was not sufficient to warrant her arrest, and the case was finally dropped, although popular opinion and belief is strong against her."

Chapter Seven

❧

TECHNOLOGY: TWO STEPS FORWARD, ONE STEP BACK

In Dickinson's day, mills and farms like these were joined by factories.

Why should we hurry - why indeed
When every way we fly
We are molested equally
By immortality
#1646

Inventions for
Pickpockets and Privy Seats

When faced with astronomic deficits or plagued by tapeworms, Americans have always shown remarkable inventiveness. The U.S. Patent office is bursting with ideas for goggles for chickens, improved privy seats, and mechanical devices to produce or maintain dimples. Amherst has been home to a number of inventors. Some, like Porter Dickinson, did quite well. In 1854, Dickinson was awarded a diploma for his corn sheller. He sold the rights to it for $6,000, a fortune at the time. In the same year, Daniel Warner, Jr., received a patent for an improved flax machine. But it was Joseph Colton who came up with the solution to a problem one would not have thought existed in rural Amherst. In 1845, Colton invented an anti-pickpocket device.

Colton was a 32 year-old tailor when his part-time career as an inventor began. Active in local politics and in the Amherst militia,

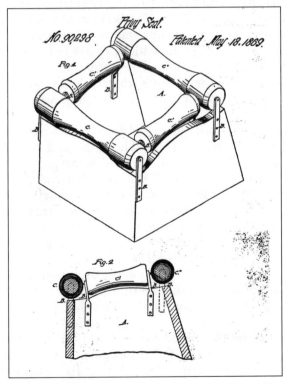

An improved privy seat invented in 1869. Rollers kept people from standing on the seat.

he was in fact the creator of the militia's uniforms. Sewn with "a black felt-bodied cap with wreath and letter A in front and pom-poms of red and white," Colton claimed they were as good in every way as those worn by the Northampton militia.

Colton's pickpocket invention was announced in the Hampshire and Franklin Express: "Mr. Joseph Colton, a tailor of this town, has invented an ingenious and effectual protection against that species of thieving so common at the present day, by which a man's money or other valuables is abstracted from his pockets. It consists of two curved plates united by hinges at the extremities, and which by means of holes in the plates, are sewed to the lid of the pocket, constituting its opening.

"While the plates are being shut a slide to which a spring is attached is forced up, which immediately resumes its place as they close and fasten them together. The pocket is surrounded by a net-work of wire so that whatever is contained in it can be neither taken out or cut out without the knowledge or consent of the owner. The model shown us was made by Mr. Boot of Amherst East Street."

Inventors from every corner of the country competed for the public's attention, including a man who created a tapeworm trap in 1854: "My invention consists in a trap which is baited, attached to a string, and swallowed by the patient after a fast of suitable dura-tion to make the worm hungry. The worm seizes the bait which is then withdrawn from the patient's stomach by the string which has been left hanging from the mouth, dragging after it the whole length of the worm … ."

The fear of being not quite dead at one's own funeral led to the "Improved Burial Case" in 1868. The coffin was provided with a ladder and a cord, "one end of said cord being placed in the hand of the person laid in the coffin, and the other end being attached to a bell on the top … so that, should a person be interred ere life is extinct, he can, on recovery to consciousness ring the bell, and thus save himself from premature burial and death."

The dangers of standing on a privy seat and possibly falling in were addressed in a patent of 1869: "This invention renders it impossible for the user to stand upon the privy-seat; and consists in the provision of rollers on the top of the seat … in the event of an attempt to stand upon them, they will revolve, and precipitate the user on to the floor."

According to the Amherst paper, Colton's Patent Pocket Book and Watch Safe successfully foiled pickpockets across the country. Colton went on to invent a "Self Acting Balance Lever Cheese Press" in 1848. This was a portable cheese maker, light enough for one to press a cheese on the run.

Those Promiscuous
19th Century Electric Poles

At the time that Emily Dickinson lay dying, Amherst was poised on the edge of the electronic age. On May 7, 1886, a Mr. Alexander from the Thomson-Houston Electric Company met with the businessmen of Amherst. He hoped to inspire enthusiasm for electric lighting, but he went away baffled. This town of educational enlightenment showed little interest in electric enlightenment.

Part of Amherst's reluctance was based on aesthetics: According to the Amherst Record, only a few years earlier the Common "was marred in its appearance by unsightly telegraph and telephone poles, and it was a very difficult matter to get them removed." The paper did not want to see "electric light poles stationed all about the streets promiscuously."

Cost was another consideration. Gas light had been introduced in 1877, yet some businesses found lighting with gas too expensive and went back to lighting their shops with kerosene. The newspaper asked, "How can these men afford electric light, which costs more than gas?" As it was, the gas rate was actually lower than in other towns in the Valley, and there was plenty for those who could afford it. Staunchly conservative, the Record proclaimed, "Amherst needs electric lights about as much as the dogs in the street need two tails each."

Until 1873, there was no street lighting in Amherst. The Amherst Gas Light Company had been formed in 1870, with Edward Dickinson as a member, but it wasn't until early 1874 that 10 gas lamps were installed. In September of 1877, the Amherst Gas Company was incorporated, with Austin Dickinson as one of the directors. This company was authorized to manufacture and sell gas. On November 1, 1877, the hat factories were lit in a "grand illumination." In 1879, gas was extended to Amherst College, and in 1881, it spread north on Pleasant Street. After 1882, all the oil lamps were changed to gas, with a total of 42 in town by February, 1889.

By that time Amherst was ready to reconsider electricity. The Thomson-Houston Company built an electric plant in the spring of 1889, and on April 13, four electric lights were lit in Amherst. The company succeeded in avoiding a confrontation over unsightly poles. The Record described them as "good looking sticks of timber, (that) with their fancy carving quite shame the less aristocratic poles planted in the back yards."

In September of 1889, the Amherst Gas Company voted to

buy the Thomson-Houston equipment. The company offered to light the town from sunset until midnight, except on moonlit nights. On December 1, 1893, nine arc-lights were lit in Amherst, and after 1894, all gas lights were replaced by electric.

The Amherst Record had gone from stating in 1886 that "we think Amherst is quite well supplied with modern improvements," thus spurning electricity, to proclaiming in 1893 that electric lights "give general satisfaction, and they are certainly a great addition to the beauty and comfort of the town."

Getting the Time
of Day in Amherst

In 1873, people in Amherst became terribly confused about what time it was. Clock towers differed from each other, and though Amherst College knew the accurate time from its clock at the observatory, it wasn't communicated to town clocks. And why was the Grace Church clock showing Boston time instead of Amherst time?

Confusion of hours, minutes, days, and entire seasons was an ancient problem. The Julian Calendar had been introduced by Julius Caesar in the first century B.C. Unfortunately, it was off by 11 minutes and 14 seconds each year. It erred by almost 1 1/2 days in 200 years. After 1,000 years it was off by a week. By 1545, the vernal equinox had moved 10 days from its proper day. This posed serious problems for the Christian Church, which used the vernal equinox to determine when to celebrate Easter.

Pope Gregory began his Gregorian Calendar with a papal bull of February, 1582. He brought the vernal equinox back to March 21 by dropping 10 days from the calendar that year. This upset a lot of people who thought they were losing 10 days of their already short lives. To complicate matters, not every country adopted the Gregorian Calendar at the same time. Britain, for example, waited until 1752. For over 100 years dates would be 10 days apart in different European countries.

To confuse matters more, the old Julian Calendar began a new year each March 25th. It wasn't until the Gregorian Calendar that the year began on January 1st. Therefore, while one country on the Julian Calendar would use, say January 5, 1700, another country on the Gregorian Calendar would call the same day January 15, 1701.

Until Galileo discovered the properties of the pendulum in about 1583, accurate timekeeping was impossible. Of course an hour more or less didn't always matter back then anyway. When the sun was directly overhead it was noon. By the late 19th century, however, it really began to matter that actual noon in Amherst would be several minutes different from noon in Boston or New York. The 12-minute difference between Boston and New York, for example, didn't matter earlier when it took three or four days to travel between them. But with the introduction of the telegraph and railroads, time within regions needed to be uniform.

This explains Amherst's confusion in 1873, when not only didn't time there agree with time in other towns, but clocks within town disagreed. The Amherst Record suggested that the town go by

Keeping time was confusing in the 1870's before standards were set. The clock at Grace Episcopal Church at the Amherst Common kept Boston time.

watchmakers Saxton and Burnell's Regulator clock on South Pleasant Street, which would coincide with Amherst College's observatory time. The town had certainly been ill-served by the clock on Grace Church which, because it had been made in Boston, ran on Boston time, a full six minutes faster than Amherst time.

It wasn't until 1883 that some sense was made of this. In that year, U.S. and Canadian railroads adopted standard time zones, making train scheduling, and a great deal more, easier than ever before.

Shakespeare
On Sewers

A century before Ed Norton of "The Honeymooners" and, more recently, the Ninja Turtles found humor in sewers, Amherst turned a satirical eye and nose to the subject.

Until 1880, Amherst had an air about it now found in only the most primitive countries. Cesspools scented the breeze, the hotel and shops on South Pleasant Street used a drain that carried a "foul mass" to the center of the common and left it there.

There is nothing inherently funny about a sewer. Typhoid fever, malaria and dysentery were just some of the killers that were prevalent in the Valley before a good system was developed. Even after the "sewering of Amherst," as it was called, children from all levels of society fell to the effects of stagnant water. Emily Dickinson's nephew Gilbert, for example, died of typhoid fever in 1883.

When the building of Amherst's sewer system was approved at the Town Meeting of September 14, 1880, Shakespeare's thoughts on sewers helped sway the vote. According to a man known pseudonymously as Smith, Shakespeare had this to say about sewerage in Stratford, 1580:

"To sewer (the town) or not to sewer, that is the question. Whether 'tis nobler in us to suffer the stinks and stenches of outrageous sink drains and cesspools, or to take arms against a sea of troubles, and, by opposing, end them? To sewer — to be pure — no more; and, by a sewer to say we end the heartache, typhoid fever, malaria, gout, drunkenness, dysentery, bald-headedness, dyspepsia, tightlacing, and a thousand natural and artificial ills and shocks which flesh is heir to, 'tis a consummation devoutly to be wished.

"To sewer; to be pure. To be pure; perchance to sleep and dream of taxes — ay, there's the rub, among those from Stratford on the north and Stratford on the south; for in that sleep what dreams come to those who oppose sewers when we have shuffled off this mortal coil, must make calamity of so long life; for who would bear the stinks and stenches that ascend from the Common, the Improvement Society's pressions ... the pangs of dysentery and typhoid fever, the insolence and delays of office holders, and the traps which those from the north and south profess to have set for them by the Center, when taxes he could escape, and his quietus make, with a seven shooter or a bare bodkin?

"Who would taxes bear, to grunt and sweat at one dollar a day to pay them; but that the dread something after death — the undiscovered country from whose bourne no traveler returns, puzzles the will and makes us rather bear the stenches we have than fly to sewers we know not the cost of. Thus taxes doth make cowards of us all."

Edgar Allen Poe seems to have had a few thoughts on the subject as well. The Amherst Record ran a lengthy poem called "The Smells" on September 8. Here, mercifully, is only the first verse:

> Sniff the breezes with the smells —
> Sink-drain smells!
> What a nauseous disgust their effluvia compels!
> How they sicken, sicken, sicken
> All the balmy air of night!
> While the winds that rise and quicken
> In the heavens, seem quite stricken
> With the dull and fatal blight;
> Saying slum, slum, slum,
> Fever-fits and ague dumb,
> Crying come, come, come,
> Typhoid heats and palsy numb;
> Swell the righteous indignation that indignantly repels
> The presence and putrescence of the smells
> And confirm the condemnation that so reasonably dwells
> Upon the smells, smells, smells, smells,
> Smells, smells, smells —
> Upon the reeking and the stinking of the smells.

Poetry helped turn the offensive tide. The day after Town Meeting approved the new sewer, two bids were received. By the end of September 1880, the digging of the village sewer was progressing rapidly.

Amherst Builds a Carriage for the President

Made from timbers taken from the Ship Constitution. Presented to General Jackson...

This fancy carriage was made by Knowles & Thayer in Amherst for President Andrew Jackson.

What is the perfect gift for an admired, two-term U.S. President when he leaves office? When Andrew Jackson left the Presidency in 1837, he was given a most exquisite carriage, as finely made as any in the country. That carriage, called a phaeton, was made by the Knowles and Thayer Carriage Company, which had a rapid rise and fall in Amherst.

Lyman Knowles had begun making carriages in his shop at the South Amherst Common in 1827. He went into partnership with Asahel Thayer in 1830, opening a larger factory on Pelham Road in East Amherst. Thayer was a deacon in the Second Congregational Church and had a good sense of Yankee trading. Together, Knowles and Thayer built one of the largest, most highly respected carriage shops in Massachusetts, if not in all of the U.S.

In the 1830s, the company employed from 100 to 150 hands in their wood-working, upholstering and painting shops. The Boston Tribune reported in 1835 that, "Coaches, Barouches,

Landeaus, Chariot Carryalls, Gigs, Stanhopes, and Fancy vehicles of any and every pattern or design, are built in this establishment, of the most perfect workmanship ... all wheels and ornamenting is done there ... . The Oak, Walnut, and Ash they consume, grows almost at their door and is of the finest quality that can be found in the country. They sold in Boston last year 110 carriages, and they have orders from all parts of the Union ... . They have made carriages for Ex-President Adams, Mr. Van Buren ... and about forty members of Congress and the Departments, and they have an order from Paris."

When Andrew Jackson left office in 1837, a group of Republican admirers from New York wanted to present him with the finest carriage that could be had. They chose Amherst's Knowles and Thayer to build it. In the days when a carriage could be bought for less than $300, this one was to be worth $3,000. Most remarkable perhaps is the fact that the oak for the carriage came from the frigate Constitution, the famous "Old Ironsides" of the War of 1812.

Knowles and Thayer used the costliest materials in lining and trimming this two-seater, and on the side panels painted the Constitution under full sail. The carriage was first used for the inauguration of Martin Van Buren on March 4, 1837. Andrew Jackson and Van Buren rode in the carriage pulled by Jackson's four, iron-gray carriage horses with brass harnesses.

Later Van Buren sent the carriage on to Jackson's house in Tennessee, along with "a quarter cask of old and excellent sherry." In 1897, much of the carriage was destroyed in a fire, but today it is being restored at Jackson's museum home in Hermitage, Tennessee.

Not long after Knowles and Thayer reached the peak of their success, the carriage makers fell victim to the Financial Panic of 1837 and closed their doors.

Ira Haskins' Famous Gold Nibs

Between the revolutionary advance of the 15th century printing press and the 20th century global information network, other smaller revolutions are easily ignored. In the 19th century, for example, the graceful quill pen was replaced by the steel-tipped pen. Most of us picture the latter as a drab tool dipped in ink by Bob Cratchit. In many places, however, the metal-tipped pen achieved the beauty and refinement of a piece of art. By 1854, Ira C. Haskins was making gold pens in Amherst. The instruments were such high quality that the U.S. Treasurer, whose signature graced U.S. currency, swore by his Haskins Brothers gold pen.

The problem with quill pens had been that they didn't last. They were also expensive, scarce, and had to be resharpened with a penknife. In 1822, a machine was developed to produce steel nibs, which were long-lasting, reliable, and came in a variety of widths and thicknesses. The steel could be gilded, bronzed, or even embossed with a portrait of Queen Victoria. The holders were anything from plain wood to silver, enamel, or inlaid mother-of-pearl.

Steel nibs had to be dipped in ink after every few words, which meant a bottle of ink had to be close at hand, as well as a sprinkler of fine sand to dry the ink. Blotting paper came into use in about 1850, around the time Ira Haskins began making his gold pens. Haskins worked on the second floor of Phoenix Row on Main Street. He and his brother Jerry C. Haskins formed Haskins Brothers and made gold pens in nearly 50 patterns.

In 1867, the firm incorporated and planned to expand production with new facilities in Shutesbury and Amherst, but this never came about. Instead, Jerry became a maker of fine custom harnesses on North Pleasant Street, where he also sold horse robes, blankets and whips. Mayhew L. Merritt joined Ira in making gold pens on Main Street.

Haskins' gold pens were sold in jewelry stores like Jonathan Rawson's store on South Pleasant, or in stationery stores like Edwin Nelson's, also on South Pleasant in 1886. In 1889, Haskins ran an ad that stated, "Haskins' Tip Top Gold Pens. Made to Suit Any Handwriting in the World. Sold on One Year Trial." The ad included a letter from F.E. Spinner, U.S. Treasurer: "Sirs: Yours is the Best Gold Pen I have found wherewith to make my signature."

In about 1893, when the western world was beginning to change from steel nibs to fountain pens, Ira Haskins retired and moved to Springfield. By the time Haskins died in 1903 the

Waterman Company in New York was producing half a million fountain pens a year.

The next revolution in penmaking came at the end of World War II. After several very messy, ink-blotted tries, the ballpoint pen became the pen for a throwaway society. Shaeffer made the first successful ballpoint in this country. Then in 1945, Baron Marcel Bich tinkered with ballpoints outside of Paris. Within a few years his company made 7,000,000 pens a day. For obvious reasons the name used for the pen in America became the "Bic."

Pen maker Ira Haskins in his carriage

The Printing Trade
and Death By Molasses

Sermons could be fiery and controversial, like those of Jonathan Edwards when he was in Northampton, or they could soothe one into a sound sleep. In 1884, the Rev. George S. Dickerman's sermon put Charles White dead asleep in Amherst's First Church, across from the Dickinson houses. When he woke up to a dark, empty church, White's only escape seemed to be a jump out of a window.

Charles White was born in 1867 in the White farmhouse, now the admissions office of Amherst College on South Pleasant Street. The farm spread over what are now college playing fields and tennis courts, east past the railroad tracks. There were apple orchards, cow pastures, a sheep run, pig yard, hen house, smokehouse, a horse barn, and a carriage house.

On October 19, 1885, Charles became an apprentice printer to John E. Williams, publisher of the Amherst Record. The printing profession was considered a lucrative one, but Charles White's diary makes it clear that he cared more for steady work than money. One of his favorite quotations reads, "... it seems to me that life is a matter of being born, living, doing your duty and dying. And the rest of it's a mystery."

His diary overflows with details of a simple life. He touches on his boyhood, apprenticeship, his courting of Sadie Weld, and his building of their house on Woodside Avenue. Charles devotes one page to living expenses for a year, beginning September, 1915. Five hundred dollars went for daughter Mildred's college bill, $40 for apples, quinces, poultry and eggs. Summing up, he laments, "Pretty expensive living, nothing left over."

Recipes, poems, taxes and death appear in no particular order: "1919 — Big Molasses Tank collapses in North end, Boston. Eleven or more dead, 50 hurt. Giant wave of 2,300,000 gallons of Molasses, 50 feet high, sweeps everything before it. One hundred men, women and children caught in sticky stream — buildings, vehicles and railroad structures crushed."

After 50 years in the printing trade, White reminisced, "I started work for Mr. Williams in the Amherst Record office to learn the printer's trade 50 years ago (Oct. 19, 1885). Was 17 years old then so that makes me 67 years old now. There is no one living now that was connected with the office then. I am the last one of the old force left. Mr. William A. Hyde retired a year and a half ago, and Mr. Carpenter died last year. Have worked all but two years in the

Record Office. The other two years I worked in Boston ... walking to and from work for 50 years, about 20,000 miles or two miles a day. Feeding press for same time, about 25,000,000 pieces, average 2,000 a day."

White was always aware of time passing, and of lives ending. Most entries are tinged with sadness, but occasionally he recalls a humorous event:

"I think it was in this year (1884) that I was locked in the First Congregational Church, Amherst; it happened like this: I had a seat in the gallery, and being the only one there I got sleepy during the sermon, and leaned my head forward on the railing and fell asleep. I was confused and felt strange and couldn't think where I was, but after a little it flashed into my mind that I had fallen asleep in Church. It didn't take me long to get down stairs and find a window from which I jumped. I didn't know but what it was midnight, but come to find out it was only a little after nine."

Charles White's own life ended in 1956, at the age of 88 years-old in St. Petersburg, Florida.

The farmhouse of printer Charles White, now the Admissions Office of Amherst College.

An Italian
Railroad Camp

John Musante, one of the few Italians who came to live permanently in Amherst.

On Friday, May 13, 1887, 85 Italian laborers arrived in Amherst to work on the Massachusetts Central Railroad. More came the next week, bringing the total to over 100 who were to help build the Amherst section of the railroad that linked Northampton and Boston. Amherst was fascinated by them and later horrified by the combination of bad luck and passion that led to a disastrous 15 hours. Within those few hours, two men were wounded and two were killed.

The Italians arrived in Amherst with notebooks and pencils, eager to learn the local vocabulary, and especially eager to learn the correct pronunciation of "Amherst." The locals repeated stories of humorous exchanges in the shops as the Italians struggled with the language. The two organ grinders who appeared also raised some eyebrows in this New England town. The Italian camp was at the west end of William A. Magill's farm on South Pleasant Street. There they had a 50 x 20 foot shanty, with two tiers of bunks on either side.

A holiday spirit permeated the Italian camp on Sundays. The men played games, cooked on outdoor fireplaces, wrote letters, read, and mended their clothing. An article in the Amherst Record described some as "sitting or lying supinely on the ground, conversing together in an unknown tongue." In commenting on the Italians' cooking habits, the writer said that "the style seems to combine simplicity and economy to a wonderful degree," and he wondered what life in their native land was like. In Amherst, the Italians were identified on the company books only by number and were known at work by American nicknames, such as Joe or Frank.

On July 6th, the newspaper reported a series of incidents which it characterized as more typical of the hilltowns than of genteel Amherst. On July 2nd, John Shea got into an argument at the Italian shanty and came away with several cuts. The next morning, Antonio Preletto, one of the workmen, accidently fell into the Freshman River and drowned.

Shortly after church services that same day, Pasquale Turso ran screaming through the train station yard toward Main Street and collapsed with a bullet wound. An inquest that afternoon revealed a confused story that began with an argument between Turso and Antonio Samorali. The railroad company's bookkeeper, Giusseppe Falbe, approached with a gun and Pasquale Turso was somehow shot. Pasquale's brother, Lenardo, went after the bookkeeper with a stick and was shot dead. The Turso brothers had come from Italy four years earlier and were described as "good, honest fellows ... and were not in the habit of quarreling with the other workmen ... their attachment to each other was something remarkable."

Falbe escaped and was not heard of again. The bodies of the drowned Preletto and the shot Turso were buried in the same grave in the southeast corner of West Cemetery on Monday, July 4, 1887.

By the end of July, more than half of the Italians moved on to their next work site on the Pennsylvania Railroad. Work for the rest of the Italians in Amherst was completed in August, and in December, 1887, the first trains traveled through Amherst on the Massachusetts Central Railroad.

Love in the Time
of Telephones

Whatever will happen to the art of writing love letters in the age of e-mail? It's clear we need new rules of etiquette, for the old books just won't do. Nineteenth century courtship seemed pretty straight forward when manuals provided form letters with titles like "From a gentleman to a lady, disclosing his passion." But in the 1870s, the telephone, like modern e-mail, suddenly made old ways of courtship obsolete, and caused endless embarrassment.

Alexander Graham Bell patented the telephone in 1876, and it was hardly more than a year before the first lines were strung in Western Mass. Bell himself demonstrated his telephone in Springfield on May 12, 1877. From the Springfield Daily Republican: "We are to have Professor Bell and his telephone Saturday evening ... stationed in the Springfield City Hall, which is to be connected with the Pittsfield Academy of Music, with Westfield as the way station.

"There will be a brief explanatory lecture by Professor Bell and then for an hour a concert of vocal solos and duets, cornet solos, and organ playing to be sent through the telephone from Westfield."

In 1880, 100 telephones were set up in Northampton, but it wasn't until late 1882 that Amherst had its first phone. However, as early as 1877, Amherst could see trouble coming. One anonymous local writer told a story of how wrong courtship could go when letter writers first attempted courtship by telephone: "The fellow lived some distance from his dear, deary, dearest. It was an awful muddy time, walking was out of the question, and a team could not be hired for love or money. After desponding for a time, and being down in the mouth for another spell, a happy thought struck him ... he would try the new fangled thing called the telephone.

"As long as he could not be near the object of his heart's best affections he thought it would be some satisfaction to hear her heave a telephonic sigh. So he chartered two and had them properly stationed and insulated. He moved his mouth up to the opening of the telephone and bawled in a slow, hesitating manner, this very sentimental piece of information with its accompanying heartfelt desire: 'All nature is looking green and beautiful, trees all leafing out, and I hope you will be next time I shall see you.'

"Then he put his ear to the opening and listened for a response, meantime beginning to glow all over, and in this disturbed state of mind he sorter put his arm around his beloved or thought he did,

Telephone, telegraph and electric poles cluttered the streets at the end of the 19th century.

but suddenly discovered it was only that inanimate telephone, as the answer to his loving outburst came: 'Oh you git out with your nonsense!'

"He sent this inquiry: 'Is the old gent at home?' not thinking that the whole family had gathered to admire the wonderful new-fangled machine, when a hoarse, gruff reply came that nearly deafened him: 'What do you mean by calling me an old gent, you yellow-haired rascal. I'll shake the hair-oil out of you, and twist your ear besides when I get in reach of you.' As the echoes of this not very affectionate outburst began to cease their reverberations in his head, our young man profanely muttered hardly above his breath, 'He's a cross old cuss anyhow,' forgetting that the telephone would betray him. 'What's that you called me, you profane polywog, repeat them words if you dare!'

"Feeling the sting of this Darwinian epithet, our young man replied to his prospective father-in-law as meekly as possible, 'I only said, don't be cross to us.' 'That's an infernal lie!' came from the paternal end of the telephone with a noise like the tumbling down of all the stovepipes in town at once, followed by, 'and if I catch you hanging round after Matilda Jane any more, I'll kick the skirts off your bobtailed store coat that you hain't paid for. No such milk sop as you is going to sneak round with any new-fangled machine to call me profane names and call it courtin', not much.'

"The future began to look dark to the young man. He threw the telephone out of gear and sighed, saying: 'Courting is dreadful uncertain business the old-fashioned way, and the telephone don't help matters any to speak of.'"

Old-fashioned love letters persisted for decades into this century, despite the telephone. At first, books on manners ignored the new technology altogether. In 1890, one such book was published in Springfield, after the telephone had been well-established. Titled *Manners, Culture and Dress of the Best American Society, Including Social, Commercial and Legal Forms, Letter Writing, Invitations, etc.,* the book included a section on "Letters of Love."

The author, Richard A. Wells, suggested, "Letters of love are generally preceded by some friendly correspondence, for Cupid is a wise designer, and makes his approaches with wonderful caution. These premonitory symptoms of love are easily encouraged into active symptoms, then into positive declarations: if the loved one is willing to be wooed, she will not fail to lead her pursuer into an ambush of hopes and fears ... . After the various subterfuges of coy expression and half-uttered wishes, there comes sooner or later, Love's Declaration."

Time will tell how modern love will get tangled in the worldwide web of e-mail — or if the love letter is really dead after all.

Chapter Eight

A FEW SCATTERED PLEASURES

Amherst, Massachusetts

I cannot dance upon my toes -
No Man instructed me -
But oftentimes, among my mind,
A Glee possesseth me...
#326

Trained Dogs and Hypnotism at the Opera House

The Amherst Opera House and Austin Dickinson's law office were in this building, now the site of Amherst Town Hall.

Where in the Dickinsons' Amherst could one go for an evening of operatic selections, a grand masquerade ball, hypnotism, musical comedy, or trained dogs? The Amherst Opera House offered all this and more in its all too brief life-span.

On November 24, 1886, it was announced that Dwight W. Palmer was going to create an opera house in the upper story of Palmer's Block, located where the Town Hall is today. A stage nearly 30 feet wide was built in the east end of the floor. A semi-circular gallery was at the west end, extending midway along the north and south sides. Palmer went to New York in early January, 1887, to purchase chairs and some of the scenery.

By January 26, the finishing touches were being made. Scene painter George Bottume of Springfield (who had painted scenery for the Northampton Opera House), worked on the scenery with Amherst artist George A. Thomas. The scenes included a street, kitchen, parlor, prison, a cottage, and a drop curtain of a Maine river. Later in the year, the ceiling was frescoed.

One of the first performances, if not the first, was "The Drummer Boy, or the Battle-Field of Shiloh." This melodrama was offered on February 2, 3, and 4, with tickets at 25, 35, and 50 cents. Following this, on the 7th, were readings by Susie D. Drew, whose voice was described as "rich, flexible ... finely adapted to humorous or pathetic, narrative or dialect."

Hypnotism, or "mesmerism" as it was then called, proved extremely popular. On February 10th, Dr. W.H. Sherman stuck his Amherst subjects to their chairs, made them dance, play baseball, and imitate Amherst College professors.

When Palmer hadn't booked performances for his opera house, he rented it to other organizations. On February 21, 1887, the Amherst Dramatic Club presented an Irish drama and a dance. It was a success, but the club complained that Palmer's rental fee of $45 per night was "a pretty round fee" for a local group to pay.

As can be seen, the term "opera house" can only be loosely applied to what Palmer was conducting in Amherst. Occasionally a popular soprano, like Clara Louise Kellogg, would be hired to sing excerpts from opera. But even she included crowd-pleasing popular songs as well. The favorite event of the season was not opera at all, but a farce called "Pearl of Savoy," seen on May 1st, 1887.

Perhaps the strangest act to hit the Amherst Opera House was Dr. Sawtelle's Trained Saint Bernard Dogs (May 27-28, 1887). It was described in the newspapers as "refined, interesting and instructive."

The colorful history of Dwight Palmer's Amherst Opera House came to an abrupt halt when Palmer's Block burned down during the famous blizzard of March 12, 1888. But the cavalcade of live entertainment continued with hardly a break, in other Amherst halls.

Ghosts and Ventriloquists
Exposed in 1834

There was great interest in 1863 when the popular ventriloquist Professor Harrington was given a farewell party at Agricultural Hall in Amherst. Ventriloquism, magic, and the belief in ghosts were a common part of 19th century life in the Connecticut River Valley. Stories of a groaning grave in South Hadley, or of the Springfield mystic who performed amazing feats while sleep-walking, added a layer of mystery to God-fearing towns.

The town of Amherst, however, exposed these humbugs in 1834 when J.S. and C. Adams published *Ventriloquism Explained: And Juggler's Tricks, or Legerdemain Exposed: With Remarks on Vulgar Superstitions.* An anonymous ventriloquist wrote this fascinating work, with an introduction by Edward Hitchcock, professor and later president of Amherst College.

The origins of ventriloquism are lost somewhere in ancient Hebrew, Egyptian, and Greek civilizations. Priests and oracles used ventriloquism to speak to gods and demons. Greece had a group called Engastrimanteis — the "belly-prophets" whose voices appeared to originate in their stomachs. Necromancers literally used smoke and mirrors to produce ghostly forms. Concave lenses and mirrors cast pictures upon the smoke produced by incense. Hippocrates thought ventriloquists were born with voice-producing organs in the abdomen, giving the art early names like "gastriloquism" and "engastrimythism."

The author of *Ventriloquism Explained* ... was alarmed at how superstitious most people still were: "Many of our honest yeomen have been robbed of their shillings to see a man eat tow, spit fire, and swallow jackknives." He felt parents and family servants added to the problem by using tales of the supernatural to frighten and control children. He believed slaves brought many superstitions about dreams, and spilled water and salt, from Africa. Sailors used the wind, stars and moon to presage good and evil, and farmers planted, or killed swine, according to the phases of the moon.

The author described a typical magic act of the 1800s by a "professor of legerdemain." The man loaded a pistol with a lady's ring and fired it. A glove was locked in a box, but when the box was opened, out flew a dove with the ring in its beak. He went on to fire a gun and catch the bullet on the end of a penknife. He swallowed a jack-knife and made an egg jump on a table and run over his body — all the while he exclaimed "Presto, Presto, etc." After drawing the sounds of an old man, a pig, and a chicken out of a small box, he closed the act by eating fabric, spitting fire, and pulling ribbons out of his mouth.

The author exposed all these feats, and then gave lengthy examples of how anyone can learn the tricks of ventriloquism, for "only God does the miraculous." He exposed sufficient information to "enable many a straggler to gain a wizard's fame, even in the sober hamlet of New England." However, the book closes with a warning against causing harm or embarrassment, for that would be a "breach of Christian politeness" and "none can calculate their soul-destroying influence beyond the grave."

Unconcerned by such thoughts, Greenfield's Penn Jillette carries on today what was exposed in Amherst in 1834. His famous comedy/magic act of Penn and Teller has published the modern equivalent of Amherst's book on trickery: *Cruel Tricks for Dear Friends*, which teaches how to "Steal Money from People You Really Love!" and "Humiliate People You Claim to Respect."

The Cat vs.
Dog Debate

People seem to have always been born with either cat-genes or dog-genes. Emily Dickinson was definitely a dog-person. She loved her red-brown Newfoundland, Carlo, and felt the only good cat was one with a rat in its mouth.

Emily's sister, Lavinia? Definitely a cat person. She took in strays and added them to what she called her "flock," giving them such names as Tabby, Drummydoodles, Buffy, and Tootsie.

Hampshire County, like all agricultural areas, was ambivalent about dogs in the 19th century. In 1895, the Amherst Record published the usual grim statistics about the sheep and poultry killed and maimed by dogs in the county: "The number of sheep killed is 168; the number injured 65. Huntington leads the list of fatalities with 22 to the credit of her dogs. Next comes Chesterfield with 11, Hadley 19, Worthington and Granby each 18. In Amherst the dogs do not go in to kill evidently, for there eight sheep were killed and 46 injured. Fowls fared better and only 88 were killed."

Perhaps to balance such grisly news, the Amherst Record published an essay called "Why People Like Dogs": "And why do people keep such lots of dogs themselves and go in such numbers to see other people's dogs? Because the dog is at once the sincerest flatterer and the most successful cheerer that the human race ever had. A good dog always gives us the feeling that we men and women are a sort of god. No other animal does anything of the kind. The cat treats us as an inferior, and the horse will treat us as a dear friend, not a divinity.

"The dog, moreover, imparts something of his peculiar gayety to us in a way that is irresistible. He mingles his suggestions of gayety with his flattery, for he not only leaves his dinner untasted to walk with us, but the mere fact that we are apparently giving ourselves the pleasure of a walk raises him into such a delirium of delight that the sight of it puts all our dumps and blues to such reproach that we shake them off in very shame."

At this same time, just 100 years ago, something new was on the horizon for cats: the cat show. The local newspaper felt it was time to give "Felis Domestica" its due: "We congratulate the cities of Springfield and Northampton on the success of the cat shows which have recently been held within their borders. We would also congratulate the feline race on the somewhat tardy recognition thus extended of its many virtues and excellencies.

"In the early ages of the world the Egyptians, the Yankees of their day and generation, held the cat in high esteem. In later years philosophers and statesmen made intimate companions of the feline race. The divine right of a cat to look at a king has rarely been called in question.

"It was not until the times when New England was sorely afflicted by witchcraft that cats, and in particular black cats, fell under the ban of public disfavor. After the witches had been hung and burned, and the black cats had been deprived of some of their superfluous lives, the feline race was gradually restored to public confidence.

"There are few things in animate nature more satisfying to look upon than a sleek well-favored cat, as she performs her toilet after discussing a satisfactory meal, or dozes before the fire with her head between her paws. There are persons who don't like cats, but as a general thing they are of dyspeptic temperament and thus incapable of appreciating a real good thing."

We can't really accuse Emily Dickinson of having a dyspeptic temperament, but, as she once wrote in a letter, her feelings toward cats were clear: "You remember my ideal cat has always a huge rat in its mouth, just going out of sight — though going out of sight in itself has a peculiar charm."

Ode to
Frank P. Wood

Popular hotel keeper Frank P. Wood was given a rousing party here by Amherst College students. Corner of North Pleasant Street and Amity Street.

The 19th century inns and restaurants of Amherst were gathering places for feasts, revelry, and all kinds of human drama. In Amherst, Wood's Dining Rooms, Gunn's Hotel and the Amherst House hosted sleighing parties, meetings of the Lafayette Hook and Ladder Company, wedding receptions, and the informal celebrations of the local students. In 1878, Amherst College students surprised Frank P. Wood, the town's most popular restaurant owner, with an evening of tributes. The crowning tribute was a reading of "An Ode to Frank P. Wood."

Wood came to Amherst in about 1876 to work as a clerk in the Amherst House at the common. Within two years he had his own restaurant on Main Street. On August 8, 1878, a dozen Amherst College students showed their affection for Wood by throwing a surprise birthday party for the 32 year-old man. The students presented him with a fine set of toilet articles, and also a rubber rattle for his newborn daughter, Clara. Frank recovered from his astonishment and treated the boys to "as fine a repast as epicurean taste could dictate."

On behalf of the students, D.E. Chamberlain of the Amherst Record wrote and recited the following ode:

Friend Wood, to you we would present,
A few small gifts to cheer your way,
While journeying o'er life's rugged road,
This thirty-second birthday.

A toilet set we bring to you,
With bowl and pitcher — firm as rocks;
A sometimes-needed shaving cup

With glass to gaze in: comb for locks.

We all remember by-gone days,
Your choice ice cream, prime oysters, too;
These little gifts but faintly show,
The friendship which we hold for you.

Our wishes are that you and yours —
(Which means your wife, and babe that prattles;)
Will still continue in our midst
When there's no further use for rattles.

This presentation rhyme I'll close
With just a parting benediction:
For kindness, always freely shown,
Accept this object of affection —
From Amherst boys, all friends to you
On this, and other birthdays, too.

In November of 1882, Wood bought Gunn's Hotel and Restaurant, on the corner of North Pleasant and Amity. He remodeled the building and met with great success, to the relief of Amherst. It seems that the previous owner, William L. Gunn, had spent much of his time in court since opening the hotel in 1877. Several suits were brought against him for the illegal sale of liquor, bad debts, for keeping a public inn without an inn-holder's license, and other problems.

In contrast, when Frank Wood sold the place in 1892, the newspaper fondly reported, "His restaurant has been headquarters for spreads of all descriptions and the boys have always found in him a genial friend, ready to help them out of innumerable scrapes."

The Perfectly Scandalous
Wine Supper of Robert J.

When 19th century humorist Robert J. Burdette spoke in Amherst in 1886, he was a smash. For an hour and a half Robert J., as he was known, entertained Amherst College students at College Hall. But the night ended in embarrassment and ironically the last laugh was on Burdette himself. It was years before Burdette found out what had gone wrong at the reception held in his honor later that night at Wood's Hotel.

Robert J. Burdette made a name for himself as a humorist and lecturer in the pages of the Brooklyn Eagle and the Los Angeles Times. He was born in Pennsylvania in 1864, and by the time of his death in 1914, he had written several books of poetry. Burdette's Amherst lecture of November 17, 1886, was met with much laughter and applause. In it he told the story of "Tom," whose precarious existence was followed from babyhood until he had developed a moustache and won the hand of a certain young lady.

Afterwards, the Amherst College seniors gave the celebrated humorist a lively reception at Wood's Hotel. The newspaper reported that "their guest was the life and spirit of the occasion which was one of those that a student enjoys and will long remember."

For the following four years, Burdette wondered why he was not asked back to Amherst. Then in November, 1890, the Chicago Tribune reported what had happened at his previous visit, four years earlier. At the reception at Wood's Hotel that night, Frank Wood had served what was called a "wine supper." The Tribune said, "The supper passed off gayly. Bob was at his best, and so were the boys. So was the wine. The wine got a little the best of it toward the end of the ceremonies, sad to say."

The next day, word spread around Amherst that several of the boys had been seen going to their rooms in a condition that was "perfectly scandalous." An investigation was held, and Frank Wood was indicted for selling intoxicants without a license. Having great affection for Wood, all the party-goers felt terrible, all except for Robert J. Burdette who was long gone.

The Amherst boys got together and hatched a plan to save Frank Wood. Since Burdette had left the area and would be none the wiser, the boys unblushingly declared that Burdette had brought the wine with him to Amherst. The hotelkeeper had nothing to do with it. Wood and the boys got away with it, until the truth was revealed in the Chicago Tribune four years later. By that time, the students had graduated and scattered.

As for Robert J. Burdette, he kept his sense of humor. He wished the boys to know that "the end does sometimes justify the means" and that they had his entire forgiveness.

Hoodlumism on the Amherst Stage

Audiences of 18th century London theatre were surprisingly emotional and sometimes violent. Theatre riots were fairly common then, and the custom was loosely translated to the New World. In 1897, Amherst was shocked when an audience rushed the stage during a performance, and an all-out brawl was only narrowly avoided.

Elijah B. Fitts had owned a grist mill and sawmill on Main Street in East Amherst in the 1870s. By 1879, Fitts left Amherst to enter show business. When he returned 20 years later, it was with his Fitts and Webster Comedy Company. On January 7, 1897, the company performed "A Breezy Time" at Town Hall before an eager audience of between 500 and 600 people.

The day of the performance, "Lije" Fitts met with many of his old Amherst friends. They swapped yarns about the old days when Fitts was a miller and the leader of the town band. He returned a bigger man than when he left, straining the scales at 320 pounds.

One of the largest audiences ever assembled at Town Hall greeted Fitts that night. Most were townspeople, and most were women, except for the first two or three rows. About 50 Amherst College students held those seats. The production included comedy, a contortionist, songs and instrumental numbers. The Amherst students joined in from the start, however, greeting the women performers with whistles and jeers, and punctuating the lines of actors with "ohs" and "ahs." During intermission, they moved their seats closer to the stage and began whistling and singing.

The second act included a cornet duet which the students accompanied loudly. The climax was reached when an actor playing a tramp appeared on stage wearing an Amherst College Class of 1900 sweater. About a dozen students attacked the stage and engaged in hand-to-hand combat with the troupe for possession of the sweater. The students got the worst of the argument and were driven from the stage. The audience was in an uproar, women left the hall, and the curtain was rung down. For a few moments, it seemed the students and townspeople would come to blows. Finally, the audience quieted down and the performance resumed. Yet, a bit later, a sentimental ballad was interrupted again by heckling from the students. The song was stopped, one student ejected, and the performance was allowed to go on.

Fitts denounced the students' behavior as "worthy of the Bowery, the worst exhibition of hoodlumism" he had ever seen in any town. He did salvage the evening somewhat by repairing to the Amherst House with his old Amherst friends. There, he told stories into the small hours about his life on the road.

The outraged report of the incident in the newspapers claimed the evening was not unique. "Students are permitted to do about what they please at theatrical entertainments given in the Town Hall." This fact was so well known that for most events townspeople were absent. Those who risked attendance usually saw "a mixed entertainment, a considerable percentage of which (was) furnished by the students."

The Crash, Bang, Squish, Roar, Hurrah, and Horribles of History

Independence Day. Is it a time to reflect on the nature of freedom, a benign day of barbecues and fireworks, or a mindless Roman Saturnalia? Americans were beginning to wonder even as early as 1826 when the 50th anniversary of the day was celebrated. Disillusioned, one observer recorded Independence Day as a day of "frying chickens, firing away damaged powder, of fuddling our noses over tavern wine."

In the Connecticut Valley, the celebrations oscillated between reverence and debauchery. By 1859, one was likely to see an early morning July 4th parade of "The Horribles." This kicked off a day described by one editor as one of "senseless, aimless, crash, bang, squish, roar, ding-dong, hurrah." Worse yet, in 1865, the all-night bonfires and noisemaking on the Amherst Common erupted into an attempt to burn down a tenement house on North Pleasant Street.

In 1781, Massachusetts was the first state to vote official recognition to the observance of Independence Day. Early celebrations were ones of great pride and patriotic fervor. Typically, bells were rung, 13-gun salutes were shot, bands played, and bonfires and fireworks lit. The focal point, however, was an oration dwelling on the colonists' fight for freedom. This was accompanied by prayers, and a reading of the Declaration of Independence.

In the Connecticut Valley, the day was not formally celebrated in the small towns. Rather, a number of towns combined for one great event. The 1857 celebration was held in Belchertown, and was one of the most impressive in Western Massachusetts. "The celebration at Belchertown," the Hampshire and Franklin Express reported, "was one of those pleasant and patriotic occasions, which heretofore characterized the people of that town. It was conducted upon liberal and enlightened principles and afforded much pleasure to all who had the good fortune to be present."

At 11:00 in the morning, local dignitaries, school children and teachers marched with the Belchertown Artillery, to the accompaniment of the South Hadley Brass Band. After assembling at the Old Church, the Chief Marshall announced the exercises of the day: music by the South Hadley Band, a prayer by Rev. Mr. Fay, music by the church choir, a reading of the Declaration of Independence, more music by the band, an oration by Homer B. Sprague of Worcester, more music by the choir, and a benediction by Rev. Mr. Blake.

Later a banquet was held, followed by more orations, poems,

and an amazing number of toasts. Seven hundred people sat down to a feast prepared by the local ladies. They listened to toastmaster S. Shumway, who began by saluting the 4th, George Washington, the clergy, the ladies, the farmers, and on and on. Eventually dozens of toasts were offered and responded to by members of the crowd, until seriousness dissolved and humor took over.

The less formal celebration improvised in Amherst two years later was, to some eyes, a less happy occasion. One commentator in the Express described it as nothing more than "an old Roman Saturnalia." Ringing bells and cannon fire ushered in the dawn. At 6:00 a.m., the most unusual of Independence Day traditions made its Amherst debut. This was a rag-tag, improvised parade called the "Resistless Battalion of Antiques and Horribles." It met with mixed reviews.

An elaborate 4th of July float.

Two hundred people assembled in the most outrageous costumes and vehicles they could concoct. They dressed as grizzled military veterans ("floodwoods and riff-raffs"), Amazons, "venerable spinsters," flouncing belles, "Indians too in barbarous costume, horrid paint, and the paraphernalia of war." There were decorated horses, and at the end of the line, a broken down wagon pulled by a cow and driven by a couple pretending to emigrate to Pike's Peak.

In normal Amherst fashion, two widely varying accounts of this same day appeared in the paper. One considered it a barbarous burlesque, another said it was a day of good humor and "heartfelt pleasure."

The Civil War brought back some of the original dignity of the day. This apparently didn't last long, for the year 1865 saw the low point of Amherst Independence Days. There were no picnics or parades that year. By midnight of the day before, the boys of Amherst had assembled on the Common. A large bonfire was built using boxes, boards, and barrel staves gathered from surrounding barns and sheds. A poem in the newspaper described the scene:

> As the hearty stroke of the College bell announced that
>   the hour had come,
> The willing bands of those youthful hands made the
>   village church bell hum.
> And its joyous tune on the breezes borne, awoke from
>   their slumbers deep,
> Full many a weary mortal who had fondly hoped to
>   sleep.
> But the bells they rang, and the fish-horn's clang from
>   all further rest did keep,
> And they wearily turned on their restless couch and
>   muttered curses deep,
> On the gallant boys who with horrid noise disturbed
>   them in their sleep.
>
> With the rosy dawn of the glowing morn, the bells
>   repeat the strain,
> And the distant hills, with the echoes fill, and return
>   on the breeze again.
> And the booming sound of the guns around in the
>   neighboring towns we hear,
> While the emblem bright of our country's might on the
>   College tower they rear.
>
> With the break of day, they hie away, content with the
>   mischief done,
> But another year they will reappear, to again repeat
>   their fun.

That wasn't the entire story, however. During that same night there was an attempt — not once but twice — to burn down a tenement building with nearly 30 people in it. Known as the "Bee-Hive" on North Pleasant Street, the building was home to a good part of Amherst's black population. Wood was placed under a bench on the porch and set ablaze. Both times D.H. Kellogg was able to extinguish it. Bonfires on the Common were one thing, but arson and the possible loss of life were quite another. State prison was suggested for the arsonists, who were never found.

By the early 20th century, Independence Day was again a more calmly celebrated holiday. In 1913, it was noted that, "The barbarities which in times past were features of the night before were altogether lacking." Special deputies patrolled the town to keep things quiet. The wild "Resistless Battalion of Antiques and Horribles" had been reduced to "the grand parade of not-too-horribles" on South Prospect Street. By then a respectable tradition, there was even a $5 prize for the best float.

In 1989, 130 years after the first Parade of the Horribles in Amherst, the 4th of July was relatively calm. The massacre in China had driven budding freedom underground, and gave our own Declaration of Independence renewed meaning.

Three Christmas Seasons
of Emily Dickinson

*Emily Dickinson as a girl,
from a painting of 1840*

Before Emily Dickinson began her slow withdrawal from the community, she took part in the winter activities of many Christmas seasons. Three stand out: a merry one when she was 15; a subdued, serious Christmas when she was 17; and a rollicking winter when, at 19, "beaus (could) be had for the taking."

Describing her Christmas of 1845, Emily wrote to her friend Abiah Root: "Old Santa Claus was very polite to me the last Christmas. I hung up my stocking on the bedpost as usual. I had a perfume bag and a bottle of otto of rose to go with it, a sheet of music, a china mug with Forget me not upon it, from S.S.—who, by the way, is as handsome, entertaining, and as fine a piano player as in former times, —a toilet cushion, a watch-case, a fortune-teller, and an amaranthine stock of pin-cushions and needlebooks ... . I found abundance of candy in my stocking, which I do not think has had the anticipated effect upon my disposition, in case it was to sweeten it, also two hearts at the bottom of all, which I thought looked rather ominous ... ."

The Christmas of 1847 found Emily in the midst of her one school year at Mount Holyoke Seminary in South Hadley. It was a time of intense religious revival, and intense pressure for the students to "give up their hearts to the influence of the Holy Spirit." Of Christmas day, Emily wrote, "Attended to our usual business today. There has been a good degree of quiet, I have hardly heard one 'Merry Christmas' this Morning —-"

Emily was relieved to return to Amherst the following year. Shortly after Christmas of 1849, we see an exuberant Emily, reveling in activities of a great Victorian winter. From a letter to Joel Warren Norcross: "Amherst is alive with fun this winter — might you be here to see! Sleigh rides are as plenty as people — which conveys to my mind the idea of very plentiful plenty ... . Parties cant find fun enough — because all the best ones are engaged to attend balls a week beforehand — beaus can be had for the taking — maids smile like the mornings in June — Oh a very great town is this!"

To her friend Jane Humphrey, Emily described a sleighride and other festivities: "A party of ten from here met a party of the same number from Greenfield, at South-Deerfield ... and had a frolic, comprising charades — walking around indefinitely — music — conversation — and supper — set in the most modern style; got home at two o clock — and felt no worse for it the next morning — which we all thought was very remarkable. Tableaux at the President's house followed next in the train — Sliding party close upon its heels — and several cozy sociables brought up the rear."

Emily Dickinson's Recipe for Black Cake

2 pounds Flour -
2 Sugar -
2 Butter -
19 Eggs -
5 pounds raisins -
1 1/2 Currants -
1 1/2 Citron -
1/2 pint Brandy -
1/2 Molasses -
2 Nutmegs -
5 teaspoons
    Cloves - Mace - Cinnamon -
2 teaspoons Soda -

Beat Butter and Sugar together -
Add Eggs without beating - and beat the mixture again -
Bake 2 1/2 or three hours, in cake pans, or 5 to 6 hours in Milk pan, if full -

The Immoral and Ruinous
Game of Baseball

The great sport of baseball had a rather rocky start in the Connecticut River Valley. Amherst College organized its first baseball club in the spring of 1859. But just over a dozen years later, the editor of the Amherst Record mounted a campaign against the sport. The newspaper complained that baseball is "not only not beneficial for exercise, but injurious to health and morals." The paper wanted to replace our national sport with cricket, which is "the best game that young men can indulge in," affording the "healthiest exercise that can be given the body."

Soon after Amherst College began playing baseball, the team captain, one morning after prayers, challenged Williams College to a game. That game was played on neutral ground, at the Pittsfield Baseball Club on July 1st, 1859. At the end of one inning, Williams was ahead, nine to one. But after 26 innings Amherst won with a whopping score of 73 to 32. This was probably the first baseball game to be played between two American colleges. A special messenger brought news of the win back to Amherst. The next day, the returning heroes were met by ringing church bells, bonfires, and a coach-and-four, which drove them through the streets. They were hailed with speeches and cheers at the college grove. The following year, Amherst again beat Williams, 70 to 30, continuing the rivalry which still exists today.

Within a year or two, several leagues were formed in Western Massachusetts. The Hampshire Baseball Club played against Amherst's Nicaean Club in 1865. This game, and most others of the period, was played on the Amherst Fairgrounds. Amherst College played other colleges as well, including Brown in May of 1866. After an Amherst victory of 29 to 13, the team returned on the Amherst and Belchertown Railroad, its small woodburning locomotive decorated with banners. The entire student body met them at the Amherst Depot.

As the popularity of the game grew, so did opposition to it. The Amherst Record's tirade against baseball in 1872 included the claim that "There is nothing in baseball requiring brain ... . We know some young men, who were once graceful ornaments of society, who have been irrecoverably ruined by contamination with the baseball playing fraternity." It was a sport "controlled and governed by professional gamblers." The newspaper urged America to make cricket the national game. It offered to organize a local movement, to distribute the rules of the game, and the paper recommended

One of the first Amherst College baseball teams.

where to buy equipment. It hoped a delegation could be sent to a cricket convention then being held in Philadelphia. Meanwhile, the town passed a bylaw stating, "No person shall play ball, or fly any kite or balloon, or throw stones or other missiles in or upon any public street in this town within one mile of the Amherst House."

But baseball only increased in popularity, officially becoming an intercollegiate sport in 1875. On a crude baseball diamond at the Amherst Fairgrounds, the season lasted from spring through late fall. In 1877, Lucien Ira Blake donated funds to build Blake Field for the college. Located on the south side of Snell Street, this was the first graded and fenced college baseball field in the country. It attracted professional teams from as far away as Ohio and Washington, D.C.

The Roller Skating Craze of 1885

In 1885, Amherst was in the midst of a phenomenal roller skating craze. The Amherst Roller Rink was located in Palmer's Hall, today the site of Town Hall. Depending on whom you spoke to, though, roller skating was either "poetry in motion" or an "illustration of the exceeding sinfulness of unfettered human nature in its search for 'exercise.'"

The first recorded roller skate manufacturer is Joseph Merlin, a Belgian inventor who moved to London in 1760 and demonstrated his invention there. The rollers were in a straight line and difficult to control. It wasn't until Joseph Plimpton of Medford, Massachusetts, improved the skate in 1863 that roller skating swept America and Western Europe. Plimpton also built the first roller rink, in 1863 in New York City.

Roller skating declined in this country after 1873, but continued strongly in London, Paris, Rome, and especially the East Indies and Australia. By 1879, America was ready for another roller skating craze, and it wasn't long before nearly every major city had from one to four roller rinks.

The Amherst Roller Rink was leased by a C. Huckins in 1885. It used the same hall that town meeting occupied in Palmer's Hall, and was open two evenings per week, usually on Thursdays and Saturdays. Roller skating in Amherst was a great social activity, and scarcely a week went by without some notice of skating events in the Amherst Record. Often the Amherst Serenade Band accompanied skaters. On March 12, 1885, there was a "Calico Party on Rollers," at which contestants wore costumes, part of which had to be calico. A band played as skaters promenaded before a panel of prominent "Amherstonians" who judged the contest. The prize was a pair of "elegant clamp skates."

Other special events included a "Bon-bon Party," where all were given candies in which were hidden paper hats. The Amherst College Polo Club once agreed to perform on roller skates for the town's amusement, and Miss Laura Chandler, "the champion fancy skater of America" performed in April, 1885. Also in that month, there was a paper costume party, where people were encouraged to wear the Amherst Record in novel ways. A five dollar gold piece was offered for the "most complete and tastiest outfit."

Meanwhile, many physicians and ministers condemned roller skating as bad for the body and bad for the soul. What was described as "the howl that has been set up by clergy" referred to the argument that "rinks are public places, open to persons of both sexes ... . No test of character is applied to those seeking admission to them. Corrupting influences for both boys and girls may be there." It was protested in Amherst, however, that the sport was entirely innocent, patronized by hundreds of "our best people," with no chance of "soiling or tinging their morals in the slightest degree."

The Rise and Fall of the Mount Toby Resort

The Victorians discovered that mountains were great places for picnics, botanizing, and romance. One of the most romantic mountains in the Amherst area is Mount Toby in Sunderland, with one of the highest local peaks and more tales per foot of elevation than most. The landscape architect Frank Waugh said of Toby, "This sweet caressing quality of primitive wildness is intangible but also unquestionable. It is spiritual." Apparently, a less spiritual "sweet caressing" went on at the peak of Mount Toby, for an old story tells of the Victorian women of Sunderland marching up the mountain and burning down a suspicious hotel on its peak.

Metawampe Club Cabin on Mount Toby, Sunderland.

By the 1840s, Amherst College was using Toby as an outdoor botanical lab. Edward Hitchcock led excursions by horse and carriage to gather unusual minerals and botanical specimens. At that time Moses Hubbard owned most of the land and had built a carriage road to a treehouse-like observation platform in the highest trees. From there, one could see Mt. Monadnock in New Hampshire, Ascutney Mountain in Vermont, and Greylock in the Berkshires.

As described in chapter five, in 1849, Edward Hitchcock, Jr., and his students ascended the mountain on a mission. Some dressed as colonials, some as Native Americans, they performed elaborate ceremonies to change the name of the mountain. Hoping to rechristen it in honor of Metawampe, the chief who signed the deeds to the whites, a mock debate was held between two students dressed as Captain Toby and Chief Metawampe. When the people of Sunderland heard of the name change, they called a special town meeting to reaffirm Toby as the mountain's only official name.

With the advent of the railroad, mountain resorts became hot destinations and places like Toby, Mount Tom and Mount Holyoke flourished. The Central Vermont built a railroad station at the foot of Toby, where travelers would arrive to hear rousing religious speeches (at a platform near Roaring Brook), and children would cavort in the playground, or watch goldfish in the fountain.

A carriage road led to a newly built, six-story tower with a hotel built into it. The hotel register (in the Special Collections of the Jones Library in Amherst), has the signatures of Emily Dickinson's brother Austin and his wife Susan, who stayed there in October of 1876. The signatures of Ulysses S. Grant and Jerusha Snapdragon take some stretch to believe, however.

In the summer of 1877, nearly 200 members of the Amherst Reform Club took the train to Mount Toby for a picnic. A contemporary account says, "It was a day and a time for old and young to enjoy themselves and they all say they did, hugely. Baskets of provisions, ice cream, etc., put in appearance ... . An old fashioned game of round ball was participated in by the old, the middle-aged, and the boys. Vocal music broke upon the mountain air and that of stringed instruments was danced to by jolly sets for two hours; but the speeches, and short, pithy remarks, from Messrs. Graves, Nash, Dutton, 'Aleck,' Kellogg, Winifred Stearns, 'Dan' (McCleary, the mountain's caretaker), Mrs. White, president of the Ladies' Temperance Union, Brailey, and E.A. Thompson, were the unique features of the afternoon.

"Many on their return spoke of the scenery of the mountain as being most beautiful just now, and many flowers, ferns, pond lilies, etc., returned with the picknickers to Amherst. The round fare was just 30 cents each for full grown members, and a more orderly company the Toby station agent said never came to the mountain."

Unfortunately, "orderly" is not the way most people described the later activities on the mountain. By the early 1880s, it had developed what was called an "unsavory reputation." Mount Toby's era as a family resort came to a close in 1884 when, supposedly, the women of Sunderland climbed the mountain and burned down the hotel.

Camels on the Common in 1877

Springtime in Amherst today is pretty tame. There are the community fairs, food festivals and commencements, but none of it is quite as exotic as what Amherst witnessed in the spring of 1877. That was the year when Van Amburgh & Company's Great Golden Menagerie and Frost's Roman Circus and Royal Colosseum came to town. Van Amburgh, known as "The Lion King," started one of the greatest circuses in the world, and the sight of his lions and camels on the common was a far cry from the usual 19th century commencement tea.

In early June, 1877, posters and ads appeared in Amherst announcing:

The Leviathan of the Road!
175 Horses, 56 Wagons, 150 Men.
Five of the World's Champion Riders:
Mlle. Clarinda Lowanda, the brilliant Brazilian
Female Bare Back Equestrienne.
George Melville, the accomplished bare back somersault
rider, who has just returned from Europe.
Wm. Du Crow, the world renowned hurdle rider,
lately from Buenos Ayres (sic).
Nap. Lowanda, emphatically the most daring
rider travelling.
George Donald, the famous English Jockey Rider.
Mons. Fontaine, contortionist or India Rubber man.

FOUR FAMOUS CLOWNS, very glib of tongue.
Van Amburgh's Great Golden Menagerie Grand
Street Parade:
The Largest Elephant in the World, The Mammoth
Bolivar!
Trained Horses, Mules, Ponies, and Camels.
Hippopotamus Hog. South American Tapir.
Australian Wombat (Only one in existence)
Two-Horned Rhinoceros.
Admission to both Circus and Menagerie 50 Cents.

Isaac Van Amburgh, born in 1811, was the grandson of Native Americans. He began his career cleaning wild animal cages in New York state when the first African animals were shown here. Van

The strange sight of camels and elephants at the Amherst Common in the 19th century.

Amburgh went on to create the first trained animal act of modern times. He astounded audiences by going into the cages and putting his head in the mouths of lions.

Dressed as a Roman gladiator in a toga, Van Amburgh took the world by storm. By combining the animals of a menagerie with clowns and equestrians, he pioneered the 19th century circus and became its first superstar. During Van Amburgh's London debut, Queen Victoria went to his circus six times within a month.

The Amherst Record welcomed Van Amburgh's Great Golden Menagerie and Frost's Roman Circus with great enthusiasm, notwithstanding that the man himself wouldn't be there, having died: "Van Amburgh's Menagerie is the oldest show of the kind travelling in this country ... . The acrobats, gymnasts, jugglers, athletes, trapeze performers, etc., are all first class." Showing the first signs of the town's concern for animals, the paper also reported, "Their menagerie is the largest, more rare specimens of wild animals, better fed and cared for, than any other show on the face of the earth."

Even Emily Dickinson took note of this circus in a letter to Rev. Jenkins' wife: "There is a circus here, and Farmers' Commencement, and Boys and Girls from Tripoli, and Governors and swords, parade the Summer Streets." There was, however, no follow-up article in the papers after the circus left town. Disaster struck in the form of a tornado that wiped out the bridge over the Connecticut River. Reports of crashing boards, horses flying into the water, of death and injuries, and a boy thrown into a tree, cancelled any news of the circus. But that's another story.

Chapter Nine

THE UNSEEN WORLD:
PSYCHICS AND SPIRITUALISTS

North East Street, Amherst, Massachusetts

Ah, Necromancy Sweet!
Ah, Wizard erudite!
Teach me the skill...
#177

The Psychic Search
for Norris Chandler

In the spring of 1844, 14 year-old Norris Chandler disappeared. Some thought the Shutesbury boy had run off to sea. But an unidentified medium claimed Norris had been murdered, and she offered to point out the spot where the bones would be found.

The birth of the American spiritualist movement — with its clairvoyants, mediums, and mesmerists — goes back to the 1840s. In Arcadia, New York, three sisters became celebrities when they claimed the spirit world was communicating through them. Margaret, Katherine, and Leah Fox talked to the other world in a language of rhythmic raps.

Newspaper editor Horace Greeley spent several weeks observing them. When he found no evidence of fraud, dozens of others came forward believing they, too, could communicate with the dead. Spiritualist newspapers and societies appeared. Seances were held in country places, at which the dead gave monologues and ghostly hands and faces floated through darkened rooms. By 1874, the New England Spiritualists Camp Meeting Association met yearly at Lake Pleasant in Montague, not far from Amherst. Newspapers often derided the Lake Pleasant gathering as a "moral cesspool."

Fully one and a half years after Norris Chandler disappeared, he had yet to be found. It was in December, 1845, that a medium who had been "mesmerized" created a sensation by announcing the boy had been murdered. She named the spot in Shutesbury where the body was, but digging there turned up nothing. She named another spot, and another, until it was thought wise to choose a different method of communication.

Aaron Chandler, the boy's father, wrote to the Hampshire and Franklin Express stating "a liberal reward will be paid to any one who will furnish to the Post Master of Shutesbury, Massachusetts, satisfactory information respecting the boy, or to the boy if he will report himself." Within two weeks, the Shutesbury postmaster received the following information:

"Norris Chandler, the lost boy, has gone to sea, and was lately seen at the Island of New Zealand, on board a whaler, by a sailor homeward bound, who brought a message from the boy to his friends ... . If further information is desired, it may be obtained in New Bedford, where the vessel in which he sailed is owned."

Whether Norris Chandler ever saw his family again is unknown. By 1850, his parents, Aaron and Polly, moved to Wendell. In 1861, they bought a farm in New Salem where, five years later, Aaron Chandler was run over by a cart and killed.

TO-NIGHT! - - TO-NIGHT!

DON'T MISS IT!

THAT WONDERFUL MAN,

J. R. BROWN,

The Mind Reader.

Owing to the interest and desire expressed by those present at his exhibition in College Hall, last Friday, Mr. Brown has been induced to give another entertainment at the same place,

THIS FRIDAY EVENING, FEB. 19.

This entertainment will furnish some valuable instruction as well as amusement.

Those who went doubting came away convinced. Says one prominent citizen, "I have never been to an entertainment where I have been so well paid."

Prof. J. H. SEELYE says:

From an opportunity with which Mr. Brown kindly favored me to test his remarkable power in mind reading, I am satisfied that his claim to possess such a power is entirely trustworthy.

J. H. SEELYE.

Prof. J. W. BURGESS says:

I had as good an opportunity as any one to observe Brown's movements here last Friday evening, and all I have to say is, that if he is a fraud I have been most completely and unconsciously duped. I think no fair and candid person could have viewed his experiments and have gone away without feeling that there is a world of power and mystery in the mental realm, of which our psychologists have not given us the faintest glimmer. JOHN W. BURGESS.

Prof. H. W. PARKER says:

Mr. Brown's method—rapid walking around the room, and moving his subject's hand hither and thither in every direction—seems to me to indicate that the subject, in the excitement of approaching that which he has in mind, gives off, unconsciously, an increase of nervous force, which is unconsciously received by Mr. Brown, but is sufficient to produce an impression of the nearness of the object sought, and finally a certainty of contact with it. Of nervous force we know little; and of course it is a mere supposition that it can be communicated from one person to another. Dr. Beard's theory that Mr. Brown is guided by muscular contractions of the subject's hand, is pretty surely known to be untenable, by those who participated in the experiments here. H. W. PARKER.

TICKETS, 35 and 50 Cents, according to location.
For Sale at Nelson's Bookstore during the day, and in the evening at the door.

Buy your tickets early if you wish to be sure of a good seat.

J. R. Brown had some of the finest intellects in Amherst convinced he could read minds.

Belief in the supernatural powers of mind readers and mediums was so widespread in Emily Dickinson's time, that scores of journals published reports of psychic experiences. By 1853, over 2,000,000 people were followers of the Spiritualist Movement in America. To be sure, clairvoyants have always been with us. Eighteenth century America saw such powers used to predict or cure illnesses. The 19th century Spiritualist Movement was taken very seriously, but by the 1850s, psychic experiments had also become popular entertainments.

In February of 1875, the Amherst Record attempted to whip up excitement for an appearance of the popular mind reader J.R. Brown. The paper described Brown's "astonishing and unparalleled power," and predicted there would not be room enough for all who would flock to the hall. Ironically, several noted academics were thoroughly convised by Brown, while the ever-skeptical people of Amherst failed to fill College Hall to have their minds read.

Brown had been born in St. Louis in 1851, and as a child had received mental impressions from other children when he grasped their hands. He attracted the attention of the press and was soon in demand "at fairs and local merry-makings." His publicity proclaimed that the most eminent scientists in New York, "after thorough examination of Mr. Brown's powers, stated that they could make nothing of him."

At Yale, Brown underwent several tests, baffling the scientists there. In one instance he read a man's mind while connected to him by a 200-foot length of insulated copper wire. The Amherst Record suggested that "our scientific men may solve the problem which President Woolsey and the professors at Yale College were unable to discover."

Brown's performance in College Hall on February 12, 1875, consisted of walking rapidly about the hall while blindfolded; finding hidden articles; and telling the name, birthplace, or occupation of members of the audience. Brown supposedly obtained a stack of photographs from local photographer John Lovell, and, while blindfolded, held the hand of a young lady and chose the photo of her "dearly beloved." This performance was described as "exciting and astonishing."

Amherst College Professor of Moral Philosophy and Metaphysics Julius Seelye said he was "satisfied that (Brown's) claim to possess such a power is entirely trustworthy." John Burgess, Professor of History and Political Science, said, "... if he is a fraud I have been most completely and unconsciously duped ... there is a world of power and mystery in the mental realm, of which our psychologists have not given us the faintest glimmer."

Apparently, the average Amherst resident was not as impressed by mind reading. Few attended Brown's first performance, and a second was cancelled when only a handful arrived at College Hall.

The Spiritualist World
of Lake Pleasant

Along with summertime picnics, band concerts, and fireworks, 19th century Connecticut Valley residents could attend annual conventions of spirits. Thousands came to see clairvoyants, mediums, seers and psychics at the New England Spiritualists' Camp Meeting Association. These conventions, billed as "The Largest in New England" opened up a hole into the spirit world at Lake Pleasant, Montague, to the disgust of nonbelievers.

It all began in August of 1874, when J.J. Richardson, a Greenfield caterer, thought he could sell a lot more ice cream if more people went to Lake Pleasant. Just that summer, the Eddy Brothers proved that people would come from all over the country to seances held in Chittenden, Vermont. At Lake Pleasant, Richardson set up 100 rented tents, there were dining rooms, the Fitchburg Band played, and people danced.

The focus at Lake Pleasant, though, was on the mediums who dazzled crowds by speaking to the spirit world. People came from many parts of New England and camped out around the lake. Hundreds of curious people from the surrounding towns were there to gape at "those queer people." One Montague woman is quoted as saying, "It is perfectly dreadful — them wicked Spiritualists are coming to Lake Pleasant! They will fiddle and dance and the Devil will cuckle! What will become of our young women: They will all be led away from our church and lose their souls!"

Though it was later claimed that the spirit world picked the Connecticut River Valley, it was Richardson the caterer who had the idea, and it was a phenomenal success. By 1907, there were 125 buildings on the grounds, including over 90 cottages, eight restaurants, and a large hotel. The New England Spiritualists' Association was hosting 2,000 people a day. There were post and telegraph offices, stores, a barbershop, police, and newspapers.

While the Spiritualists firmly believed in spirits, they did not believe in a deity. God and the Bible were made up by men, who made of woman "a satellite to man while she would be his equal." So persuasive were the mediums and psychics, that when the Methodists tried to convert Lake Pleasant to a Christian meeting place, they lost a lot of their members to the Spiritualists and abandoned the site.

Money, rivalry, and arson all played a part in the dwindling of the movement. In 1882, Jonathan Roberts, the Philadelphia editor of the paper "Mind and Matter," visited Lake Pleasant. The

Mary and James Kellogg of Amherst bicycled to Lake Pleasant to see mediums and psychics.

Directors of the camp asked for his arrest after he "grossly insulted the President of the Association and insulted Judge Patton by loud and obscene language, too vile for record or publication." Roberts sued the Association for slander. In 1884, a roller skating rink was set up in direct competition to the dance hall. Someone burned down the rink, and thus returned dancing to profitability.

The natural decline of the movement in the 20th century increased in momentum with the fire of 1907. A cottage lamp overturned and exploded. Within three hours, 112 buildings were destroyed. Some floated personal property in boats on the lake, some simply threw things in. The bucket brigade could do little. While the New England Spiritualist Camp Meeting Association would never be the same, spiritualists still met at Lake Pleasant well into the 1950s.

And what did Amherst think of the psychic world of Lake Pleasant? The Amherst Record once referred to the place as "A Moral Cesspool."

The Life of a Homeless Palm Reader

John McLean lived in a barn and read palms in the streets of Amherst.

When winter arrives and the holidays approach, we often think of those who are homeless, and we are, perhaps, a little more charitable than at other times of the year. Looking back at Emily Dickinson's Amherst, we find an unusual example of year-round kindness toward one homeless Amherst man. John McLean, a kind but eccentric man, was considered the only authentic fortune teller in town.

John McLean was born in the parish of Ballintoy, county of Antrim, North Ireland, in about 1840. He himself wasn't sure of the date. John arrived in Amherst in about 1867 and worked digging the foundation for Palmer's Block, the building later supplanted by Town Hall. He found that odd jobs on a farm or work as a hod carrier didn't suit his uneasy mind, and he began hauling things for people in a wheelbarrow. For his uncle Archie McGowan in Granby, he hauled numerous loads of apples, potatoes, old clothes, furniture and even a goat, through the Notch in the Holyoke Range.

McLean eventually became a well-known figure on Amherst's streets, as he began his eccentric collecting habits. From morning into the night he collected old clothes, shoes, hats, umbrellas, old wagon wheels, and the little tin spoons given away with ice cream.

Amherst had a certain affection for John, who had free run of the streets and back lots. In 1898, he lived at Mrs. William Kellogg's house on North East Street. By 1900, he was turning the hand press for printer Henry McCloud and doing odd jobs at his house.

For a number of years after the turn of the century, John lived in Arthur Bardwell's barn on North Pleasant Street. There he slept inside a high circular nest of discarded clothes, magazines, and derby hats.

McLean seemed to enjoy telling fortunes and entertaining children with old stories. He would offer to read one's palm for nothing, though he usually went away with a dime or a quarter.

On July 4, 1901, a cannon fire cracker lacerated McLean's hand badly, putting him into the hospital. The town began a subscription list to pay his hospital bills, and many of the most prominent Amherst families contributed.

John McLean lived to a ripe age, dying in a tolerant Amherst. It can also be said that McLean died with a certain amount of dignity, for he had saved enough for funeral expenses and a headstone.

Speaking to the Dead
at the North Amherst Post Office

More than 65 years ago on March 30, 1930, Adin Field died in North Amherst. Field hasn't been heard from since, which isn't the case for his father. Adin's father, Phineus, appears to have communicated with him from beyond the grave on February 16, 1891.

In the 1890s, Adin Field got swept up in the Spiritualist Movement at Lake Pleasant in Montague. North Amherst seemed particularly taken with seances, for in addition to Field, physician William Dwight and postmaster Forester Ainsworth were devotees of the psychic world of Lake Pleasant. In fact, Forester Ainsworth, who was also librarian for the North Amherst Library, a lawyer and a justice of the peace, became a medium. It was through Ainsworth's hand that Field received a letter from his dead father.

Ainsworth became so involved in the movement that he and his wife rented a cottage at Lake Pleasant each year during the Spiritualists' Camp Meetings. In 1889, he met Dr. Henry Slade there. Slade was a well-known medium of his day and he surprised Ainsworth by agreeing to perform private seances in North Amherst the following year. Ainsworth's detailed records of those seances have disappeared, but that period apparently served as his apprenticeship into the realm of "automatic writing."

Ainsworth's friend Adin Field took part in that 1890 series of seances with Slade and wrote of it later. For a week in April, people came to the North Amherst Post Office to see Slade. When Field saw him on April 17, this is what happened: "Slade took his seat on the east side of the table and I sat on the west side near the window. He took two slates, placed a pencil between them, and with his right hand held them under the table, his left hand grasping the top of the table ... I did not touch the table. Soon we heard writing. When the sound of writing ceased the slates left Slade's hand, came into my lap, remained there a few seconds and then came upon the top of the table.

"I could detect no movement in Slade's arm and shoulder, as would be required in throwing or tossing the slates into my lap, and certainly no hand was visible as they moved through the rather circuitous route from my lap to the table." An unconvincing message to Field on the slate said only that he had spirit friends that would help him achieve success.

The following February, it was Ainsworth who acted as medium for Field in the North Amherst Post Office: "Mr. Ainsworth and I sat down near the stove. We did not discuss the matter of spirit

Dr. Henry Slade held seances at the North Amherst Post Office.

communication, nor any subject of that character. In the meantime I told Mr. Ainsworth that I had a small farm in mind that I had thought of buying, but was undecided. Almost immediately his right hand and arm began to shake. He grasped a pencil that lay on his desk, found a sheet of paper, and without any volition on his part wrote the following:

'My dear son:

'The time for you to act has not quite arrived. Be patient for a short time and you will see the way opening. You can then better determine how to act and what to do. Your first duty is to attend to your mother; she needs unusual care, and it will not be long before you will see what we mean by the advice to wait. Let your confidence be undisturbed, and in due time you will see that it has not been misplaced.

Father'"

Taking his father's advice, he fortunately didn't buy the farm. Shortly afterwards, death and illness in the family made expansion too risky, and thus the dead father's advice seemed to be wise. He continued to see mediums at Lake Pleasant, but with mediocre results. Field's ultimate opinion of communication with the dead was that, yes we can talk to the dead, but they aren't any smarter than when they were alive.

Chapter Ten

AMHERST VS
THE OUTSIDE WORLD

"Greetings from Amherst, Massachusetts"

*If I could bribe them by a Rose
I'd bring them every flower that grows
From Amherst to Cashmere!*
#179

The Exile
of Perez Dickinson

Amherst College conferred an honorary degree on Dickinson cousin, Perez Dickinson, an exiled Civil War hero.

When the Civil War broke out on April 12, 1861, there were many who happened to be living on the wrong side of the battle lines. For Northern families living in the South, or vice versa, their lives and all they had worked for were suddenly in jeopardy. Some were considered traitors, and a few became heroes. Perez Dickinson, from Amherst but living in Tennessee when the war broke out, became one of the Valley's Civil War heroes. But he did it without firing a shot.

Perez Dickinson was born in 1813, and was the first cousin of Emily Dickinson's father. He was educated at Amherst Academy and entered Amherst College with the class of 1831. By 1830, however, some of Dickinson's family left Amherst for Knoxville, Tennessee. There, Perez simultaneously headed an academy and completed his education at the University of Tennessee. Amherst College later conferred an M.A. degree on him in 1888.

Perez was immensely successful in the South. In 1832, at a time when there was no railroad or telegraph there, he joined with his brother-in-law to establish one of the largest merchant businesses in Tennessee. Cowan and Dickinson began in the days of barter and hauling by wagon, and grew with the age of steam engines and commerce.

In 1845, Perez married Susan Penniman of Boston. Susan died little more than a year later, then within a few months their only child, Lucy, died. Perez never remarried. He faced the most dramatic part of his life, and of the life of the country, alone. When the Civil War came, he spoke out in favor of the Union side, though he was surrounded by Confederates, many of them old friends.

In 1861, the governor of Tennessee granted Perez permission to visit the North on business. Upon returning to the South in October, he was arrested and accused of having been born in Massachusetts and of going to the North to communicate with Northerners. Perez was ordered to take an oath of allegiance and fidelity to the Confederate States, or forfeit all his property and go into exile.

One Knoxville newspaper immediately came out in his support: "Thus a man who has spent his life here — acquired by industry and business talents, a fortune — a man whose relatives sleep in these graveyards — a man who has committed no offense, but the one committed by his parents in allowing him to be born in Massachusetts, is forced to leave his property and abandon his home of adoption and choice, and go into exile. He has less than a week to get out of the State ... . From such oppression and tyranny, may God deliver the people of this distracted and ruined country."

Dickinson refused the oath and steadfastly refused to leave Tennessee, daring anyone to touch his property. Perez became a hero to those back in Massachusetts. The Amherst Record praised his opposition to "Southern bluster and bravado" and proclaimed, "All honor to this noble son of Amherst."

This stalemate was broken when General Ambrose Burnside took Knoxville from the Confederates in September, 1863. Perez went on to become the founding president of Knoxville's First National Bank, and an outspoken advocated for Blacks during Reconstruction. Amherst warmly welcomed Dickinson whenever he visited, as he had done even during the war, in 1864. When he died in Knoxville in 1901, Perez Dickinson was honored in both the North and the South.

Amherst and the Armenian Massacres

H.H. Goodell, president of the Mass. Agricultural College, gave an impassioned speech to help save starving Armenians in 1896.

Tracy Kidder, Pulitzer Prize-winning Connecticut Valley author, called Amherst "the kind of place that has a fine school system and a foreign policy." Town Meeting often grapples with issues of international scope, yet this is nothing new. From the first class of Amherst College in 1821, Amherst was known for the missionaries it sent to deal with problems all over the world. The townspeople, too, rallied to foreign causes, and one of the most emotional examples occurred in the 1890s. Amherst considered the Armenian massacres of 1894-96 the greatest crimes of the century.

Armenia began an active struggle for independence from the Ottoman Empire in the 1860s. The growth of Armenian nationalism brought the wrath of Sultan Abdul-Hamid II. This culminated in a series of barbaric massacres beginning in 1894. Nearly 200,000 Armenians were slain within two years, earning the Turkish leader the title "The Red Sultan."

The Amherst Record implored the town to help the Armenians, quoting an estimate that over 300,000 were in danger of starvation. A mass meeting was announced for Thursday, February 12, 1896, at Town Hall. "Our neighbors, Springfield, Pittsfield, Adams and Northampton are giving freely. It is now our turn," the paper said. Money was to be raised to provide food, cooking utensils, clothing, and shelter.

An enthusiastic crowd gathered at Town Hall to hear several speeches. The president of the Massachusetts Agricultural College, H.H. Goodell, gave an impassioned opening address. He graphically described the persecution of the Christian Armenians by the Moslem Turks. The Amherst College Choir sang, then the citizens of Amherst drew up three resolutions. They expressed their "profoundest indignation at these outrages against humanity ... the atrocious outrages against womanhood, and homelife." Copies of the resolutions were sent to the Secretary of State and Representatives in Congress.

An Amherst Fund for Armenian Relief was begun, with a goal of raising $500 within 30 days. L. Dwight Hills was treasurer of the fund, and several local businesses and ministers helped collect donations. Within five days they raised $300.

Amherst was of two minds about the character of The Red Sultan. Sounding vaguely like the criticism of Ronald Reagan in the 1980s, some felt the sultan was a "charming gentleman ... a bad king, but a good man with excellent intentions." But most felt he was "a cold-blooded murderer of the innocent, a liar and a perjurer."

More devastating massacres of Armenians took place in 1909. Then, during World War I, more than 1,000,000 Armenians perished as the Turks deported them to the Syrian desert. Armenians were never to achieve the independent state they hoped for, despite the support of many countries and many towns like those in the Connecticut River Valley.

"Dog" Meat in Amherst

Newspaperman Charles Morehouse thought the "invigorating atmosphere" of Amherst was a good place to raise quality meat.

As the 19th century progressed, Amherst and similar towns changed from a local barter system to a cash-based economy. Increasingly, farmers turned to cash crops, becoming less self-sufficient, and relying more on food brought in from elsewhere by local merchants. In 1883, editor Charles Morehouse blasted Amherst's meat markets in the pages of the Amherst Record. Calling their goods "shoddy" and "dog meat," the editor made accusations that threatened the town's calm and prosperous exterior.

Morehouse blamed both the greed of butchers, of which there were four in town, and the tight-fisted townspeople, who chose inferior imported grades when they could afford the better local meat.

The tirade brought up a fascinating issue in New England history. As early as 1813, many Amherst farmers were sending cattle to Boston and other markets in order to raise cash to educate their children. The bulk of the local food supply was still grown locally in 1820, though, with as little as 25 percent of it available to export. This changed rapidly, and by the 1850s, some farmers were fattening 100 head of cattle each season to export, with herds of 40 to 50 common. At the same time, an increasing proportion of the region's food came from out of the area.

As the frontier moved westward, meat, wheat and corn production moved west as well, where they could be grown more economically. Chicago, centrally located as a railroad terminus, became the center for the collection and slaughter of livestock. Cincinnati slaughtered such a quantity of hogs that it became known as "Porkopolis."

In the opinion of Charles Morehouse, Chicago beef was not to be compared in quality to meat fatted by Amherst farmers. The western slaughterhouses preserved their meat with a free use of chemicals. This ruined the flavor and made it possible to send it on "a fashionable tour to Great Britain and Europe where the peasantry no doubt consider American beef a dainty morsel."

Amherst butchers claimed they couldn't find enough locally produced meat for market, and what they did find was too expensive. Morehouse countered with a claim that from two to six dozen railroad cars of livestock were being shipped from the Amherst depot to the Boston market in Brighton every week. That Amherst ate mostly Western beef could only mean that local butchers were making higher profits on the inferior meat.

Morehouse felt the only economically viable option was to take care of one's health by eating the best food. After all, said Morehouse, "Amherst enjoys a world-wide reputation of being one of the loveliest and most healthful spots on the face of the earth ... where students improve in health each year of their college course, and where broken down constitutions regain their former vigor in this locality of picturesque surroundings and a moral, invigorating atmosphere."

The Panic
of 1873

When the Stock Market crashes, as it did in 1929, and more recently in October, 1987, the effects are instantly felt in virtually every town in the U.S. and in worldwide markets. One of the worst financial panics in U.S. history occurred on September 18, 1873, on what was called Black Friday. At first, Amherst considered it a remote, New York event, to which the town would be immune. The Panic slowly spread, until every town including Amherst was eventually drawn in, and the country went into a five-year Depression.

The Fearing Hat Factory, a bleak building in the Amherst landscape, suffered in the panic of 1873.

On Black Friday, the banking firms of Jay Cooke & Company of New York, Washington, and Philadelphia, closed. Cooke had lost enormous sums by overextending credit in the building of the Northern Pacific Railroad. On that September 18th, the Stock Market tumbled. Soon other New York and Philadelphia banks closed. Crowds of depositors gathered at bank doors in New York, and detectives had to be called out to protect them from pickpockets.

The Panic extended south and west, with hundreds of banks closing. One Detroit banker said, "There's a light ahead; there's help in God; there's wealth in Jesus; there's power in prayer." His desperate words didn't help and factory cutbacks and closings followed.

In the face of this, the Amherst Record blithely claimed that "We shall feel the effects of the panic very slightly as compared with those towns which depend largely upon manufacturing for their prosperity." The town was concerned instead with the apple and potato crops, and with the yearly Cattle Show. Rev. Herrick of the North Amherst Congregational Church preached on the beauty of nature and railed against Amherst's concern with the "almighty dollar." To raise funds for upholstering the church pews, the Ladies of College Church held a tea party, serving oysters, ice cream and tea.

But the Panic did come to the Connecticut Valley. By November 12, newspapers were filled with ads like photographer John Lovell's: "Panic! Reduction!! Reduction!!! Ready cash will do wonders at the Amherst Picture Gallery." J.M. Waite & Sons' ad read: "Ladies' Misses' and Childrens' Furs will be sold at Panic Prices for Cash. A large Stock of Buffalo, Wolf and Fancy Robes and Horse Blankets, at prices that cannot be beaten."

The Fearing Hat Company hoped business would remain as good as ever, having just imported 9,000 hats from Italy and having expanded their facility. But factories and mills in Lowell, Fall River, Wilbraham, and throughout the state were in trouble. Many Canadians in Holyoke returned to Canada because of the scarcity of work. In Amherst, J.R. Cushman & Son announced they would close their leather company on January 1, throwing 25 men out of work.

The barbers in town decided to close their shops on Sundays, farmers had difficulty selling tobacco, and the number of homeless people passing through Amherst was on the increase. Even Emily Dickinson referred to Jay Cooke and the Panic in her letters.

In 1873, the Massachusetts Central Railroad had been designed to pass through Amherst to Northampton, but the Depression put a stop to it. A map in Beers Atlas of that year optimistically shows the track that wouldn't exist for many years. (It displays it, by the way, in the wrong part of town.) It wasn't until 1878 that the Depression ended, the railroad was revived, and hard times were over.

Amherst vs.
New York City

John E. Williams, in doorway, argued in print with the editor of the New York Sun about which was the better place to live, New York or Amherst.

In the 19th century, prosperous rural towns like Amherst sometimes pointed a smug finger at the evils of big cities. John Williams, an editor of the Amherst Record, printed an attack on the New York Sun, accusing the newspaper of sensational journalism and of catering to "the vices of the vicious." Williams got more than he bargained for, however, when the Sun's editor picked up the gauntlet and counter-attacked. The exchange pitted New York City against the "placid and comparatively uneventful community that is shut in by the Hampshire Hills."

John Williams' complaints against the New York Sun, printed on December 10, 1884, accused the paper of seducing the "vast sensational masses that feed their shallow natures on momentary excitement ... delighted with the latest sensation and latest romance in society." This issue is of course still alive today, with people like Rupert Murdock and the tabloids the frequent targets.

Some of the headlines Williams found objectionable included, "Preparing to Jump Off a Bridge," "Tragedy in a Courtroom — A Jealous Lover Fires at his Sweetheart and Then Shoots Himself in the Heart," "She Says She Was Kissed in an Uptown Store," and "Mother Baum Runs Away." He accused the Sun of shining on "all the vilest of the living vile ... all the iniquity of New York City." That the writing style made all this irresistible reading caused Williams even more consternation.

To the surprise of Amherst, the editor of the Sun read the Amherst Record and came back with a rebuttal and his own accusations. The editor claimed not to be immoral but to have a larger moral philosophy than peaceful Amherst, which was not as complex and varied as New York. Moreover, if the events of New York took place in Amherst, he felt Williams would readily report them, however sensational. As it was, the Amherst Record was restricted by the tedium of the town's peaceful ways. He considered the following Amherst news items to be utterly dull: "No death has occurred since November 12," "Chicken thieves are said to have vigorously plied their calling lately hereabouts," "William Pharough, a well-known citizen of this village recently slaughtered a hog," "Dr. Dunbar, whose trial and acquittal on a charge of abortion are fresh in the public memory, was married last week to an Athol woman."

John Williams' response to this was to back down, saying the Sun's criticism was not unjustified. After all, he said, "news is bought and sold and has a relative value, like any other commodity." He admitted that if terrible murders or frightening escapes of wild circus animals were to occur in Amherst, he might write thrilling accounts himself. He concluded with, "For a newsy, independent, perfectly wreckless and very reliable sheet give us the New York Sun."

Do Not Go West, Young Man

Levi Stockbridge of the Massachusetts Agricultural College argued that Amherst farm boys should stay home.

With the help of Horace Greeley's cry to "Go West, Young Man," the draw of Western land was irresistible to many, especially after the Civil War. But in the Connecticut Valley, the advice of Levi Stockbridge, president of the Massachusetts Agricultural College, was "Do not go West, young man," unless you want to live "in a house not as good as a New England pig pen."

Within two generations after 1800, the great Western expansion was complete. New territories reached the West coast, most of which was acquired by war or the threat of war.

In Amherst, as in many Eastern towns, the population seemed restless. Of the craftsmen working in Amherst in 1850, only 20 percent remained in 1870. The easy conclusion is that they all went West. It would seem, too, that the hilltown migration would be mainly away from their rocky fields to the Western farmlands, but such was not always the case. Church records in Shutesbury, Leverett, and Pelham reveal that as agriculture declined in the hilltowns, the population wasn't drained primarily by the West. Most were attracted by the more prosperous cities in New England where industry was growing.

Though Amherst had some industrial growth, many migrated to the booming Massachusetts mill towns, or urban centers in Connecticut and New York. Others did go West, including some of the men who worked for Amherst toolmaker Truman Nutting. Aaron Ferry went to Ohio in 1841 with his wife Judith. They struggled with poverty and homesickness until he developed a brick-making business. Eli Nutting went to Buffalo, where he noticed a lot of Easterners going West, but also a lot of Westerners going East. He himself returned to Worthington and then moved to Conway, where he made woodworking planes.

Nathaniel D. Goodell made a successful transition to Sacramento, where he became an architect. But his brother, Noble, returned to Amherst after only one year.

In recommending to his students that they not go West, President Stockbridge described the huge "bonanza" farms of Southern Minnesota, the Dakota Territory, and Montana. Begun by speculators on tracts of as many as 70,000 acres, wheat was virtually the only crop grown. Most of the settlers were Norwegians, but there were "some Yankees living in this country who do most of the business and 'skin' the foreigners." It was mainly a money-losing business, according to Stockbridge.

With the scarcity of wood and water out on the plains, no school or churches, and houses worse than pig pens, Stockbridge advised his students in New England to stay home.

The Suffering of Native Americans, Blacks, and Asians

Before the ashes of the 1992 L.A. riots could cool, Newsweek magazine described the trauma as "the deadliest urban upheaval in this century, scarring the face of the city and the nation's soul." That the violence swept up several races meant "the old vocabulary of race no longer applies." The magazine concluded, "The unrest in L.A. underscored the importance of finding new ways to think about ethnicity, crime and poverty." The old ways go back a very long time, as a look at the Amherst summer of 1888 shows.

Amherst has always had a social conscience that goes beyond its pastoral boundaries. Like most New England towns, it was begun as a Christian parish, so it's not surprising that its first acts of social outreach came from the churches.

Amherst's First Congregational Church was very active in missionary work in the 19th century. In 1888, the church invited Rev. C.J. Rider, the secretary of the American Missionary Association, to speak about issues the town hoped to address. Foremost in their minds was the treatment of African Americans, Native Americans, and Asians.

Rev. Rider began by giving the group population figures on minorities: "Instead of four million negroes, there are today eight millions in the United States. In the mountain region of the South there are two millions. On the western frontier are 300,000 red men. With the Chinese on the Pacific coast, these three nations, the Blacks, the Indians, and the Chinese, there are 10,425,000 people which can be reached only through such an organization as the A.M.A."

Rider claimed that 28,000 children were being excluded from schools on Reservation land. In a Federal Court House on a major Reservation he saw "Indians of all ages herded together like cattle. The superintendent in showing me over the institution pointed out the gallows where the eight ropes were dangling and, as he said, they could swing off eight Indians by a single touch of the spring, but they had hung but six at a time." In speaking of the treatment of the Indians, he believed "the government of the United States would have much to answer for in the final day of reckoning."

Of conditions in the South, he noted there were "90,000 mothers in Tennessee who can neither read nor write. More murders are committed in one day in Kentucky than occur in six years in Vermont."

As a leader of a missionary movement, Rider naturally approached such problems from a religious perspective: "What they need is the gospel and the christianizing influence of our free institutions."

During that same summer of 1888, Amherst also took part in a relatively new experimental program. Eight children from Brooklyn were sent from the city for a rural experience in Amherst. The Amherst Record thought this "most worthy charitable work ... . Some are orphans, others have no father living and only their widowed mother to support them ... . They are not barbarians as some people may wrongly suppose ... . Some of the families in Amherst who have got interested in the work say they have enjoyed the little ones' company as much as the latter have their visit in the country."

How successful such efforts were is difficult to measure. The Amherst paper, nevertheless, was optimistic about local efforts to solve national problems: "Everywhere in this broad land are kind and humane people, willing to devote their time, their energy and their money to alleviate suffering, prevent crime, and elevate those who, through no fault of their own, are less fortunate and less favored than themselves and millions who have enough of everything and to spare."

Evidence of the often overlooked ethnic mix of Emily's Amherst: a Chinese laundry in the basement of the building on left, Main Street.

Chapter Eleven

NATURAL AND UNNATURAL DISASTERS

"A Factory Hollow, North Amherst, Massachusetts"

The Lightning showed a Yellow Head -
And then a livid Toe -
The Birds put up the Bars to Nests -
The Cattle flung to Barns -
Then came one drop of Giant Rain -
And then, as if the Hands
That held the Dams - had parted hold -
The Waters Wrecked the Sky -
    #824

The Day the Local Papermaker
Fell into a Vat of Boiling Bleach

Reuben Roberts, first owner of the Roberts Paper Mill. Both his son and grandson died horribly in his mill.

Of all the ghastly ways Emily Dickinson's contemporaries met with accidental death, one of the most agonizing had to have been the way Sylvester Roberts died. In November of 1849, while practicing the gentle craft of papermaking, Roberts fell into a cauldron of boiling bleach.

Daniel Rowe of Montague built the first paper mill in Amherst in about 1795. Located on the Mill River in North Amherst, he sold the mill to Reuben Roberts and Benjamin Cox in 1806. In 1839, Sylvester Roberts, Reuben's son, bought into the family business, which by 1848, was to grow into two papermaking mills on the same river.

In the early 1800s, most paper was made from bleached cotton rags which were collected, sorted, washed, and bleached. Then they were shredded to a fine pulp. A water-powered Hollander machine did the shredding with knife blades in a tub of water.

The pulp, like a creamy batter, was poured into a vat and a wire screen was carefully dipped in. As the screen was raised a thin layer of pulp adhered to its surface. This was drained, and the film of pulp was flipped onto a felt cloth.

A "post" of 144 sheets was stacked about two feet high, each sheet separated by a piece of felt. A large press forced more water out of the pile of sheets and felts. The sheets were separated and hung in a drying loft. Because the sheets had an absorbent surface, they had to be coated with a sizing to make the surface smooth.

Water-powered wooden rollers were then used to glaze the surface to make a more uniform texture. Trimmed and finished sheets were packed either into quires of 24 sheets or reams of 480 sheets.

When South Hadley paper mills began producing writing paper in large quantities, the Roberts Company turned to making inexpensive paper for newsprint and wrappers. Instead of cotton rags, straw was used, and much of this short-lived paper was shipped from Amherst to Albany for newspaper printing.

On Monday, November 13, 1849, Sylvester Roberts bleached straw in a large cauldron. He stood on a plank laid over the top of it, and attempted to raise the straw out of the liquid by pulling down on a rope attached to a block and tackle. The rope snapped and Roberts fell headlong into the boiling bleach.

His obituary stated, "The flesh was almost literally scalded from his body, and he lingered in great agony till Tuesday morning. He was a highly respected citizen, and his loss will be severely felt by the community."

This was the second such tragedy to hit the Roberts family within three months. On August 28, Sylvester's 18-month-old son William had died in a similar scalding accident at the paper mill.

Eighteen Hundred
and Starve to Death

Every year, the people of the Connecticut River Valley anticipate another lush summer, but such a pleasurable season can't always be taken for granted. There have been years when summer never seemed to come at all, and the Valley went from a cold spring to a cold fall, then back to winter. For Amherst, 1873 was one of the coldest years on record, and to make matters worse it was also a hurricane year. Yet, when old-timers in Amherst gathered to talk of that year's weather, they claimed that it was balmy compared to 1816. That was the year known as "eighteen hundred and starve to death."

Weather records specifically for Amherst go back only to 1836. To understand how bad 1816 was, we can look at newspaper accounts or weather records kept elsewhere, for it was a disastrous year throughout America and Europe.

Following a very cold December, January and February of 1816 were unusually mild. Far fewer fires were kept in parlors than normal. March began cold, then warmed to the point of causing great floods along the Ohio and Kentucky Rivers.

April began warm, but grew colder as days passed. The month ended with wintry blasts of snow and ice. In May, buds and flowers froze and ice formed half an inch thick on ponds. Fields were planted and replanted with corn as sprouts came up and died.

June was among the coldest ever known at this latitude. Frost and ice killed much that was green, and nearly all fruit was destroyed. Vermont had 10 inches of snow, Maine seven, and Massachusetts three.

July brought only more frost and ice. Most of the corn crop was destroyed, except for some on the hill farms. August was, if possible, even worse. Ice was again forming to a depth of a half inch. The little corn that had matured froze and much of it was cut down for fodder. It seemed that nearly everything green had been destroyed. Papers arriving here from Europe reported similar stories of a summerless year.

The mildest weather of the year came in the first two weeks of September, but then it was a quick return to frost and ice. By November, enough snow fell to make good sleighing. The year ended with a mild and comfortable December.

The year 1816 had been one in which frost and ice were common in every month. Very little vegetation matured in the Eastern and Middle states. Food prices rose drastically and many families feared for their futures.

Shot Dead
on the Amherst Common

By one of those odd quirks of fate, Stillman Rice met his death on the Amherst Common in 1822. Rice was born in 1798, and he attended Dartmouth Medical School in 1818. He lived for a time in Leverett, and upon becoming a doctor he settled in Enfield, Massachusetts. Rice was planning to marry a young Enfield woman when he found himself to be in the wrong place at the wrong time.

Amherst had its first militia company soon after 1740, but it wasn't until 1792 that a federal law created mandatory service. Every free, able-bodied white male between 18 and 45 years old was required to enroll in the militia as of that date. In Massachusetts, men were required to attend three training days each year, one in May and two in the autumn. Each man was to furnish his own arms and equipment, which usually included a flint-lock musket and a bayonet. Each was to bear all expenses, without pay.

A certain amount of laxity prevailed among members of Amherst's North Company and South Company. Training days were usually only half days until the War of 1812 made the men more conscientious. The President requisitioned Massachusetts troops to serve in the war, but Governor Strong refused. He did, however, order troops to prepare to defend the state's borders.

The gathering of the local regiments occurred alternately at Hadley, Amherst, and Belchertown. The regiments included the Old Hadley Light Infantry, and the Northampton and Belchertown artillery companies. At one time, there was a calvary company known as the Amherst Horse Company.

In 1822, the troops met at dawn at the East Amherst Common for inspection and training. The orderly sergeant called the roll and noted the names of absentees, who were to be fined later. After drilling, the companies got in formation to be marched to fife and drum tunes played by the combined musicians of all the companies.

They marched to the customary place, the south section of the Amherst Town Common, now part of the Amherst College campus. After inspection, the weapons were stacked, guards placed over them, and the men given a break. At this point, with townspeople gathered around enjoying the festivities, someone approached the weapons and asked the guard if he could handle one of the unloaded guns. He casually picked up a rifle, aimed it at the crowd and pulled the trigger.

Unfortunately, that particular gun was loaded. The young Dr. Stillman Rice happened to be passing through Amherst. While watching with the crowd, Rice suddenly dropped to the ground, to the shock of everyone. He was taken to a house next to where the Town Hall is today, and he soon died. The body was brought out to be viewed, under the guard of the Old Hadley Light Infantry.

The impact of the tragic accident was so great that training day was suspended and the soldiers returned to their homes.

A Tornado Sent Fred Into a Tree

On June 14, 1877, a tornado lifted little Fred Cook into the air. But instead of landing in the Land of Oz, Fred was caught by the branches of a tree and later retrieved. The tornado had destroyed the covered bridge over the Connecticut River, which linked Northampton and Hadley. Eleven people from Northampton, Hadley, and Amherst went down — or in Fred's case up — in the disaster.

In the 18th century, Northampton and Hadley had been connected only by ferry. One was operating at the Hockanum section of Hadley by 1658. The first bridge over the river in that area was completed in October of 1808, making possible the beginning of stage coach travel between Amherst and Northampton. A flood washed away this bridge in 1826, and a wooden covered bridge replaced it.

In 1873, the Massachusetts Central Railroad planned to build a railroad bridge alongside the covered bridge. The Financial Panic of 1873 delayed its completion. The tornado of 1877 destroyed both this partially built bridge and the old covered bridge in a matter of minutes. Unfortunately, as storm clouds gathered, many

Three bridges — a trolley, a carriage, and a railroad bridge — replaced the covered bridge that blew down at the Connecticut River in 1877.

people had sought shelter in the covered bridge moments before the tornado brought it down.

The newspaper reported that, "Clouds of dust, limbs of trees, and missiles of every description filled the air, accompanied with rain and hail, driven by a mighty tempest and wind. For a time extreme darkness prevailed. A loud roar was heard for a moment, then a few sharp cracks, a terrible crash and in a twinkle, the ruins of the old bridge lay in the river."

Along with 11 people, six teams of horses went crashing into the river. Fortunately nearly everyone survived, including Amherst's constables, William W. Smith and L.A. Williams. It was Constable Williams who dragged out the only fatality, Widow Catharine Sullivan, who breathed twice and died in the constable's arms. Fred Cook was taken out of the branches of a tree unscathed.

An iron bridge replaced the old covered one in 1878. Then on October 11, 1839, the Calvin Coolidge Memorial Bridge was dedicated. Its demise was already predicted, however, in the Amherst Record. It was thought that the river might cut through the bend the bridge spans, leaving the new bridge uselessly crossing an oxbow while the river flowed by, some distance away.

The Terrifying
Apple Glacier of 1878

As apple blossom time returns each May, it is sobering to look back to 1878 when a bountiful apple season ended in disaster. At least, the Rev. Henry W. Parker painted it as a disaster. Parker, the first resident chaplain of the Massachusetts Agricultural College, sent a bogus report to the outside world of the devastation of what became known as the Apple Glacier.

Amherst has always had an affection for apples. The Dickinsons grew them and Noah Webster had an orchard on Main Street. George Atkins began the first large commercial orchard in Amherst in 1888. Professors F.A. Waugh and F.C. Sears set off an apple planting boom in the Valley in 1908 when they planted 1,500 trees on the northern slope of the Holyoke Range. By 1946 there were about 1,000 acres of apple trees in Amherst alone.

In October of 1878, after an astonishing apple crop, Rev. Henry Parker wrote to the New York Tribune of the devastating consequences. Adding to the abundance was the fact that thirty years earlier the planting of apple trees had become so fashionable that every house, garden, meadow, hillside, park and roadside bloomed with apples. The first sign of trouble came in the summer of 1878 when the trees became one conglomerate mass of fruit. The snapping of large boughs echoed like gunfire, frightening mothers and children. Fruit began to fall day and night until "the increasing pomonic shower became as intense as the drumming of hailstones on a roof."

Cider and vinegar mills struggled to keep up with the load, but avalanches of apples interfered with the work. The mill horses struggled round and round, neck-deep in apples until they disappeared in the mass. Only the surface movement of apples indicated where horses still pushed on underneath. People filled their cellars with apples, then the lower story, their attics and their barns. The immense weight of apples throughout the Valley crushed the lower layers of fruit until juice began to flow from windows. The lowest stratum of apples became semi-fluid to a depth of from one to seven feet.

According to Rev. Parker, the entire mass, as far north as Vermont, began moving at once, very much like the action of a glacier. "Sheets and streams of the fruit were sliding or rolling down declivities, and over the roads, swales and streams were fast filling and slowly flowing." At a rate of from five to 10 miles a day, the narrow Connecticut Valley was filling from brim to brim. The Hatfield and Hadley meadows had overflowed and the swollen

Connecticut River was said to contain three percent alcohol as far as Middletown, Connecticut.

Inhabitants had left the valleys and were crowding such peaks as Mount Sugarloaf in South Deerfield. The glacier was a sloping wall, 700 feet high, with an unusual color from the mix of Baldwins, Jersey Sweets, Tompkins and Country Kings. A young geologist explored the Apple Glacier, wisely taking along a Saint Bernard. He described the sub- and centro- acceleration, with a terminal, crescentic, double line of vertical revolution, antero-posterior, and postero-anterior. Venturing back a second time, he himself unfortunately made a postero-anterior revolution and disappeared out of sight, his dog following. It was believed, however, that he would eat his way out.

Rev. Parker's moral was "when everybody else is planting one thing then the wise must plant something else, or sell out and depart" before the likes of the next terrifying Apple Glacier.

The Sad Death
of Ira Cook

Ira Cook helped found the First Baptist Church in 1832, and died a strange death five years later.

No one should have to die the way Ira Cook did. Ira, whose life had rarely held much joy, died hanging from his heels in 1879.

Ira Cook was one of the founding members of Amherst's First Baptist Church. In 1832, at the age of 20, he helped begin the church at the Amherst Common. Five years later, though, he was "cut off as a dead branch," as the records put it.

In mid-1837, from this building which now houses the Peter Pan bus terminal, a church committee was sent out to visit Cook. It seems that Cook was accused of an unnamed breach of church rules and hadn't appeared at the church for several weeks. The committee tried unsuccessfully to bring Cook back.

Pastor Lovell wrote to Cook and visited him, hoping Cook "would return and walk orderly with the church." Cook refused to return unless an apology came from the church. Lovell found Cook "alienated, & manifesting unchristian feeling." He was then, according to the pastor, "exhorted to return to God & to the church with penitence & reformation, & warned that if he did not soon return he must be cut off as a dead branch." Cook was put out of the church in September, 1837.

Ira married Theodicia Church in 1840. Their son Alfred was born in July of the next year and died two months later of "bowel inflammation." Daughter Mary Jane was born in 1842, then Clara Maria arrived in 1844. In just less than a year, Clara Maria died of cholera.

In 1842, Cook had sold his father's land on Bay Road, then in 1861 he lost all his Amherst property to creditors. The end came in February 1879, when the Amherst Record ran the following report: "Ira Cook, 66 years old, a native and former resident of this town, was found dead, his body hanging to the high picket fence which surrounds the state farm connected with the lunatic hospital at Northampton, on Saturday morning, by some boys.

"Mr. Cook has been in poor health since he was hurt by being run over and nearly killed by a pair of bulls which he was driving at the Agricultural College farm, several years ago. He owned a small place about a mile and a half west of the hospital in Northampton, and being a widower was cared for by his son-in-law and his family.

"Between 5 and 6 o'clock last Thursday evening he went with a pail of eggs to the village, where he disposed of them, and is supposed to have been on his return when he became bewildered, and, on reaching the high picket fence, half a mile from the hospital, undertook to jump over the pickets, when he caught one of his heels and was thrown with his head downward ... and died a terrible death, hanging to the picket fence, which bears the marks of the unfortunate man's struggles to release himself.

"This is a warning to all not to climb picket fences, especially on a dark night."

The Great Blizzard of 1888

When the worst blizzard of the 19th century hit on March 12, 1888, the headlines shouted, "Snow and Blow, A Manitoba Blizzard Let Loose in Amherst. Everybody and Everything Blockaded. No trains. No mails. No meat. No business. No travelling." The famous Blizzard of '88 was both exhilarating and frightening. Families were separated, some folks died, laborers were stranded, animals starved, and disastrous fires broke out. One of the worst of those fires destroyed a good part of the center of Amherst.

Ironically, it was fire, not snow, that caused the most damage during the Blizzard of 1888.

Sunday, March 11, was cloudy and windy. After nightfall, the snow began and continued through the night. By mid-day on Monday, the wind whipped the storm into a blizzard of icy, stinging flakes. Snow came from all directions and it was nearly impossible to see more than a few feet. It blocked freight trains from Palmer, and trains from Brattleboro, Vermont, had to turn back. Another was derailed just before reaching the Amherst Station. Within a day or two, the Amherst meat markets were low on supplies, and the hotels and boarding houses were reduced to serving codfish balls and canned goods. Mail could not get through and telegraph service ceased when poles and wires snapped. Local artist

Elbridge Kingsley was eventually successful in getting a telegram through to his friend Clifton Johnson in New York. "Am snow bound," it said. "No trains running. Coming as soon as possible."

Farmers who happened to be in town couldn't return to their farms, where soon the supplies of feed became dangerously low, and their cattle suffered. Many people who worked in Amherst's shops and factories couldn't return to their homes. Three young woman factory workers spent Monday night at the Hills Hat Company on Railroad Street, and others stayed in nearby homes. None of those living at South Amherst was able to make it home for several days.

Many narrow escapes were reported and in Chesterfield, David Damon never made it home at all. The 33 year-old man lost his way in the storm and crawled up to a stone wall, not many yards from his house. His body was found four days later.

Harriet Richardson of Hadley wrote a personal account of the storm to Clifton Johnson, who was studying art in New York. She wrote over a four-day period as the gale blew outside her door. On Monday, March 12, she wrote that the storm was "Tumultuous enough to be quite joyous and exhilarating." The next day she noted, "The storm soon became so violent that all pleasure in it gave way to dread, and anxiety for the safety of those of our family exposed to its fury ... the snow deepened, the drifts piled higher, and the wind blew on. At two in the afternoon the two milk sleighs, with two horses each attached came slowly wallowing into the back yard, horses and men completely covered with clinging snow and both well nigh exhausted."

The sleighs had been trying to get back to the farm for three hours, but lost their way in Fort Meadow Swamp. With the sleighs safely in, Harriet continued to worry about the two children, Harry and Nettie, hoping they had remained at school and weren't stranded out in the drifts. After a four-hour struggle, the children had taken shelter in a house along the way.

One of Amherst's worst fires occurred during the blizzard, leaving the center of town drastically changed. At three in the morning on Tuesday, March 13, a nurse sleeping in a room over Hill's Restaurant on Main Street smelled smoke. It came from the building next door, Palmer's Block, located where the Town Hall is today. Palmer's Block burned to the ground, taking with it Hill's Restaurant to the east, the Cooper house, just south of it, and threatening the Grace Church parsonage. Firefighters didn't have a chance in the midst of the blizzard. The fury of the fire was such that windows across the way on Main Street were shattered.

Palmer's Block was one of the most important buildings in town. Businesses there included John Mullen's Meat Market, Sing

Lee's Chinese Laundry, J.S. Thomas's Fish Market, and H.O. Pease's Tailor Shop. The District Court met there, and on the second story was Emily Dickinson's brother Austin's law office. Dickinson's law library, in the family for three generations, and an archive of valuable papers were lost. The entire third story contained the Amherst Opera House, which had only recently been renovated.

The Cooper house was one of the oldest in town, and was probably built by General Zebina Montague, prominent Amherst merchant and member of the General Court.

In the days that followed, news reached Amherst of destruction as far away as Chesapeake Bay. Many lost their lives there, and more than 100 vessels capsized or sank. Ten foot snow drifts paralyzed New York City, and from Connecticut, news came of the many elderly people and children who perished in the greatest blizzard of the century.

Blowing the Teakettle
Through the Roof in Pelham

In January of 1891, a terrible explosion destroyed the kitchen of Joseph Powell's home in Pelham, killing his wife and knocking part of the house off its foundation. This tragic blast of nitroglycerin was caused by the carelessness of a boarder who worked in a little-known Pelham industry — asbestos mining.

At least as early as 1873, asbestos was mined on Butter Hill in Pelham. In that year, James and John Murray of Boston opened a mine there and began blasting out the mineral. Asbestos has been known since ancient times for its resistance to fire, but it didn't achieve commercial importance until the 19th century. Hundreds of tons of asbestos were mined in Pelham, and sold for grinding into paint and for asbestos papers.

The mine on Butter Hill was bought by another set of Boston partners in 1890. They hired a Mr. Merrill to oversee the operations, and he boarded with Joseph R. Powell on Enfield Road. In blasting the rock, Merrill used nitroglycerin cartridges called the "Miner's Friend." These six-inch long, very powerful explosives were made by the Hecla Powder Company, which provided Merrill with a circular on their safe use.

Using the cartridges in winter was difficult because they froze below 42 degrees and had to be thawed before using. Merrill told the agent from the Hecla Company that he knew how to safely thaw the explosives. The company sent him a circular, warning, "Do not put cartridges on boilers or hot iron plates." Nevertheless, on Thursday morning, January 8, 1891, Merrill placed three nitroglycerin cartridges in the coal stove of the Powell home. In the kitchen at that time were Powell's 65 year-old wife, and their daughter-in-law, Mrs. Nelson Powell.

A powerful explosion blew the stove "to atoms," as the newspaper put it, blowing the teakettle standing on the stove through the ceiling. Windows and doors shattered and the walls shifted off the foundation. Neighbors quickly gathered and found Mrs. Powell with her limbs crushed and body torn open, surrounded by fire. She died within hours. Her daughter-in-law was badly injured, but she survived. Merrill was barely hurt, having been out of the room at the time.

The local papers hesitated calling it an accident and preferred to label it "gross carelessness" on Merrill's part. Judge Strickland ordered Medical Examiner D.N.B. Fish to investigate the causes of the disaster.

The Bursting of the Dam at Hadley Falls

Immigrant mill workers who lived near the dam at Hadley Falls.

California's floods, mudslides, fires, and earthquakes make New England's winter ice and spring potholes seem pretty tame. With half of California declared a disaster area in 1995, the Connecticut River Valley may be tempted to feel comparatively safe. But dams breaking, rivers overflowing, and people drowning have been part of the regular cycle here for generations. One such calamity involved Irish immigrants who had just come to the Valley to escape the Irish Famine.

The most famous of local floods happened in May of 1874, when a dam along the Mill River in Williamsburg burst. In just over an hour 145 lives were lost, and houses, shops, streets and livestock were washed away. But an earlier flood, when Emily Dickinson was in her teens, is equally fascinating. Caused by a poorly engineered dam on the Connecticut River, it says a lot about a time in Emily's life when transportation and business were changing radically.

It was the 1840s, and the age of the canal was coming to a close as railroads took over the landscape. Wealthy Boston investors brought the Industrial Revolution to towns like Lowell and Lawrence and were about to pour money into the Connecticut Valley. The Boston Associates eyed the factories already in Chicopee and saw a potential for massive amounts of water power from near-by Hadley Falls. In 1847, the Associates began buying all the land surrounding the dam site.

A ready population of laborers was found among Irish immigrants. Hundreds were housed in shanties, while they built the dam and a series of canals around it. The first crisis occured in January of 1848, when the laborers' wages were cut from 75 to 70 cents a day. The Irish workers rioted until the Northampton militia arrived. From the Hampshire Gazette: "A serious riot occurred at Ireland — the 'New City' at Hadley Falls — last evening, between seven and nine o'clock. On Monday week, the Irish laborers, three or four hundred in number, employed by Boody & Stone in constructing the great dam, in consequence of a reduction of wages, refused to work.

"Yesterday a small number, a dozen or more, concluded on pledges of protection, to go to work, at the terms offered. The other Irishmen in consequence threatened vengeance upon them. Fearing that their shanties might be torn down as threatened, the chief engineer, Mr. Anderson accompanied by a constable and a number of other individuals, repaired to the ground to protect the few who had gone to work from their infuriated compeers. The latter soon came upon the constable and his associates, armed with clubs and other weapons of Irish warfare, and commenced an attack.

"The constable, Mr. Theodore Farnham, in attempting to arrest some of the leaders in the riot, was knocked down with a club, the blow of which gashed his lip to the bone, and he was then trampled upon by the maddened crowd, until he was almost senseless. Mr. Anderson, the Engineer, was struck in the face ... . The windows in a temporary grocery store were also broken in."

Before the Connecticut was successfully dammed, the Irish workers suffered another crisis. A cholera epidemic, caused by unsanitary living conditions in the shanties, killed many laborers within a few weeks.

By November, 1848, the dam was complete. A mammoth structure for those days, it measured 1,000 feet long and 30 feet high. Hundreds lined the banks of the river to watch the water rise behind the dam. At about noon on November 19, a spurt of water was noticed leaking from the base of the dam. Several men took a flatboat out to try to stop the leak, but at 3:20 the water started rushing through and they had to flee to the shore. They barely made it when the dam gave way with a roar said to have been heard in Granby.

Throughout the disaster, messages were telegraphed to Boston: "The dam is leaking badly." "We cannot stop the leaking." And finally, "Dam gone to hell by way of Willimansett."

Water swept over Main Street, and over South Hadley Falls. The only fatality was a horse drowned tied to a post. Embarrassed but undaunted, the engineers went back to work. Their more substantial stone and boiler plate dam on the Connecticut was completed in October, 1849.

The Sarcastic Response
to the Brickyard Fire

A bucket brigade from the Amherst Fire Department spent the hours after midnight trying to save the Marcy & Gardner Brickyard in South Amherst. It was August 20, 1896, and after three wet and grimy hours, the men had saved the boarding house, but the sheds where bricks were made were lost. Four days later, their hard labor won them only ridicule in a critical article published in the Springfield Union.

The South Amherst brickyard had its origin in the fall of 1886, when the land was first tested as a possible brickyard site. William F. Williams owned a farm on East Street and had been negotiating with parties from Connecticut and Palmer, Massachusetts, for possible sale of the farm. To test the clay underlying the farm, barrels of it had been sent to Philadelphia for examination and for the making of trial bricks. The clay was deemed of fine quality for producing the best kind of brick. Holes were bored 10 to 15 feet deep over a large tract of the farm, and it was concluded that the deposit was practically inexhaustible.

Negotiations for the sale of the farm fell through, but Clayton Alexander of Palmer was successful in arranging to lease 10 acres of it in a good location. It was situated between the parallel tracks of the New London Northern Railroad and the Central Massachusetts Railroad, where they were between 500 and 600 feet apart. This gave the brickyard access to a north-south rail line, and an east-west line.

Alexander built a boarding house for workmen, barns for teams of horses, and a shed for steam-powered brickmaking equipment and the firing of bricks. Unfortunately, in 1892, Alexander's company became insolvent, and Marcy & Gardner of Palmer took over the business.

The success of Marcy & Gardner was interrupted in August, 1896, when the fire broke out in the main building. It began at 9:00 at night, but the brickworkers were able to quickly extinguish it. At midnight, however, the fire roared up once more and was soon beyond control. An alarm was sounded in Amherst and 15 firemen gathered at the engine house on North Pleasant Street. They made their way to South Amherst in two wagons and attacked the fire with a borrowed steam pump, a bucket brigade, and axes. They were able to save only the boarding house and some cordwood.

Under the circumstances — the fire being two miles from the water supply — Amherst felt it did pretty well. The Springfield Union, however, disagreed. In an article described locally as "a series of inexcusable falsehoods and lame attempts at wit," the Union made the Amherst Fire Department look like the Keystone Cops. In a "burst of sarcastic eloquence," the Union referred to Amherst's new fire alarm as "a cow bell." The Amherst Record indignantly complained that the Union even got the colors of the firemen's coats confused.

The Amherst Record's rebuttal admitted that the department was poorly equipped, but protested that "chronic fault-finders" shouldn't expect to find a city fire department in a small town that paid its firefighters only 12 dollars a year.

Marcy & Gardner ignored the debate and quickly began rebuilding the brickyard, which later became the Amherst Brick Company.

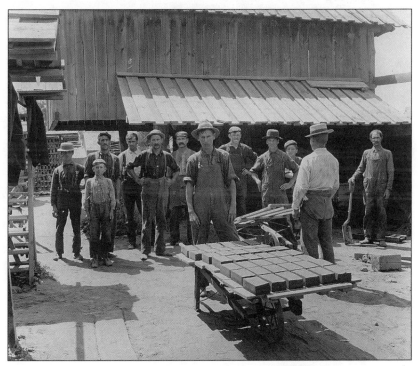

The Amherst Brick Company, South Amherst. There were four brickmakers in 19th century Amherst, one of which supplied the bricks for the Dickinson Homestead in 1813

Chapter Twelve

POETS, ARTISTS, LOVERS, AND PARSONS OF THE VALLEY

"Freshman River" by the light of the moon

The Poets light but Lamps -
Themselves - go out -
#883

The Other Unknown Visionary
of the Dickinson House

The more we look at the Emily Dickinson Homestead, the more fascinating the story of a single house becomes. Emily Dickinson was not the only visionary to be associated with the solid, brick home. David Mack III, whose family shared the house with the Dickinsons for seven years, was a radical transcendentalist who set out to change an entire society. While Emily quietly revolutionized poetry within the walls of the Homestead, David Mack went out to loudly revolutionize the way people live and work.

David was the son of Deacon David Mack, Jr., who had brought his family to Amherst to manufacture and sell straw hats. In early 1833, Deacon Mack bought one half of the Dickinson Homestead. In this condominium-like arrangement, the Macks lived on the west side of the house and the Dickinsons on the east side. Emily was not yet three years old when the Macks moved in, a move which began lifelong friendships between the Dickinson and Mack children.

David Mack III was born in 1804 and he graduated with the Yale class of 1823, along with Emily's father, Edward. David married Lucy Maria Barstow in 1835, and spent several years studying law with his uncle Elisha Mack in Salem. He and Lucy established a school for girls in Cambridge, where they met the great transcendentalists, including Emerson, Hawthorne, and Alcott. It was in Emily's Connecticut River Valley, however, in the Northampton village of Florence, that Mack helped found a utopian community.

To the list of radical utopian communities of the day — among them Brook Farm, Fruitlands, and Hopedale — can be added the Northampton Association of Education and Industry. A more middle-class, less literary community than the others, much less has been written about it. It grew out of the Northampton Silk Company, which died by 1841, after the mulberry speculation bubble burst. The factory in Florence was sold to a group who gradually transformed it into a utopian community. The group was against slavery, conventional religion, and materialism. It attempted to do away with race and sex discrimination, and the drudgery of 12 hour factory days.

David Mack had flirted with the idea of joining Brook Farm, but instead he became one of the founding leaders of the Northampton Association in 1842. The group continued to make silk, plus added a grist mill, book club, library and lyceum. But it was the school run by David and his wife that produced what little

The Dickinson home spawned more than one visionary who affected the wider world.

financial success the community enjoyed. As Thoreau had done in Concord, the Macks took the children out of the classroom into the woods and fields to learn botany and biology first hand. Trips to Mount Holyoke were taken to gather minerals. In an unusually humane gesture for the day, no corporal punishment was allowed. The school became so popular that non-community families sent their children there.

Among the community's members were black leaders and former slaves Frederick Douglass and Sojourner Truth. William Lloyd Garrison and Wendell Phillips spoke there, and Nathaniel Hawthorne corresponded with David Mack about the utopian movement.

In 1845, the community began its downward slide under the pressure of financial troubles, and criticism from within and without.

Amherst College was among those who lost money invested in the Association. In that year, the Macks went to a water cure in Brattleboro, Vermont, then on to Belmont, Massachusetts. There David was active in civic affairs and founded the Belmont town library.

While it is unlikely that David Mack lived for any great length of time in the Dickinson Homestead while Emily was there, it is certain that he often visited there. His ties to the Homestead and Amherst were strong, and after his death in July of 1878, his remains were brought to Amherst for burial.

Sylvester Graham, the Philosopher of Sawdust Pudding

The eccentric nutritionist, Sylvester Graham, went to school in Amherst before trying to change 19th century eating and sexual habits.

Back in 1823, Amherst Academy expelled a young man when he was accused, but not convicted, of assaulting a woman. He went on to found the first movement to fully recognize the benefits of fruits and vegetables and the harm of meat and white flour. This was Sylvester Graham, remembered now mainly for the cracker that bears his name. But was Graham an "eccentric and wayward genius," as one contemporary thought? Or was it true, as one 19th century newspaper put it, that "a greater humbug or a more disgusting writer never lived"?

Born in West Suffield, Connecticut, in 1794, Graham attended Amherst Academy at the late age of 29. His arrogant personality alienated the younger students who quickly got him thrown out on a false charge of criminal assault. From Amherst he went to Rhode

Island where he had a nervous breakdown, and married the daughter of a sea captain.

At the age of 36, after a failed attempt to become a minister, Graham became a professional reformer. He first attacked alcohol, and he himself refused to drink anything stronger than water. Graham did allow his wife to drink wine and gin, which he considered beneficial when she was ill and needed strength to nurse an infant.

Graham sought to revolutionize the diet and sexual behavior of the country. By 1835, his lectures in Philadelphia and New York had become so popular that he moved to Northampton, a base from which he could conquer the northeast. At this point, his views on sexuality caused such controversy that some lectures got out of hand. He believed sexual desire irritated the body and caused disease, and that the remedy was to marry, get the urge out of one's system, and let it fade.

It was reported that so many women were fainting at his lectures, that Graham dropped the sexual focus and concentrated on vegetarianism. This was hardly an improvement, for his views on food led to riots in Boston.

By the 1830s, the American diet was based largely on meat and white bread. Fruits and vegetables weren't thought to contain much nutrition. Graham turned that around, became a vegetarian and trumpeted the benefits of homemade bread made with whole grain wheat — which became known as Graham flour.

What seems logical today led to a very bad year for Graham in 1837. He was scheduled to speak in Boston at Amory Hall, but the owners feared the place would be burned down. Boston butchers were angry at Graham for telling people they ate too much meat, and bakers were after him for advocating making one's own bread. No other Boston hall would book Graham, so he turned to the Marlborough Hotel, the first temperance hotel in America.

When the mayor warned that there were not enough constables in Boston to protect the hotel, the owners barricaded the first floor against an angry mob. Meanwhile Graham's followers took over the third floor, from which they poured down buckets of lime on the protestors. Harper's Magazine reported, "The eyes had it, and the rabble incontinently adjourned."

Though there were so many Grahamites that some hotels served only a Graham diet, many newspapers were skeptical and often cruel. In 1851, the Northampton Courier printed an article titled, "Dr. Bran — his dignity and consistency": "The people of Northampton were amused one day last week by seeing this philosopher of sawdust pudding trundled on a wheelbarrow from his house to the barber's house, he being infirm and unable to walk the distance ... the doctor stands a chance to recover and will be able before long to do without the wheelbarrow ... his best physician is the keeper of the hotel hard by his dwelling with whom he luxuriates on beef and mutton."

Graham died less than a month later at the age of 58. The Amherst newspaper was kinder to Graham when it printed his obituary: "He has left behind him several works on physiology, hygiene theology, etc., ably and powerfully written. As a public speaker he was rarely equalled, and he possessed great clearness of perception and vigor of intellect."

Not many realize that the popular Sylvester's Restaurant in Northampton was the brick home of this wayward philosopher.

Artist
Orra White Hitchcock

Emily Dickinson wrote that at the funeral of Orra White Hitchcock, a hen and her chicks tried to fly through the window as the minister prayed. This singular event marked the end of the life of a remarkable, largely unknown Connecticut Valley artist.

Orra White was born in South Amherst in 1796. Her father, Jarib, was a justice of the peace in 1805, and in 1818 he signed a substantial pledge to the original endowment of Amherst College. Orra was educated at home, at the Misses Wright School in South Hadley, and finally at a private school in Roxbury, Massachusetts.

Orra began drawing at an early age, and by the time she was 11 was doing landscapes, flowers, and imaginary scenes. In 1813, at the young age of 17, she became preceptress in charge of female students at Deerfield Academy. In 1814, she was asked to star in Edward Hitchcock's drama "The Emancipation of Europe," at Deerfield. (He became principal of the academy in 1816.) By 1818, Orra's drawings began to be published. Her "View of the Falls on the Connecticut River at Gill, Mass." appeared in the Philadelphia magazine called Port Folio, and it's thought that her color sketches were published in a book of medicinal botany. In that year, too, Orra taught at Amherst Academy, where later Emily Dickinson would study.

In 1821, Orra White married Edward Hitchcock in a tavern that stood at the corner of Amity and North Pleasant in Amherst. Their life together began in Conway, where Edward was a minister from 1821 to 1825, and continued in Amherst, where Orra devoted herself to illustrating Edward's scientific works. Her watercolor herbarium, based on his botanical collections, were justly admired by scientists. Edward became a widely known geologist and one of the most influential presidents of Amherst College.

Orra's most important works are her hand-colored lithographic views of the Connecticut River Valley. Orra loved the "pure & fresh air" of Amherst, as her husband put it in his memoirs, and when compelled to be in New York City felt as if she were doomed to a prison. Edward credited most of the 232 plates and 1,134 woodcuts in his works "to the pencil and patience of my beloved wife, aided in later years by my daughters." She illustrated his lectures in botany, geology, zoology, and anatomy, even creating a 70 foot long drawing of an Iguanodon.

One of the few personal facts known of Orra's life is that she wore false teeth, which she unfortunately swallowed in a fall on Main

Street. (They remained lodged in her throat for three weeks until, as the Amherst Record reported, the teeth "passed into the stomach, where they lay for a week, and passed off through the bowels.")

The Hitchcocks' daughter Jennie was a close friend of Emily Dickinson's sister, Vinnie (they were schoolmates at Ipswich Academy in 1850). On May 29, 1863, Emily wrote the following to her cousins Loo and Fanny Norcross: "Jennie Hitchcock's mother was buried yesterday, so there is one orphan more, and her father is very sick besides. My father and mother went to the service, and mother said while the minister prayed, a hen with her chickens came up, and tried to fly into the window. I suppose the dead lady used to feed them, and they wanted to bid her good bye.

> Life is death we're lengthy at,
> Death the hinge of life."

Rattling the Chaplain's Teeth:
Harlan Fiske Stone

Harlan Fiske Stone seen while at Amherst College. He fomented rebellions in Amherst and went on to become Chief Justice of the Supreme Court.

One of this country's greatest jurists, Chief Justice Harlan Fiske Stone, grew up in Amherst. He had been born on October 11, 1872, in New Hampshire, and his family moved to Amherst in 1874 in order for Harlan to get a good education. Somewhere between his earliest years and his years of distinguished service to the nation, Stone displayed an incomparable appetite for hot-headed rebellion. In fact, his usually glossed-over time at the Massachusetts Agricultural College was ended by his abrupt expulsion for shaking the college chaplain "until his teeth rattled."

After graduation from Amherst High School, Stone entered Mass Agricultural (now UMass) in 1888. Despite the fact that he was a "townie" and commuted from his family's Mill Valley farmhouse, he found time to plunge into the tradition of "rushes," wherein freshmen and sophomores clashed. Sometimes a single student was dragged out of bed, paraded in his nightshirt and dumped into a fountain. Other times dozens joined in noisy rumbles. After one such fracas that disturbed the chemistry lab, Stone was singled out and warned by President Goodell to stop such behavior or else face severe reprimand.

The following spring, Stone's freshman class was harassed by the sophomores, or perhaps it was the other way around. At any rate, the freshmen borrowed the college fire hose as their weapon, and the result was one ruined hose and the beginning of Stone's probation. The following fall, Harlan Stone was back in good standing, but not for long.

In March of 1890, tension between the classes grew, as did resistence to the college's rule of compulsory chapel attendance. During chapel prayers on the morning of the 19th, Chaplain Charles Swan Walker led the hymns, and prayed that "we love our enemies ... never avenge ourselves ... (and) know that righteousness is better than malice." Someone gave a signal and suddenly all four classes were on their feet, tumbling over one another toward the exit.

Chaplain Walker jumped in and grabbed Stone by the back of the collar. Stone made the fatal mistake of shouting, "Take your damn hands off me!" and then, as he later said, "I turned and grabbed him and shook him until his teeth rattled. I continued shaking him till I suddenly discovered who he was!"

President Goodell called Stone and two others before the faculty. Stone asked for leniency, but Goodell pointed out that while Stone had been on probation the year before, he was guilty of no fewer than five violations. On March 25, 1890, the faculty voted to throw Stone out of the college. The student body rallied to Stone's defense and petitioned for his reinstatement. Stone personally asked to be readmitted, but it was too late. In later years, Stone confounded his critics by becoming one of the great men of the century, but not before one more spirited college episode.

The Gates Rebellion of 1894:
Harlan Fiske Stone, Again

After Harlan Stone was expelled from the Massachusetts Agricultural College, his father was outraged. Frederick Stone told his son, "Your school days are over. You're through! From now on it is the farm for you." Instead, Harlan went on to Amherst College where, in 1894, he was the mastermind of the Gates Rebellion.

Stone entered Amherst College during an enlightened time under the liberal Dr. Julius Seelye. President Seelye helped create the unique Amherst System, whereby students were given the privilege of self-government under their own Student Senate. Stone worked well at Amherst; he studied hard, became class president, and helped dissolve the custom of "rushing."

When Dr. Merrill Gates succeeded Seelye in 1890, he was heartily welcomed as the first Amherst president to come from academia rather than the clergy. The students soon became cynical, however, when confronted with a rather pompous, name-dropping man, adorned with a high silk hat. In the spring of 1892, President Gates began one of his lectures on political ethics with, "When I was in Washington, I and the President ... ." In an act of impolite bravado, the unimpressed students hurled catcalls, shuffled chairs and stamped their feet. Gates picked up his hat, left the hall, and did not return that year. Harlan Stone considered Gates's conduct as an educator as "the most outrageous imposition during my college course."

The Amherst System received its severest test in 1894. The faculty temporarily suspended an unnamed senior who persistently cut classes. The action was followed by a letter to the boy's father. The audacious youth intercepted the letter and tore it up. President Gates happened to run into the boy's father during the Christmas holiday and expressed regret that his son had been suspended. This came as a shock to the bewildered father. Gates, no doubt embarrassed, sought out the son and suspended him for the rest of the year.

Stone was livid — not because of the deserved suspension, but because the faculty handled the punishment, not the Student Senate, which he felt had jurisdiction. The president wouldn't budge an inch, the Senate wrote angry letters, and the newspapers fanned the flames. The college sought the advice of ex-President Seelye and some of the alumni. The students made their case in speeches in Boston and New York, then on March 20, 1894, they requested that their Senate representatives resign in protest.

Students continued to interrupt Gates's lectures, and they

began carving graffiti on college buildings. Stone later stated that beneath Gates's showy exterior "were only a shallow intellect and shallow character. When this opinion became widespread, Gates was doomed."

Gates had lost the support of the students, faculty, trustees and alumni. In the spring of 1898, he left the school for a leave of absence, and on June 9, he sent a letter from Cambridge, England, offering his resignation.

A Civil War Hero
Back From the Dead

William S. Clark showed up in Amherst four weeks after being declared killed in the Civil War.

Under the heading "Another Hero Gone," reports were printed of the death of Amherst's William S. Clark. It was at the Civil War battle of Chantilly, on September 1, 1862, that Clark was numbered among the 38 killed. The Hampshire and Franklin Express said, "He has lived a noble man, and has died a hero." Yet four weeks later, the dead war hero arrived in Amherst entirely alive and healthy.

Clark's eventful life began in Ashfield in 1826. He studied at Amherst College, and taught at Williston Academy in Easthampton (while Austin Dickinson was a student there). After earning a doctorate in chemistry in Germany, Clark became professor of chemistry and instructor of German at Amherst College.

With the outbreak of the Civil War, Clark eagerly enlisted in the 21st Regiment of Massachusetts Volunteers. He was attached to the command of General J.L. Reno and received a commendation for bravery at the battle of Roanoke Island. When he briefly returned to Amherst in June of 1862, he was welcomed home as a hero. A large crowd met him at the railroad depot with three rousing cheers. E.F. Cook brought out his four-horse team for the occasion to carry Clark and his wife in style. Clark didn't stay to bask in glory, though, for, as the papers reported, "The rebels are to be whipped and he means to have a hand in it."

After the erroneous report of his death at Chantilly, he was eulogized in the Amherst newspaper in glowing terms: "The whole community will mourn his loss, for he was esteemed, admired and beloved by all who knew him ... . His heroic conduct at the battle of Roanoke is still fresh in the minds of our readers; and his gallant charge at the battle of Newbern, will never be forgotten. His heroic deeds and his manly character will ever be remembered by a grateful and sorrowing public."

There was little chance of Clark being forgotten, for in early October he was the featured speaker at a meeting of the Hampshire Agricultural Society. He told the audience about his harrowing experiences while a prisoner in the rebel camp, and his "miraculous escape from their clutches."

William S. Clark went on to become the first president of the Massachusetts Agricultural College in 1867. Clark's real fame, however was earned while in Japan. In 1876, he became the first president of Sapporo Agricultural College on the northern island of Hokkaido. Clark was adored in Japan and his advice, "Boys, be ambitious!" has become so much a part of Japanese culture that even today Clark is a folk hero throughout Japan.

Eugene Field: Poems of Innocence, Poems of X-Rated Experience

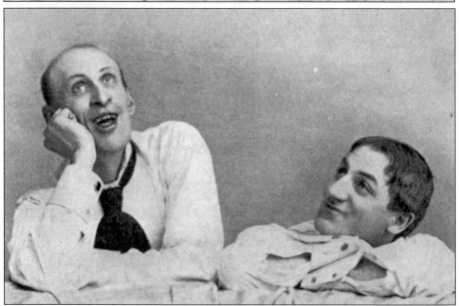

Francis B. Wilson and Eugene Field as Cherubs. Eugene Field (top: right, bottom: left), the great children's poet, also had his witty and salacious sides.

The name Eugene Field means little to most young people today. If they recall that he wrote "Little Boy Blue," most confuse it with the Mother Goose rhyme, "Little Boy Blue, Come Blow Your Horn." But Field's poem is far more chilling. It's a poem about a boy's death. Field's career was like that: sentimental and romantic in appearance, but underneath something else. His was a life touched by death, and controversy, but always infused with a wild and bawdy sense of humor.

Eugene Field, though considered a midwestern poet, had strong Amherst ties. Born in St. Louis in 1850, he was sent to live in Amherst at the age of six, after his mother died. He and his brother Roswell lived with their uncle Thomas Jones for nine years in a large white house on the corner of Amity and Lincoln Streets. One of Field's first poems was written in Amherst, a poem about his dog Dooley and the Emerson house, now the Historical Society's Strong House Museum:

> O, had I wings like a dove I would fly,
> Away from this world of fleas;
> I'd fly all around Miss Emerson's yard,
> And light on Miss Emerson's trees.

Many of his later poems were based on incidences and people from Amherst. Those memories included the theatre he and his friends set up in Lucius Boltwood's barn in 1865.

Field went from Amherst schools to Monson Academy, Williams College, and Knox College in Illinois. His guardian at Knox was another man who had lived in Amherst, Professor John Burgess.

Field met with great success as a newspaperman in Chicago and as a writer of children's verse and satire. Audiences reacted emotionally to his "Little Boy Blue," tearfully questioning if the dying boy was Field's own son. The poem made Field's career, but also made for an accusation of plagiarism. It was among several poems other poets claimed to have submitted to Field for publication, only to see them changed and published under Field's name.

Field's wry humor came out in such nonsense pieces as "Tempting Turkey": "What a Big Fat Turkey it is! It must have eaten lots of Worms and Caterpillars to be so Fat. It is stuffed with nice stuffing made of Old Crusts and Spoiled Biscuits. The gravy Looks Quite Tempting. It does not look like Tobacco juice, does it? The Innards of the Turkey have been chopped up and are in the Gravy. Unless the Cook was very Careful while Chopping up the Innards, there is a Piece of her Finger in the gravy, too."

The ironic and only recently published bawdy verse of Field may come as a shock. Even more scatalogical than Mark Twain's similar efforts, his first such piece, a mild example, was "Slug 14." Field read it at the Printers' Banquet in Missouri in 1876. In it, Field described the fatal mistake of an unfortunate newspaper typesetter:

> *Why, sir, when there came in a wedding report,*
> *You ought to have seen that "lead-pounder" cavort!*
> *He got so confused, and so reckless besides,*
> *That for "kissing" he set "the groom pissed on the bride."*

Field was hard at work on "The Love Affairs of a Bibliomaniac" when he died on the morning of November 4, 1895.

Mittie Hall Anderson: From the World of Slavery to the Founding of a Church

In 1869, Mittie Hall Anderson was born to parents who had only recently been slaves. They were living in Raleigh, North Carolina, at a time of turmoil just after the Civil War. From such a beginning Mittie Anderson eventually owned her own home in Amherst, and helped found a black church. Her story is a classic one of struggle against the odds: Mittie was black, and a single woman. She came North where she faced abuse, but then became an admired part of the Connecticut Valley for over 50 years.

By the 1880s, agencies existed in the South to send young black women North for positions as domestic workers in private homes. When Mittie was about 17, she and a friend went through such an agency and were placed in Northampton. Because of sexual advances made by the owner of the house she worked in, Mittie left.

By the turn of the century, she was working as a housekeeper in Amherst. Mittie Hall worked for Laura A. Ward on Northampton Road, and Charles Fennimore on Hazel Street. By 1905, she had bought a home on McClellan Street. Meanwhile she had become very active in Zion Chapel, a church affiliated with Amherst College. There she presided over a kindergarten for black children and the children of Amherst College faculty. When the African Methodist Episcopal Church on Woodside Avenue laid its cornerstone in 1910, it was Mittie Hall who had the honor of breaking ground for the church. Later when the church quickly paid off its mortgage, Mittie was there too, helping raise the necessary funds.

Next door to Mittie Hall on McClellan Street lived Alexander Anderson, a tender for a mason. He lived with his two sisters, Rebecca Thompson, a widowed laundress, and Susy Belle Anderson, a professional singer. By 1912, Mittie and Alexander married. The church played a major role in the life of their family. On the recommendation of Booker T. Washington, Susy Belle Anderson gave a Town Hall recital to raise funds for the church.

Among the many families Mittie Hall Anderson worked for were the Waughs. Dorothy Waugh has many fond memories of the two days each week that Mittie spent with her family: "She was industrious, thorough, always good-humored, had great insight into human character, and was an amusing storyteller. Her principles were high and her understanding and logic regarding life and its attitudes and responsibilities were clear and just.

"When my sister Esther was preparing to be married, we use to laugh with Mrs. Anderson as she repeatedly found things around the house for Esther. 'Miss Esther, your mother doesn't use this

Mittie Hall Anderson helped found one of the early African American churches in Amherst. (Watercolor by Dorothy Waugh.)

knife very often. I don't see why you shouldn't take it' or 'this dust brush' or 'this pan.' Then we would all laugh together. Mrs. Anderson was great fun."

Mittie Hall Anderson died at the age of 83 in 1954. She is buried in Amherst's Wildwood Cemetery.

Chapter Thirteen

❧

WOMEN: HARASSMENT, VIOLENCE, AND FREEDOM

Mrs. Musante, Peanuts, Fruit and Candy, Amherst, Mass.

Mrs. Musante, Amherst, Massachusetts

My second rank - too small the first -
Crowned - Crowing - on my Father's breast -
A half unconscious Queen -
But this time - Adequate - Erect,
With Will to choose, or to reject,
And I choose, just a Crown -
#509

Sexual Harassment
and the Apostles of Nastiness

In 1893, Amherst found itself in the midst of a number of cases of sexual harassment. The town was criticized as a place where "immorality prevails to an alarming extent ... the streets are not safe for an unprotected girl or woman after nightfall." A front page story in the Amherst Record called such critics "Scandal Scavengers" and "Apostles of Nastiness." The paper claimed there was more imagination than truth to such stories, but that view soon evaporated in the face of the activities of George Smith.

The pseudonymous George Smith came to Amherst from Prescott, a town that now lies under the Quabbin Reservoir. He worked as a laborer and lived in a tenement on South Prospect Street. The following 1893 notice in the Amherst Record refers to Smith:

"A certain young gentleman temporarily employed in town has developed 'mashing' proclivities which have proved annoying to several respectable young ladies and may get him into serious trouble if he does not reform his conduct while on the street."

On April 21, 1894, Smith was arrested by Sheriff D.A. Tillson. Accused by an East Amherst woman of indecent exposure, he was tried in Northampton several weeks later. "Since his arrest," the Record reported, "rumors have been in general circulation connecting Smith with a number of unsavory occurrences during the past year."

Smith was also under suspicion of stealing an Amherst College student's valise while working for Charles Utley's moving company. Sheriff Tillson searched Smith's tenement unsuccessfully. In addition to theft and indecent exposure, Smith was charged with stealing a family Bible of G.W. Lincoln of Prescott and put under $200 bond.

Two other assaults on women occurred during this period, both in North Amherst. One, in December of 1893, resulted in an arrest. The other, a "felonious assault upon a young lady," in August of 1894, went unsolved.

In all of the above incidences, the Amherst Record implied that the cases were isolated and attributed to one or two outsiders. The paper revealed the names of the victims but, true to its policy, it left out the graphic details commonly reported today. After Smith's conviction, the paper summed up his case in an article called, "Exit Mr. Smith": "It may be stated without fear of successful contradiction that George Smith of Amherst is an all-around bad man. He is no specialist in crime, but whenever he sees one of the ten commandments laying around loose he gives it a kick or a punch and fractures it in some way. Had it not been for Smith, Amherst would have been remarkably free from crime during the year just past."

Among his crimes, the paper noted, "he appropriated a bicycle and took it out of town where he disposed of it ... he stole a cow from a pasture, hired a man to slaughter it, and with his family made away with part of the beef."

The paper's conclusion may reveal that the judge considered Smith's thievery more serious than his sexual harassment: "Judge Fessenden sentenced him to one year in jail on each of the two charges of larceny and sentence was suspended in the case for indecent exposure. Probably the town will see and hear little of Smith during the next two years."

George Smith, in fact, never returned to Amherst.

A charcoal kiln in the town of Prescott supplied coal to surrounding towns. Prescott also exported a very sick man who preyed on Amherst.

They Risked Jail for the Freedom of a Black Girl

Henry Jackson was willing to break the law to keep a black girl from slavery.

When Henry Jackson died in 1902, obituaries and editorials throughout the Valley lauded this 83-year-old black man. He was considered one of Amherst's most respected citizens, particularly admired for his "industry, honesty and intelligence," and it was said that no one thought "any the less of him on account of his color."

Though one editorialist could find no higher accolade than to say there was no man "whiter" than Jackson, it was not just his ability to make it in a white world that earned him respect. In 1840, Jackson was willing to break the law and suffer imprisonment to keep a young woman from the possibility of being sold into slavery.

Henry Jackson was born in North Amherst in 1818. He had some education in East Amherst before beginning his career as a teamster and bank courier for the merchants and businessmen of the Valley. Long before the railroad reached Amherst, Jackson hauled goods from Springfield, Northampton, Millers Falls, and elsewhere. He was the link for the Amherst palm leaf hat makers to the railroad connections to market.

Before banking developed in Amherst, Jackson was entrusted with merchants' profits and payrolls for trips to banks in Greenfield and Northampton.

Though slavery was illegal in Massachusetts, in 1840, it was still legal to capture escaped slaves in the state. And there was fear among free blacks, too, that they might be taken into the South and sold into slavery.

Angeline Palmer was a black servant about 10 years old, working in the home of Mason Shaw of Belchertown. Mrs. Susan Shaw was about to take Angeline to the South when Henry Jackson heard of it. He, one William Jennings, and Angeline's half brother Lewis Frazier, planned to capture the girl and save her from danger in the slave states.

Angeline was allowed to visit her aunt, who worked for the Hezekiah Wright Strong family on Main Street in Amherst. Rumors of a capture attempt circulated, and Deputy Sheriff Frink escorted her back to Belchertown. Jackson, Jennings and Frazier followed and entered the Shaw house after Angeline was left there by the sheriff. There was a brief struggle as Mrs. Shaw and the neighborhood women tried to hold onto Angeline, but she was successfully taken out of the house and brought to Amherst.

Sheriff Dwight stopped their wagon on the road, but admitted he had no authority to detain them. Mrs. Spencer Church took in Angeline at Amherst until Henry Jackson could secretly take the girl to the town of Colrain. Charles Green sheltered her there without the authorities' knowledge.

Jennings, Frazier and Jackson were each arrested after several weeks and charged with assault and forcible abduction. The Northampton Gazette reported that "the sympathies of the people are almost wholly with the colored persons."

The trial in Northampton proved that charges of abuse, breaking and entering, and taking the girl without her consent were untrue. Though they were found guilty of the abduction, the court offered to let them off if they revealed where Angeline Palmer was hidden. The men refused, and gladly served their three months in jail.

Sympathy for their actions was indeed widespread. The men were allowed daytime freedom, and their jail food was supplemented by generous contributions by people on the outside.

One report of their release in June, 1841, stated, "they were met by the congratulations of all classes, coupled with commendations for their display of pluck in taking Angeline from possible harm to a safe place."

Committed to an Insane Asylum for Her Religious Views

In March of 1866, Elizabeth Packard walked into the offices of the Hampshire and Franklin Express in Amherst and announced the publication of her new book. The astonishing story told in it spread quickly: Mrs. Packard had been declared insane for her religious ideas, and placed in an asylum by her husband. The book was titled, *Marital Power Exemplified in Mrs. Packard's Trial, and Self-Defense from the Charge of Insanity; or Three Year's Imprisonment for Religious Belief, by the Arbitrary Will of a Husband, With an Appeal to the Government to So Change the Laws as to Afford Protection to Married Women.* Mrs. Packard's book was a bombshell aimed at her respected husband, a Sunderland minister, and the entire male-dominated judicial system.

Theophilus Packard attended both Amherst Academy and Amherst College, graduating in 1823. In 1839, Packard married Elizabeth Ware of South Deerfield, and they lived in Shelburne where he was a preacher. It was after the family moved to Manteno, Illinois, that the marriage broke down and became the subject of newspaper articles from Chicago to Boston.

Theophilus was an immovable Calvinist, believing in man's total depravity and that God had foreordained some to be saved and others to be damned. Elizabeth came to believe that humans have free will and are accountable to God for their actions. She also thought slavery was a national sin. Her husband considered these views "the vagaries of a crazed brain."

Early on the morning of June 18, 1860, Elizabeth Packard prepared to take a bath. When she saw her husband approach with two physicians and a sheriff she hastily tried to dress. With Theophilus wielding an axe, the group smashed through a window and entered the room. She sprang into bed, "in a state of almost entire nudity," where, upon taking her pulse, the physicians declared her insane. Thus complying with the 1851 Illinois laws, Theophilus then committed his wife to the Jacksonville Insane Asylum.

Elizabeth Packard was taken from her six children and kept in the asylum for three years. While there, she wrote a 700-page allegory about her situation called *The Great Drama.* The asylum trustees sympathized with her and let her out, into the hands of her husband who then imprisoned her in their home. Elizabeth was allowed to see no one, the windows were screwed shut from the outside, and the doors were kept locked.

Reverend Packard's next plan was to return to Massachusetts

After spending time in an asylum in Illinois, Elizabeth Packard fought her husband, who wanted to place her in the Northampton Lunatic Asylum (above).

where he could have his wife placed in the Northampton Lunatic Asylum. Just two days before they were to leave Illinois, friends of Mrs. Packard delivered to the court a suit asking for her release under the Habeus Corpus Act.

The trial began on January 11, 1864, and it disclosed facts that the public found "most wonderful and startling." For example, one of the doctors who certified Mrs. Packard insane on religious grounds stated, "Three-fourths of the religious community are insane in the same manner ... I would say Henry Ward Beecher, Horace Greeley, and like persons are insane."

Another doctor thought she was insane for 15 reasons, including, "Her viewing the subject of religion from the osteric standpoint of Christian exegetical analysis, and agglutinating the polysinthetical ectoblasts of homogeneous asceticism." He left the stand amid roars of laughter.

On January 18th, when the jury found Elizabeth Packard sane, cheers arose from every part of the courtroom, and women waved their handkerchiefs. Even before the verdict was read, Theophilus Packard had "left the state, bag and baggage, for parts unknown."

Reverend Packard had taken the children to his sister's house in South Deerfield. A number of people there believed the story he told of his flight from an "insane" wife. Within a short time, the Sunderland church installed Packard as minister. Elizabeth's own father, Reverend Samuel Ware, lived in Sunderland and hardly knew what to make of the situation.

A great groundswell of support for Elizabeth developed as major newspapers picked up the story. She moved to her brother Austin Ware's house in South Deerfield and published more books and pamphlets. Elizabeth then successfully petitioned the Massachusetts Legislature to make it virtually impossible for a husband to commit a healthy wife to an asylum. She later helped change laws in Illinois, Iowa, and Maine.

These events forced Reverend Packard to leave the Sunderland church. Elizabeth Packard's effect on the care of the mentally ill was quite extensive, but, despite her accomplishments, her own mental stability still remains in question. There is evidence that she believed she embodied the Holy Ghost, and was herself partially divine.

Amherst's
Brilliant Women

Helen Hunt Jackson, born in Amherst, was a renowned writer, and one of the few who recognized Emily Dickinson's genius early on.

How was it that Amherst, within a patriarchal, somewhat Puritanical valley, could have fostered such brilliant women? This rural town, known mainly for its all-male colleges, brought us, among others, poet, novelist and Indian rights activist, Helen Hunt Jackson, editor and writer, Mabel Loomis Todd, and, of course, Emily Dickinson. One clue lies in the attitudes of two of the most important men in Dickinson's life: her supposedly stiff and stern father, and her much maligned mentor, Thomas Wentworth Higginson.

The often quoted line about Edward Dickinson is Emily's comment that her father's heart was "pure and terrible." This almost military facade of his cracked many times, such as when he begged Emily not to read the many books he bought her, knowing full well she would anyway.

Most remarkable, perhaps, is an obscure essay Edward Dickinson wrote and published anonymously in the New England Enquirer on December 22, 1826. Years before Emily's birth, while still a bachelor, he wrote passionately about the need for women to have access to education. He stated that "you can judge the state of civilization ... by knowing in what estimation their women are held."

In towns where women grew up "ignorant and uneducated ... taught only the rules of the most ordinary house-work, and void of a taste for reading; their ideas confined to the kitchen and the dairy room," one found women dull, uninteresting and even vulgar. In villages where women's education was thought to be important, Emily's father said, "you find the neatly painted dwellings, the tasty gardens, handsome fences and outhouses, the snow-white church" and women with cultivated minds and good taste, good manners, and good morals.

While Dickinson didn't go as far as to encourage women to enter professions such as law (as he had), or to become great writers, he hoped education would produce "an ardent desire to extend their charity to the poor and destitute, to relieve the distressed, to comfort the afflicted."

Thomas Wentworth Higginson, on the other hand, went far beyond young Edward Dickinson. The eminent literary man is often seen as bewildered by Emily Dickinson, not recognizing her genius until after her death. Yet in other ways Higginson was one of the most enlightened men of his day, and his views on women's education may have had at least as much of an effect on Emily Dickinson as her father's. Dickinson considered herself a student of Higginson, who was a leading editor, and a crusader for the rights of blacks, women, and the poor. Emily signed some of her letters to him, "Your scholar."

Higginson lectured in Amherst on women's education and suffrage on December 3, 1873. In a town of male colleges he argued for coeducation. As for other women's rights he observed, "according to our laws, paupers, idiots, lunatics, and convicts are disenfranchised because they are such, and women because they are women." Higginson boasted of women who had made it in the professions, and Emily and other Amherst women were fully aware of his words.

With Edward Dickinson's cautious encouragement, Higginson's (and others') forthright feminism, and the brilliance they were born with, several Amherst women shook a world that prefered being shaken by men.

Why Women Shut Down
the Hills Factory

Women hat factory workers spent wearisome hours steps from the Dickinsons' door.

In 1905, the women factory workers at the Hills Hat Company in Amherst went out on strike. This long-buried incident is remarkable for many reasons, one being the women did it spontaneously, without union leadership. More telling were the reasons for the strike: The presence of one Japanese man in the hat factory, and what his presence meant, caused such fear that the women walked out. The story has some surprisingly modern parallels.

When Leonard M. Hills began palm leaf hat making in Amherst in 1826, it was a simple process. Women sewed the hats in their farmhouses and Hills sold the hats from a shop. By the end of the century the Hills family had established the country's largest palm leaf and straw hat factory.

In a complex of brick factory buildings, about 200 women and 100 men worked, earning from $9.00 to $15.00 per week. By and large, the workers were from local old New England families, unlike the textile factories in the eastern part of the state. Those factories hired a succession of cheap laborers, as Irish girls replaced Yankee girls, then French supplanted Irish, and Polish followed French.

The Hills Company resisted hiring immigrants, but could not avoid the competition of hats imported from overseas. The company found it couldn't produce hats from raw products and pay the wages Yankee women wanted. They began importing partially-made hats from abroad and doing the finish work in Amherst.

By 1905, however, the company had a severe employee shortage. Ads increasingly appeared in newspapers. Still, the company simply couldn't attract enough local women to sew hats 58 hours a week at the wages they were willing to pay. The factory owners saw three options on the horizon that many companies today face under present trade problems. The company could create a factory run completely by Japanese, it could sell out to a foreign corporation, or it could go into bankruptcy. The Hills Company chose the first option.

The company planned to build a new electric powered factory in East Amherst in which workers would be Japanese. As a start, one Japanese man was brought in and trained with the understanding that he would train the Japanese to be hired at the new factory. Seeing this as a threat to their livelihood, the women of the Hills Factory walked out. The company faced a terrible crisis: Already unable to hire enough women, they now had no women, and large orders began backing up.

The strike was successful. The Japanese man was let go, plans for a factory run with Japanese laborers were abandoned, and the women went back to work.

The Hills Company couldn't continue in the same way with the local and world economies changing drastically. Foreign competition brought cheaper straw hats, and that style of hat went out of favor as horses and carriages gave way to automobiles. After many struggles, the Hills Company went out of business in 1935.

Amherst and the Dickinsons'
Fight Against "Gross Brutality"

It was a terrible situation, one which so enraged Amherst that a mob attacked a man's house with rotten eggs. In what should have been a lovely spring of 1876, a girl ran from her home and was secretly hidden by her minister. As the details surfaced, Emily Dickinson's brother Austin became involved, and Emily herself wrote a poem about the villain at the story's center. The issue that led to all this? Child abuse.

Rev. Charles Lothrop moved to Amherst with his children in 1865, after the death of his wife. There, he lived as a minister without a pulpit, married Mary Ward Underhill, and became a member of the First Congregational Church. For years, his house on Boltwood Avenue, near College Street, hid the tragic story until one of his daughters could no longer take the beatings.

In April, 1876, 18 year-old Mary Lothrop witnessed her father's abuse of her step-mother at the dinner table. When Mary protested, Lothrop knocked her down and beat her until bruises rose on her skin. For some time Mary had been confiding in Rev. Jenkins, the minister at First Church. That night she ran to Jenkins' house in a near suicidal state and refused to return home. As she later testified, "I intended to go to the cemetery where my own mother was buried and lie down on her grave, thinking if I did so that I would die before long."

While Jenkins was hiding Mary in his house, he called in lawyer Austin Dickinson and Edward Hitchcock, Jr., of Amherst College as advisers. Shortly, local newspapers were printing angry editorials and the letters of those involved, detailing the sorry affair. Under the headline "A Ministerial Wolf" the Amherst Record reported, "The irregularities in Mr. Lothrop's family have been known to several parties in town for some time. Last fall his oldest daughter, Anna, ran away from home, and has since supported herself by teaching music in Newton. Mr. Lothrop claims that she is insane, and it is said he has repeatedly tried to procure her committal to an asylum. It is charged that he has repeatedly horse-whipped them all, and seems to have kept the family upon insufficient and disgusting food."

For Lothrop's part, he did admit beating Mary with a riding whip and knocking her "gently" against a window casement, but he denied beating his wife. Of his daughter he said, "through much study she has become mentally unsound ... . Her mind is disordered by novel reading." As for charges of making his family eat meat that

Boltwood Avenue, where, sadly, a minister regularly abused his children.

had gone bad, he claimed "it was only tainted enough to give it that delicate flavor which many greatly prize." He gave no explanation for forcing his daughters to eat their pet rabbit, "watered with tears," as he threatened them with a horse whip.

Edward Hitchcock recorded Amherst's reaction in his diary: "Of course the town was excited as soon as it heard of the matter, and on a dark evening a great crowd of students surrounded the house with tin horns & eggs, making a hideous noise. I felt it was outrageous ... . So I made for the locality & as the noise was so tremendous that I couldn't be heard, I at once took away every tin horn ... . I sent the students to their rooms & threatened the town people if they didn't leave."

News spread to Springfield, where the Republican reported, "The town witnessed a disreputable performance Monday night, when the students and some of the townspeople serenaded Rev. C.D. Lothrop, accused of cruelty in his family, with horns and 'devil fiddles,' amid yells of 'chicken meat,' 'boiled rabbits,' etc., adding the final indignity in a shower of rotten eggs."

Lothrop wrote a letter to Austin Dickinson and Rev. Jenkins accusing them of estranging "our children from us" and asking for a "fair, honest, impartial tribunal." He referred to "gross slander" and said "our household has been thrown into deepest distress and danger, now that we are hooted at in the streets and mobbed in our home." Showing some insight into this kind of abuse, the Amherst Record noted, "Mrs. Lothrop, as is often the case, sustains her husband in everything."

Austin's reply to the letter said, "You understand very well how your daughter came to be at Mr. Jenkins', and the pitiable plight in which she arrived there, for we told you within eighteen hours after. She is under no constraint or advice to remain there. She will not, under the circumstances be turned into the street from there. If, in stepping in as we did to save her life, we have done you any legal wrong, your counsel will point you your legal remedy."

Interestingly, the court system never became involved in the case; it was purely a matter for the church to deal with. Members of First Church brought formal charges against Lothrop for "conduct unbecoming a christian," and began a trial in July of 1876. The trial lasted until October, and though Lothrop was repeatedly called to testify he did not do so until the last day of the trial. He read a statement denying the charges.

As reported in the Record on October 18: "The last act in the Lothrop drama was performed at the First Congregational Church last Thursday evening, when the members present voted 35 to 10 to excommunicate Mr. Lothrop for gross brutality in his family, and unchristian conduct ... ."

Lothrop immediately moved to Salem where he began a libel suit against The Springfield Republican. The reports don't reveal what became of his wife and daughters. It wasn't until 1879 that the libel case was tried. At least a dozen people from Amherst were called to testify in Salem and the Amherst Record quipped "the streets in this village were nearly deserted yesterday." Amherst was outraged when Lothrop was initially awarded $1,000 in damages, which the Republican appealed.

Emily Dickinson made it plain that she was indeed in this world when she commented on this case in a poem she sent to her brother's house:

In Petto

A Counterfeit — a Plated Person
I would not be —
Whatever Strata of Iniquity
My Nature underlie,
Truth is good Health — and Safety — and the Sky,
How meagre, what an Exile — is a Lie,
And vocal — when we die.

Under this poem, Emily wrote a single word: Lothrop.

When "Sarah Jane Doffed Her Bonnet" and Got the Vote

From 1879 to 1920, Amherst was engaged in a long debate over the right of women to vote. The very first vote cast by a woman in Amherst symbolized Amherst's contradictory feelings. It took place in 1879 when Amherst women were allowed to take part in the election of school committee members for the first time. Louisa B. Marsh stepped up and cast the first ballot, which led to the election of Mary E. Stearns. But Stearns, ironically, was ardently against women voting, and she declined to serve.

Three years later, a long article appeared in the Amherst Record deriding the women's rights movement. The writer, "A.G." from Newport, wrote about "the inconsistency and absurdity and fallacy of Woman Suffrage." He claimed that the movement was based on "antagonism between the sexes which God and nature never designed. It would degrade true womanhood, demoralize society and revolutionize our whole social fabric."

A spirited reply came on September 20, 1882, from "O.H.K." The writer could not agree that "evil must follow the elevation of female to equality with males." On the contrary, it would be a natural progression "from the debris of primitive ignorance into a higher state ... . And if Sarah Jane wants to doff her bonnet and enter the political arena, the great American Eagle must submit to hold that bonnet."

The movement went through hard times for many years, with bills for limited women's suffrage defeated in Massachusetts in 1901, 1902, and 1903. By 1903, women from nearly every prominent family in Amherst belonged to the local branch of the Massachusetts Association Opposed to the Further Extension of Suffrage to Women. In September of 1905, Amherst women were asked to organize a branch of the Connecticut Valley Equal Suffrage Association, but little interest was shown.

Charles S. Walker wrote in 1905 that "the women of Amherst have been indifferent, and have scrupulously avoided politics ... . Women's success (is) in making good citizens by training their boys in their own homes and by teaching them in the public schools." He felt women shouldn't jeopardize this situation by participating in elections.

By the time the women's voting rights amendment was ratified in 1920, Amherst had changed its tune. An article in the Springfield Union on November 14, 1920, boasted that Amherst women showed remarkable abilities as business managers and they certainly deserved the vote. The article claimed that one of Amherst's best postmasters had been Clara S. Hill. It pointed to the success of the Beston sisters' millinery store on Pleasant Street, Pearl Davenport's inn on North Pleasant, Mrs. Harold Ward's tea house called "The Lilacs" on Bay Road, and Mrs. W.D. Herrick's school for invalid children on South Prospect Street.

Domestic Violence
in Emily's Pelham Hills

The year 1992 was the most violent year on record for families in Massachusetts. Murders of women and children as a result of domestic violence reached an all-time high. News of this arrived exactly 100 years after a terrible case which took place in Emily Dickinson's beloved Pelham hills. There, a man who had murdered within his own family was set free.

In late March, 1893, Governor Russell pardoned Marion Montgomery, who, 10 years earlier, had killed one child and wounded another in Pelham. The editors of the Amherst Record were outraged: "If ever an executive has laid himself open to the charge of an abuse of the pardoning power that executive is William E. Russell ... . A murderer who is thoroughly hanged can never profit by the tender heart or brain of an executive."

Two days after Christmas in 1882, an unusually lurid headline had appeared in local papers: "The Annual Pelham Murder. An Innocent Boy Killed by His Father. Envy Stronger Than Love — A Pistol Shot For a Kiss." Eva Augusta Montgomery, who had refused to live with her abusive husband, sat in her father's house with six-year-old daughter Eva. Her estranged husband entered the next room, where he shot their four-year-old son George in the head, then went after his wife and daughter.

Montgomery placed his revolver against his daughter's head, but the gun misfired. The next shot wounded the girl severely in the neck. Before he could kill his wife, Montgomery's father-in-law Horatio Marsh subdued him.

Horatio Marsh had tried to earn a living in the weaving mills of Chicopee, then as a farmer, and as a day laborer. He went to the Midwest more than once for a fresh start. It was in Iowa that daughter Eva Augusta was raised. At school there she met Marion Montgomery and began a relationship her parents tried to discourage.

At the age of 17, Eva and Marion eloped. The couple struggled to survive, sometimes living with her parents, sometimes living on their own. In 1879, the Marshes followed them to Kansas where they found their daughter and her children living in poverty. Montgomery had traded a team of horses for a billiard saloon, which he stocked with 45 gallons of whisky. The place was shut down, and both families left Kansas for Pelham. Illness and a cyclone helped defeat the farm they rented together. In 1880, Horatio Marsh and Marion Montgomery temporarily left their families behind to earn some cash in Colorado.

Surviving pictures of Pelham often show pleasant scenes like this of a camping trip in the Pelham hills. However, the town at one point was known for the "annual Pelham murder."

While the men were away, Eva worked in a mill until her health failed. A young local man, Irving Cary, was then taken in as a boarder to help with expenses. Montgomery returned and tried to convince Eva to leave her family, which she refused to do. Montgomery said if she would no longer live with him he would kill himself and would "kill all the rest of them." He came back a few nights later with a knife, which Eva succeeded in getting away from him.

Aware of the danger, Horatio Marsh sent Montgomery on a wild goose chase to Chicago by telling him Eva had taken the children there. In October, 1882, Montgomery returned again. He left his horse at a stable in Belchertown and arrived at the Marshes with Constable William Burnett. An argument erupted as he attempted to take the children away, Horatio all the while insisting Montgomery and the constable leave the property. Montgomery went for his gun, but was stopped by Eva's mother.

At Christmas, Montgomery returned with presents: a gold ring for Eva and a sled for four-year-old George. On December 26, he asked Eva once more if she would live with him. When she refused he went into the kitchen where, according to the Amherst Record, he "took out his revolver and had but to turn to his left to face little Georgie standing on his new sled, saying 'papa kiss me.' The father answered with a shot of his revolver, and the boy instantly fell dead." The community was thoroughly angered when Montgomery wasn't hung but was sent to prison for life. People would have prefered that "Judge Lynch would pronounce the sentence and the people would execute it." The community was angrier still when, 10 years later, the Governor set Montgomery free.

The Amherst Record did, in its own way, apologize to the town of Pelham for its original report of the crime, which had appeared under the title, "The Annual Pelham Murder." "We believe that the citizens of Pelham, especially the older citizens, are peacefully disposed," the paper said, "and while there are, perhaps, as many petty quarrels among neighbors, and now and then a case of bigamy comes to the surface and reveals a bad state in the marital affairs of some of the poorer class, as happens in many other places, still such things are expected to happen and no town or city amounts to much unless something of the sort arrests the attention of the rest of the world."

A Very Personal Ad
for a Loafing Scoundrel

In the 1990s, some go courting in column after column of personal ads. In the 19th century, personal ads were used for quite opposite reasons: When a marriage broke down, some men vented their anger by disavowing their mate in print. With little money or influence, few women could respond. But in 1854, Sarah A. Jones published some well-chosen words after her husband placed such an ad, and she found herself cheered in newspapers eager to see women vindicated.

Tied as they were to men financially, and responsible for virtually all child-rearing tasks, 19th century women found great difficulty in leaving a marriage. When the wife of Amherst's Elias Cook did just that in 1865, he printed the following notice: "My wife Jane Ann Cook, having left my bed and board without just cause, I forbid all persons harboring or trusting her on my account after this date, as I shall pay no bills on her contracting."

When Lizzie Hunt of Leverett left her husband Wilson at about the same time, Wilson printed virtually the same notice. When the wife of Leverett's Asa Wood left, he used the same language, but added embellishments: "Whereas my wife Cordelia Wood has left my bed and board without just provocation, I hereby forbid all persons trusting or harboring her on my account as I shall pay no debts of her contracting after this date. She also took with her a bunch of keys, for which a liberal reward will be paid."

It was in the winter of 1854 that Leander Wetherell, the editor of the Hampshire and Franklin Express, printed the words of one of the few women who were able to reply to an ad like the above. He published Sarah Jones' letter in full. Wetherell couldn't help, however, adding an editorial introduction that was admiring, yet a bit condescending.

"Women's Rights Vindicated — Edward H. Jones having advertised his wife Sarah A. through the columns of the Stamford, Ct., Advocate, as a contumacious absentee from his downy bed and ample board, she takes up the broomstick in self-defense, and 'carries the war into Africa' with an earnestness and vivacity truly Napoleonic."

Sarah Jones' astonishing letter reads, "To the Public — Whereas my husband Edward H. Jones, has falsely advertised that I have left his bed and board and that he will pay no debts of my contracting, etc., this is to inform the public that the aforesaid Edward H. Jones had neither bed nor board for me to leave, he having been living at the expense of my father; and further, under the pretence of procuring money to pay his way to Birmingham, Connecticut, he borrowed a dollar of my father, and with that paid for his lying advertisement against me and even after this dastardly act, he took all the money I had, and borrowed every cent in my mother's possession, and left the town.

"For the past three months he has been kept from nakedness and starvation by the exertions of myself and relatives; he squandered in dissipation, all the money his inborn laziness would allow him to earn. The scamp need not have advertised that he would not pay debts of my contracting for the public well know that he does not even pay his own.

"He is a lazy, ungrateful, loafing scoundrel; not content with living at the expense of my relatives and borrowing their money, he publishes an outrageous lie. His bed and board indeed! If left to himself his bed would be nothing but a board, and I should not be much surprised if the bed he dies on were made of boards, with a strong crossbeam overhead."

Chapter Fourteen

PROSTITUTION, SCAMS, AND GROSS IMMORALITY

Amherst House. Amherst, Mass.

Amherst House, Amherst, Massachusetts

> *I know some lonely Houses off the Road*
> *A Robber'd like the look of -*
> *Wooden barred,*
> *And Windows hanging low,*
> *Inviting to -*
> *A Portico.*
> *One - hand the Tools -*
> *The other peep -*
> *To make sure All's Asleep -*
> *#371*

Getting Rich Quick: A Century of Scams

In the 19th century, editor Edward Carpenter thought the people of Amherst were so gullible they would fall for any scam that came along.

Emily Dickinson's grandfather lost a fortune in the founding of Amherst College. Her father invested in risky, money-losing railroads. While both men let their passion outrun their business sense, they at least had the willpower to resist the plethora of bad, often wacky scams that tempted their neighbors.

In the 19th century, Edward Carpenter of the Amherst Record said of Amherst people, "They have been ready to rise to almost any kind of bait if the hook wasn't too plainly in sight." Back in 1830, South Amherst's Timothy Smith began the doomed business of raising mulberry trees and silk worms. The mulberry craze attracted so many followers that even the Second Congregational Church, in need of a new building, invested in the business. The church was eventually built, but with no help from the silk worm.

In the 1880s, Amherst and her neighbors eagerly bought gold and silver mines in the West. The Starr-Grove Silver Mines Company in Nevada was supposed to equal the value of "the mines of King Solomon." William S. Clark, former president of the Massachusetts Agricultural College, used all his influence and enthusiasm to draw a lot of local people into this particular disaster with him. It became known as a "permanent investment."

Between 1887 and 1896, hundreds of local people were taken in by various insurance investment schemes, taking nothing but experience away with them.

After nearly a century of experience as an "easy mark" (as the Amherst Record was to characterize the town), Amherst was taken on yet another ride. The news coming from St.Louis in 1896 dumbfounded the town. Professor Clarence D. Warner had been a great friend of both students and faculty at the Massachusetts Agricultural College during the last years of Emily Dickinson's life. A year after he left Amherst in 1895, people who knew him began to hear of stories printed in the St. Louis Post-Dispatch. The paper charged Professor Warner with swindling insurance companies in a series of arson and fraud schemes. Amherst at first refused to believe the charming professor was this con man. People eventually conceded that Warner might have been an example of "The Strange Case of Dr. Jekyll and Mr. Hyde."

Mass. Aggie was glad to get Clarence D. Warner as a professor of mathematics and physics in 1884. The talented man held a Ph. D. from Johns Hopkins University, and he soon distinguished himself in Amherst, mainly doing research in meteorology.

The number of fires in houses Warner owned seemed unremarkable at the time. After his move to St. Louis he was asked to accompany the Peary Arctic expedition as meteorologist. Just before he was to sail, however, a fire broke out in his house. He wrote to Lieutenant Peary that he had to remain in St. Louis to adjust his insurance.

In March of 1896, the Daily Hampshire Gazette in Northampton listed the Warner buildings that had burned in and around Amherst. One was a house owned by Warner's wife on Amity Street. He collected insurance money on this, on his house on Sunset Avenue, a South Hadley ice house, and a house he owned at Dwight Station, Belchertown. In 1893, he also collected insurance claims for three injuries.

In addition, Professor Warner allegedly masterminded a very complicated cigar scam shortly after moving to St. Louis. It was a confusing shell game wherein cheap Pennsylvania cigars were exchanged for combinations of real estate and cash. Warner claimed his partner skipped out with all the company's assets.

In October of 1895, Warner pressed his luck and became trapped in a sting operation. On a single day he went to two insurance companies and took out very large accident policies. Posing as a wealthy real estate tycoon, Warner bluffed his way into two policies that would guarantee a high lifetime income were he to become disabled. Within half an hour of signing both policies, Warner was injured while riding a trolley car. Armed with two statements from doctors, he attempted to collect.

One insurance company, however, decided to have a detective named Matthews follow Warner. Matthews moved into Warner's boarding house, claiming to be an investor from Mississippi. He and Warner hit it off, and soon the professor confided his schemes to the undercover detective. Warner even proposed that Matthews sign an affidavit to the effect that Matthews had witnessed Warner's accident on the trolley.

The Gazette reported that when the insurance company confronted Warner with documents provided by the detective, Warner "turned as white as a sheet and nearly fainted away, the perspiration rolling off his forehead and dropping to the floor ... the scene was intensely dramatic." Warner agreed to drop his claims, and even gave the insurance man a cigar as he left the office. Warner's wife later appeared at the same office declaring she would kill Detective Matthews. The insurance companies let the matter drop.

Warner's former Amherst neighbors had to read the Northampton papers to keep up on the story, for none of the details appeared in the Amherst Record. The paper did point out how well-liked Warner had been, and hoped he would be vindicated. The Record published a letter Warner wrote to his Amherst creditors, in which he promised to pay all his debts. He would have done so earlier but for "a severe accident which I received late last fall." He attributed all the stories about him to "the work of blackmailers."

The Amherst Record failed to follow up on any of this. It even ignored Professor Warner's other great scheme to produce 28 pounds of butter from two gallons of milk in Mexico.

Lake Pleasant, a Moral Cesspool

Lake Pleasant, shown here with its Fountain of Youth, was the site of many spiritualist camp meetings.

The Spiritualist Movement had its Connecticut Valley center at Lake Pleasant, as described in Chapter Five, and many in Dickinson's era took the movement very seriously. It grew out of the ideas of Emanuel Swedenborg, who communed with spirits, and Franz Mesmer, who developed mesmerism. The movement spread over the Western world and attracted many distinguished figures, such as Mary Todd Lincoln and Sir Arthur Conan Doyle. Mediums like Henry Slade and Daniel D. Home became sought-after celebrities.

A vigorous attack of the movement was launched, however, by Rev. H.W. Eldredge, who angrily claimed Lake Pleasant had become "a moral cesspool." In the late summer of 1882, Rev. Eldredge of Turners Falls said of Lake Pleasant, "Here fat mediums, harpies in human form, practice their deception upon bereaved and heart-broken women in the sad hour of sorrow. For years

Spiritualism has been allowed to exert its baneful influence among us, and, as a result, this quiet, moral region has abounded in more scandals and outrages, in more murders and incendiarism, in more horrible and unnatural crimes than can be shown in any other section of equal size and population in America."

During a particularly fiery sermon, Eldredge claimed he would rather see a son of his dead than see him a Spiritualist extremist. Unfortunately, the minister's young son died very shortly afterwards.

The Lake Pleasant Spiritualists published an article in the Gardner News pointing to the coincidence as a judgment from Heaven. Eldredge's angry response in the Greenfield Gazette said that if Spiritualism were the only alternative to his son's death, then "I thank God a thousand times that he is gone."

Today's renewed interest in channeling and reincarnation is evidence that the Spiritualist Movement — bogus or not — has never really lost momentum.

Advising the Minister
to Jump in the Sea

When Edward Owers told the people of North Leverett that he had "buried his wife," they thought he simply meant he was a widower. There was much more to the story, however, and as it was revealed, Leverett, the town just north of Amherst, burned with anger. According to reports, the man's conduct had "well nigh rent the little Leverett Baptist Church in twain." The reason, sadly, was that Owers wasn't merely any man, but the trusted minister of their church.

When Rev. Edward Owers began his ministerial duties in the 1890s, people believed his half-truth that he had buried his wife. The Baptist Church on North Leverett Road was shocked to learn that yes, his wife had died, but Owers was no widower: he had another wife living whom he had abandoned. The living Mrs. Owers tracked the minister to Leverett, but was turned away from his door. She went to the town's selectmen for help and was accompanied by one of them to the parsonage. There, Rev. Owers declared that if his wife didn't stay away from him he would "horsewhip" her.

The Leverett correspondent to the Amherst Record responded in no uncertain terms: "We would advise the Reverend Gentleman (?) to tie a millstone about his neck and cast himself into the depths of the sea. We should be glad to render all needed assistance."

Rev. Owers' troubles continued when he was summoned to the county courthouse in Greenfield on Christmas Eve, 1895. Some of Leverett's best-known citizens testified against him and he was convicted of assaulting schoolboy Lester Waterman. He was fined 10 dollars.

Owers had been before the courts twice before for non-support of his wife, but those efforts were fruitless. State authorities were notified and Mr. Stone, superintendent of the Out-Door Poor, made an investigation. Stone concluded that, "Mr. Owers should support his wife, and ought to be punished if he refuses. If the whole family will go back to England, from whence they came, the Commonwealth will pay their expenses."

Owers was again arrested, and taken before Justice Gunn of Montague. The Leverett correspondent granted that while Mrs. Owers was no angel, "there is no excuse for Mr. Owers to abandon her in the way he has, trampling under foot a mother's heart in taking from her her own children."

The fate of the minister and his wife remains a mystery. They receive no further mention in reports from Leverett. The last admonition from the Leverett news correspondent warns Rev. Owers that "the way of the transgressor is hard."

Leverett, with its Congregational Church, farms, and (on right), a box factory.

The Russian Count, the Heiress, and All the Spicy Particulars

When the New York Herald printed a story under the headline, "Amherst's Romance," it promised to expose the "Full and Spicy Particulars." It was February 1871 and the facts that came to light involved a varied cast of characters: a mysterious Russian Count named Eugene Mitkiewicz, the Amherst College Professor of Greek, William S. Tyler, and the professor's wealthy niece, Carrie Lester. It was a story as passionate and exotic as any Gothic novel, and for a time both the town and the college were consumed by it.

Carrie Lester was described as "a bewitching young lady of twenty-three" who had come into a large fortune upon the death of her father. Professor Tyler, her mother's brother, had become her guardian, and both she and her mother moved from New York into Tyler's Amherst home on Tyler Place. Tyler was one of Amherst's highly respected senior professors. He was an 1830 graduate of the college, and he went on to write the history of the school. Tyler firmly controlled Carrie's affairs, and taught her to address him as "father."

Carrie and her mother travelled frequently and, in 1863, fate brought them to Washington, D.C. It was there that the 15 year-old Carrie met Count Mitkiewicz. The Count was Secretary of the Russian Legation and was described as "a regular lady killer." It was love at first sight. Bliss was not theirs, however, because Carrie, being a minor, would need Tyler's consent to marry, and Tyler, it was alleged, had plans for the heiress.

Though Tyler was an esteemed member of the Amherst faculty, his annual salary was only $2,000. Tyler also had an unmarried son, an unsuccessful lawyer named Mason, whom Tyler hope to match with Carrie, and thereby keep her fortune in the family. Tyler spent five years maneuvering toward this by intercepting letters between the lovers and trying to prove that the Count was an imposter.

The Count hoped to liberate Carrie from her guardian and sent the following telegram from New York to her on February 2, 1871:

> To Miss Carrie Lester, Amherst, Mass.:
>
> I will be with you, in spite of hell, tomorrow. Can you see me? Answer.
>
> Eugene

Professor William S. Tyler was pitted against the mysterious Count Mitkiewicz in a fight for Tyler's niece, Carrie Lester.

When the Count reached Palmer by train, he learned that Tyler and four other Amherst College professors were waiting for him at the Amherst depot. He outfoxed them by taking a carriage instead of the train, and he registered at the Amherst House before they realized what had happened.

The Count audaciously knocked on Tyler's door but Mrs. Tyler answered and turned him away. He returned to the hotel, crying "I cannot, I cannot stand this; for there is murder in my heart!" Tyler and his entourage of college professors confronted the Count at the hotel, but failed to toss the man out of town.

Tyler then threatened to call out a mob of 250 Amherst College students, but even this failed to impress the Count. The students and townspeople alike had by this time become swept up in the affair.

The Count sought to liberate his lover by offering $500 to anyone who could get a note to her. A message eventually made it to Carrie, by way of a Tyler family servant, and she flew to the arms of the "lady killer." The New York Herald said, "'Twas affecting in the

The Russian Count Eugene Mitkiewicz (shown here as a boy), nearly caused a riot when he wooed Carrie Lester in Amherst.

extreme." However, Professor Tyler burst in on them in the parlor of the hotel and a public scene ensued that lasted over three hours. The lovers declared their devotion, both proclaiming they would take their own life if they could not marry. Tyler invited them back to his house for tea.

The scene at the Tyler house started out pleasantly enough, but it quickly got out of hand. Carrie's mother declared the marriage would never take place. Carrie said she would run off. Professor Tyler ripped her from the Count's arms, threw her to the floor and tried to choke her. Carrie's mother screamed; the Count coolly lit a cigar. Tyler ordered his son, Mason, to throw the Count out of the house, but Mason was by that time reduced to quivering jelly.

The Count returned to the hotel, whereupon he fainted dead away. Later that night he received this letter:

> My loved one, my only hope, my salvation. —You are right in calling them murderers. They choked me, and held me down on the floor, to hide my agonizing cries. I will never give you up. You are my only hope. Do come to me. I am dying to be in your loving embrace once more. Do not leave this place. My heart is broken, and I do not wish to live, only in the presence of him I love. Your broken hearted,

Carrie

The Count paced the floor all night. The next day he returned to the Tyler house, where somehow an agreement was reached that a marriage would take place in one year. Tyler insisted on one stipulation, however. He wanted proof that the Count was not an imposter, that he was not the swindler that the newspapers claimed he was.

The Tylers ushered the Count off to Europe and Carrie remained in Amherst. During the waiting period it was said that "Miss Lester reads French novels to pass the time away," and that the Count's brandy bottle was labelled "Forty drops every fifteen minutes until you drive dull care away."

After a waiting period of one year, the sensational romance of Count Mitkiewicz and Carrie Lester was punctuated by marriage. They were, in fact, married twice, and neither time was Carrie's guardian, the angry Professor William Tyler, present.

On May 1, 1872, the Amherst Record reported that the Amherst Romance had ended at last: "The marriage of Count Eugene Oscar Mitkiewicz, third son of Count Ivan Ivanorriez Mitkiewicz, Ex-Councilor of State of the Russian Empire, and Miss Caroline Martha Lester, only child of the late Ralph Lester, Esq., formerly a banker in Rochester, New York, took place at the residence of the Catholic clergyman, Rev. Francis Brennan, at two o'clock yesterday, Mrs. Lucius Boltwood being bridesmaid, and Mr.

Peabody of Mass. Agricultural College, groomsman.

"At three o'clock p.m., a second ceremony, in accordance with the forms of the Episcopal Church, Rev., F.H. Allen officiating, took place at Grace Church ... . The bride was given away by the Hon. Lucius Boltwood, in the presence of a dense throng of interested spectators ... . The Count has long pressed his suit in the face of many obstacles and extreme opposition, but his persistent efforts have at length been crowned with success and his dearly cherished hopes become realized.

"The Count furnished cake, wine, and cigars to his gentlemen friends after the marriage, in one of the private parlors of the Amherst House. At five o'clock the wedding party took cars for Boston, where they will be guests of the Tremont House for a short time. An immense crowd assembled at the station to see the last, for the present, of the Count and Countess who have made the Amherst Romance."

Three weeks later Carrie, now calling herself Countess Caroline Martha Mitkiewicz, returned to Amherst from her bridal tour to visit her mother. But none of this laid to rest the bubbling controversy over the Count's character, and the behavior of Professor Tyler. In fact, as the Amherst Record was announcing the couple's marriage, it was also adding fuel to the fire. It noted that the Count "claims that he has proved beyond a doubt his title to nobility and that he is in every way worthy of his lively bride." Many in Amherst had come to believe that the Count had been persecuted by Professor Tyler, who had hoped the wealthy Carrie would marry his son, Mason.

However, the Record claimed to have indisputable proof that the Count was a fraud. The newspaper had received letters from the proprietor of a hotel along the Pacific Railroad, west of Omaha. He said that during the previous February, the Count and 16 Englishmen were snowbound in his hotel. The Count claimed he was an attache of the Grand Duke Alexis, and that he was short of funds.

He obtained $1,200 from the hotel in exchange for a check he wrote on the Bank of London. The check was later returned with a letter from the bank manager stating, "I have to inform you that a person calling himself Count Eugene Mitkiewicz had a very insignificant account here for a short time which was closed nearly two years ago."

The newspaper further said that Carrie had been supporting the phony Count and would have to continue to do so. Oblivious to this, the couple travelled, and from time to time returned to Amherst. Then in 1901, the following obituary appeared: "The death of Count Eugene S. Mitkiewicz has revived the memories of

Amherst people, who recall the eccentricities of this brilliant soldier of fortune. He was always fighting, always charming, always a delusion. He seems to have been possessed of a marvelous hypnotic power. He cast a spell over the innocent girl and the women of the world, over the hotel clerk and the bank president ... . Could this erratic genius have been confined to legitimate channels and his great powers have been directed by conscience, the world would have found a hero whose deeds would have blessed mankind."

Lewd and Lascivious Behavior in the Valley

From the earliest days, the Massachusetts legal system has had an obsession with sexual offenses. In the 18th century, over three fifths of the crimes prosecuted were crimes of immorality. How society prosecuted "unclean actings" and "sinful dalliance" from the 17th century into the 20th reflects how we feel about sex, and its relationship to religion and violence.

Enfield, where Rev. McElroy had to resign for "gross immorality" in 1887.

While sexual deviancy has always been with us, relatively little space is given to it in general histories. Buried under the heroic accounts of the Plymouth Pilgrims is the case of Thomas Graunger. In Plymouth, execution was the sentence for treason, murder, witchcraft, arson, and sexual crimes, yet the colonists were surprisingly lenient in applying it. Thomas Graunger's was the only sexual crime case for which capital punishment was the sentence in Plymouth Colony. In 1642, the 16 or 17 year-old servant from Duxbury was accused of "buggery."

His punishment bears the haunting echo of ancient Biblical law. In William Bradford's words, "Horrible it is to mention, but the truth of the historie requires it ... first the mare, and then the cowe, and the rest of the lesser cattle, were kild before his face, according to the law, Livit: 20.15, and he him selfe was executed."

In the laws of 17th century Massachusetts, homosexuality was punishable by death: "If a man lyeth with mankinde as he lyeth with a woeman, both of them have committed abhomination, they both shale surely be put to death (1641)." Between 1692 and 1780, a man could be whipped for wearing women's clothing, and a woman for wearing a man's.

Fornication was strictly punished in the 17th century, usually by whipping. In 1670, when Rebecca Allen of Northampton was found to be with child, she said she had been raped by an Indian. The accused Indian was caught, but he later escaped. Rebecca Allen was sentenced to be "well whipped on the naked body, when she is capable of receiving correction, she now being forward with child."

In that same year, Thomas Welles, Jr., of Hadley was accused of "unclean actings with the negro wench, servant of Mr. Russell." It was evident that there was "sinful dalliance between them in the barn." His sentence was to be either whipped by his father in the presence of the constables, or to pay a fine. He chose the fine.

In the late 17th century, it was common for couples who had a child too soon after marriage to be prosecuted, but by the mid-18th century married couples were no longer fined for these early births. In the 19th century, prosecutions for sexual crimes no longer dominated Massachusetts courts. Liquor-related offenses far outnumbered them, but sexual crimes of ministers were exposed with increasing regularity.

For example, life in the peaceful, lost town of Enfield was shattered in March of 1887 when the terrible deeds of its Congregational minister were revealed. The 1880s were a time when churches had become alarmed by what was labeled "New England Heathenism." Conferences were held to determine its causes, and most often rum and foreigners were blamed. When "heathenism" of Enfield's own Rev. Edward P. McElroy was discovered, he was dealt with swiftly and the episode was then quietly swallowed by history.

The town of Enfield was originally called Quabbin, when it was the southern part of the town of Greenwich. In 1816, Enfield became a separate township, deriving its name from Robert Field, an early settler. The Enfield Congregational Church was founded in 1787, exactly 100 years before the Rev. McElroy affair.

Edward P. McElroy was installed as minister of the Enfield

church in 1884. He served for two years to the apparent satisfaction of the congregation, then on March 23, 1887, the Amherst Record ran a story headlined, "A Minister in Disgrace." McElroy had been forced to resign for reasons of "gross immorality." According to the newspaper, the minister confessed to "debauching some of the youth of the town. The crime is pronounced of the most base and repulsive in the whole category, the details of which are too vulgar and indecent to print."

When the church demanded a written resignation, McElroy complied, adding that he intended to leave the ministry. He wisely left town quickly, avoiding the wrath that would certainly have come had he lingered. Only a few knew of his whereabouts. McElroy's wife had died earlier, and no other family remained except his elderly father, for whom he was responsible.

The village of Enfield was "considerably agitated" according to the report. In the view of the Amherst Record, it would be charitable to suppose that the minister's mind was imbalanced "or that he is insane." In conclusion it declared that "if a public whipping post was in use, we should say place the culprit there and publicly administer about a hundred lashes on his bare back in unutterable disgrace."

While the most gory details of violence often appear in 19th century newspapers, sexual matters were handled very gingerly, if at all. Many cases, in fact, were handled by church parish committees and never reached the courts. This tragic episode has been scrupulously avoided by every history that has since been written about the area. A historical sermon published during the town's centenary in 1916 merely lists McElroy as a minister, but misspells his name.

Enfield went out of existence on April 28, 1938, to make way for the Quabbin Reservoir, whose waters have almost succeeded in covering the dark episode of Rev. Edward McElroy. In all the books that have been written about the lost Quabbin towns, Enfield is painted as a quaint New England village, with no mention of his name to spoil the picture.

Emily Dickinson's Amherst was very much a part of Massachusetts' Puritan sexual heritage, overtones of which still survive. In fact, today the old Puritan phrase "lewd and lascivious behavior" is still used in the courts, and adultery, a misdemeanor in most jurisdictions, is a felony in Massachusetts.

Small-Town Prostitution
and Amherst's Poco

Among the many social evils of the 19th century, one of the most pernicious was prostitution. Often hushed up, and always controversial, prostitution was a problem that no one in the Connecticut Valley, from poets to poor farmers, could ignore. After a lengthy surveillance, Amherst's deputy sheriffs Tillson and Bell raided a "notorious resort" in Hadley and arrested three women and a man on November 22, 1896.

During America's colonial period, prostitution flourished despite some violent opposition. Boston became a center for it and in 1734 and 1737, mobs severely damaged and closed down two houses. The problem increased as urban centers grew, and as war conditions provided willing soldiers and sailors who were away from home. Opposition by tradesmen and laborers grew when it became obvious that the women did not necessarily come from elsewhere. Some were members of their own families.

Brothels had come to be connected with taverns, and to be centered especially in growing seaport towns. In Boston, reformers hoped to prevent women from becoming prostitutes by keeping them busy with household crafts. Thus, spinning and needlework became mid-18th century crazes. The first organized anti-prostitution group in this country was the American Society for the Prevention of Licentiousness and Vice and the Promotion of Morality, formed in the 1820s.

The group's philosophy relied on the old explanation of the "fall" of woman. Later, Susan B. Anthony, an early crusader against prostitution, astutely saw poverty and industrialization as contributing factors. Most community leaders, however, were against public discussion of the problem, fearing that even discussing it would swell the ranks.

In the mid-19th century, the majority did not favor abolition of prostitution, but rather state regulation, which was the case in Europe. Even doctors (who were alarmed by the incidence of venereal diseases), and police were among those favoring regulation. The acceptance of prostitution, while certainly not universal, was such that on the eve of the Civil War one could purchase a guidebook to the better "bawdy houses." Titled *A Directory to the Seraglios in New York, Philadelphia, Boston, and All Principal Cities in the Union*, it was similar to those published in Europe. It listed addresses, amenities, and recommended women.

Though a fact virtually unknown today, prostitution was widespread in Emily Dickinson's Valley. The Orient House in Pelham was, for much of its history, a health resort. Yet in August 1863, the following notice appeared in the Hampshire and Franklin Express: "Doctor" Luke K. Blair, formerly of Pelham, is under $500 bond by the Northampton Police for making the Orient House at Pelham a place of Prostitution."

In 1869, two "disorderly houses" were raided, one in the Plainville section of Hadley, and one in Northampton. In early December the Amherst Record described the circumstances: "This (Hadley) house, it is stated, has been the resort of disorderly characters for some time and has received a liberal patronage from Amherst and Northampton parties. Complaint was made by Amherst parties to the selectmen in Hadley, and they presented the matter before the court authorities in Northampton and secured a warrant for the arrest of the inmates of the house.

"It is understood that the man who conducted the house has made his headquarters in Amherst and had been warned by Amherst college authorities to keep off the college grounds. At the district court session held in Northampton on Friday the prisoners were arraigned for trial. The three women found in the house were convicted; one was sentenced to one year in Sherburn, one to four months in the house of correction, and the case of one was continued for sentence. The hostler was discharged.

"At an early hour on Friday morning officers raided a house on Market Street in Northampton and arrested as disorderly characters three girls found living there; a fourth girl was arrested the same day. Two of the girls were mere children, 14 and 16 years of age. All were convicted and sentenced by the district court."

In 1892, students at Amherst College published a lovely book called *Amherst Sketches*. One of the pieces describes a man with a "fat, jolly face" known only as Poco. He went from college to college selling and buying used clothing, to the delight of impecunious students. Within five years of this affectionate portrait, Poco was arrested for dealing in something quite different from clothes.

Samuel Warriner, an Amherst student and a minister's son, wrote the sketch of the mysterious Poco. The word "Poco" was college slang for "an old-clothes man," derived, according to Webster, from the Italian and Spanish word for "little." In the minds of Warriner and his friends this wandering peddler became a romantic Amherst character: "What would a modern college be without its Poco? No merchant, unless it be John the peanut vendor, is more widely patronized; and none, I wager, takes more solid enjoyment in fleecing the luckless student.

"I have often wished for a chance to peep into the den of this

The Orient Spring House, one of several places in the Amherst area used for prostitution.

veritable junk-dealer. What a genuine 'Old Curiosity Shop' it must be! Every style of clothing since the good old times of homespun; coats of all cuts, from the modern Prince Albert to the old blue 'swallowtail' with its tarnished brass buttons, all waiting to be dipped into the fountain of youth, and recover once more their long lost color and shine.

"How anxiously the periodical visits ... are awaited by the bankrupt student! Well, here he comes now in person. You could not mistake him. His very air is that of a 'gatherer and disposer of other men's stuff.' If you have any doubt, those old 'gym pants' over his arm are conclusive proof. Suppose we try to strike a bargain. It will be an interesting operation. Poco is not one of these one-price, cash-down dealers. For such slow, iron-clad methods he has a lofty disdain. A scientist in his way, he starts cautiously, with a significant glance at a miserable rent in the unlucky trousers, which in spite of my care is persistently conspicuous, he offers with a most sacrificing air 'just twenty-five cents.' With the craft of an old angler, he dangles the bait before your face. But you are too wary a fish to be caught thus easily, — have perhaps been fooled before. 'Feefty cents.' The mute pleading is too much; half out of pity you yield, and Poco with an effusive obeisance departs, leaving you to reflect on the possibility of having been outwitted after all."

The dark side of Poco's business came to light in the following newspaper article: "Last Thursday evening (January 7, 1897), Deputy Sheriff Tillson and Officer Graves made an important capture in the person of Max Latter, who is charged with keeping the house of ill-fame which was recently raided at North Hadley, its occupants being sentenced to imprisonment. Papers were issued for Latter at the time of the raid but he kept out of the way and has not since been seen in Amherst.

"Thursday evening the officers learned of his presence in town and captured him at the Boston & Maine depot as he was getting on board the last train for Northampton. He was taken to the Amherst lock-up and confined over night. Friday morning he was summoned before the district court in Northampton and held in $500 bonds to await the action of the grand jury. He succeeded in securing bonds yesterday.

"Latter is known to the students as 'Poco,' his headquarters being at Hartford whence he makes periodic rounds of the colleges, buying up old clothes."

The Demise of
a Disreputable Sneak

When George Newell checked into a hotel in Schenectady with another man's wife, he took the precaution of registering under an assumed name. Unfortunately, Sam Redding, another Amherst man, happened to be in the same hotel and he confronted George. It was a hot July day in 1884, and things were about to get hotter for George Newell, as he became known in the Connecticut Valley as "a disreputable sneak."

George W. Newell was a music teacher in Palmer's Block facing the Amherst Common, the same building where Emily's father and brother had their law office. Newell was also choirmaster of the Methodist Church, and in his choir was Ella Thurber. Henry M. Thurber of East Street rented an organ from Newell for his wife Ella to play. The Amherst Record reported that "the intimacy between Newell and married women has been observed by our citizens and commented upon in this village for months," but that Newell had been getting away with it because the husbands failed to stop him. One husband, Henry Thurber, decided to do something about it.

Thurber, a hard-working carpenter employed by John Beston, Jr., usually left his house at 6:30 in the morning and didn't return until evening. Thurber claimed he and his wife never quarreled in their eight years of marriage, and that to make her work load lighter he often brought home restaurant meals. It was common knowledge though that Newell often entered the Thurber house when Henry was at work, that he took Ella out for carriage rides at all hours, and that Ella saw Newell in his music rooms daily. All of this was presumably for the purpose of "making music."

When Ella's father Andrew Hunn died in July of 1884, she inherited several hundred dollars. On July 15th, one week after the Belchertown funeral, Thurber went home after work and discovered his wife had left, taking some clothing and several photographs. Thurber confronted Newell in the street, but Newell claimed to know nothing. Thurber went to Sunderland (where he had friends) seeking his wife, then returned and confronted Newell again.

Newell took the strange step of offering to help Thurber find Ella, even volunteering to pay the expenses, to help clear his name. The following morning brought an odd sight at the Amherst train station. Ella Thurber's husband and her lover set off together to find the missing woman. Thurber got off in Belchertown, and Newell went on to Palmer, both agreeing to meet back in Amherst later. Instead, Newell went to South Deerfield and then disappeared.

On Friday night, July 18th, Sam Redding happened to stay at the Ellis House in Schenectady. At 2:30 in the morning a fire broke out in the hotel, and as Redding rushed out of his room he ran into George Newell. The next morning Newell was gone. Redding checked the register and found that Newell and Ella Thurber had checked in as "George Winfield and wife, Jonesville, Mass." The clerk said that Newell and a short, stout woman dressed in black and wearing blue glasses had taken the 11:00 a.m. train for Amsterdam, New York.

Amherst citizens lost no time in prying out every detail. They dutifully wrote to the hotel to verify that Newell, a father of 10, a "genuine shouting Methodist, one of the roaring enthusiasts," had indeed occupied the same room with Ella Thurber. Rev. Daniels of the Methodist Church preached against "the apostles of lust and lewdness," blaming the situation on the Spiritualist Camp Meetings held each summer at Lake Pleasant in Montague.

Ella Thurber returned to her husband in early August, but was received in "a very cool manner." Thurber told her to leave town forever on the noon train, which she apparently did. By 1886, Henry Thurber had moved to Springfield and George W. Newell had moved to Albany.

Stephen Burroughs:
Imposter, Seducer, Counterfeiter

Just as the real 19th century is only vaguely understood by us, the Dickinson circle inherited myths about the 18th century. Legend had it that in the 1700s, the scoundrel Stephen Burroughs held an angry mob from Pelham at bay by preaching an inspired sermon from a hayloft. Burroughs, who had been impersonating a minister, later admitted the story was greatly exaggerated, yet even without the veneer of legend, Burroughs's life was incredibly strange.

Stephen Burroughs was born in 1765 in Hanover, New Hampshire. His father, a minister, managed to get him into the seminary of Dartmouth College. After stealing watermelons at Dartmouth, Burroughs, like an early Orson Welles, threw the town into a panic by announcing that hostile Indians were attacking. This neatly covered up the watermelon theft. Later, when a pregnant widow claimed Stephen as her seducer, he made the first of his many escapes into the night.

In the spring of 1785, armed with a bundle of his father's old sermons, Burroughs temporarily filled the pulpit in Ludlow, Massachusetts, under the assumed name of Davis. This phony Rev. Davis was later hired to preach in Pelham for a total of five months at $5.00 per Sunday.

Unfortunately, while delivering a funeral oration in a crowded Pelham parlor, someone noticed how old and stained Burroughs's sermon notes were. Rumors spread about this incident and about certain liberties he was taking with women in the Pelham congregation. When an old college acquaintance arrived in Pelham and called Burroughs by his real name, Burroughs hurriedly left town, taking an advance on his salary with him.

While breakfasting in Rutland, Burroughs was surprised by a crowd of pitchfork toting Pelhamites. Burroughs jumped out a back window, and in the chase supposedly broke the arm of William Conkey with his own cane. He then heaved a rock at the head of Dr. Hinds.

Burroughs helped create the famous legend of his entrapment in a hayloft, and his escape by an impromptu sermon, by publishing a wild satire of the event in 1823. He quoted himself as preaching, "Then said the Lord, I will give them a minister like unto themselves, full of all deceit, hypocrisy and duplicity ... . Then rose up Stephen the Burronite, of the tribe of Puritans ... and went forth to Pelham, sorely oppressing the Pelhamites, taking from them ten shekles of silver, a mighty fine horse, and changes of raiment, and ran off to Rutland."

After preaching in Attleboro and Danbury, Connecticut, he was arrested in Springfield for counterfeiting. Burroughs was sentenced to the pillory and three years in the Northampton jail. After setting the jail on fire, he was sent to Castle Island in Boston Harbor, from which he made a daring escape.

In 1790, Burroughs was arrested in Worcester for assault and attempted rape. He was whipped, placed in a pillory, and jailed. Burroughs mysteriously disappeared and went on to become a teacher and librarian, keeping less than one step ahead of the law all over the east coast. This legendary imposter, seducer, counterfeiter, and escape artist went to Canada after 1800, and died in 1840.

Sending Missionaries
to Shutesbury

Shutesbury, considered by many in Amherst to be in need of a missionary effort

Let it first be said that Shutesbury is probably as fine a town as any in the Connecticut Valley. It is undeniable, however, that the town had more than the normal number of cases of polygamy. Far more than one might — or might not — expect in a 19th century New England town. Whatever the causes, Shutesbury was at one time considered a "dark corner" where missionaries were sent, as if to a strange foreign land, to evangelize the populace.

On July 19, 1880, a deputy sheriff from Greenfield arrested a Shutesbury man "for being too much married or having more wives than the law of the commonwealth allows," as the newspaper put it. The Amherst Record referred to the incident as "the same old Shutesbury complaint," but didn't follow up on the story, when a more tragic situation took over the front page.

On August 8th, another case of polygamy in Shutesbury was revealed as part of a larger story of rape, murder, and attempted suicide. While admitting their report of it contained "sickening details," the Amherst Record ran it nonetheless, as an example of why Shutesbury was in need of a missionary campaign. Leaving out the "sickening details," and the participants' last names, this is what happened:

When Jarvis was 16 years-old he married a young woman from Palmer named Mary. It was said that on the day of their marriage, July 11, 1876, both were drunk. Only a few days later Mary left Jarvis. The following December, Jarvis also married Sarah of Turners Falls. The couple lived with his father and had a child, before Jarvis was arrested for polygamy and sent to the Greenfield jail for a year. Sarah and the child eventually moved in with her father at Turners Falls.

Jarvis tried to get Sarah to live with him again after he was let out of jail, but she refused. Somehow Jarvis managed to get the baby back to Shutesbury. In August, Jarvis, Sarah and her sister, Jennie, went on an outing to Montague's Lake Pleasant. There they met Sarah's friend George. When they left the lake for Shutesbury, Sarah refused to ride with Jarvis and went with George instead. On the way they had a "good time, and although it was Sunday, fired their revolvers, raced horses, talked and made considerable loud noise." The girls changed wagons more than once along the way.

While Sarah was in Jarvis's wagon, he persuaded her to go to Zabina Tillson's farm under some pretext. On the way, Jarvis raped and murdered Sarah in the woods southeast of Shutesbury center. Jarvis then shot himself several times, but was able to continue to the Tillson's.

When Mrs. Tillson saw him she exclaimed, "Are you Drunk?" "No," he replied, "but I have killed Sarah, shot myself and can't live but a few minutes. Get me some water." But Jarvis did live to be tried for his crimes.

After the arrest came the inevitable debate in the press about morality in Shutesbury. The Amherst Record noted that only 25 years earlier, missionaries attempted to edify Shutesbury. Greek missionary George Constantine, then an Amherst College student, had organized a campaign to Shutesbury, but the effects didn't last. It was hoped that Constantine would return to lead the town "upon the path of fair morality."

Another editorial bluntly blamed alcoholism, prostitution, terrorism, and greed, for making laws unenforceable in Shutesbury. To its credit, Shutesbury defended its reputation by citing its two flourishing Sunday schools, and the hardworking Baptist and Congregational churches. The question Shutesbury posed was this: "Are there not as dark corners and as degraded families in some of the neighboring villages as in the town of Shutesbury, where some recent and sad exhibitions of depravity have been noticed in the newspapers?"

Throwing Bricks at Emily Dickinson's Pallbearer

The postmaster in small New England towns was not always a loved local character. Appointed by the government in Washington, often as a political pay off, they were sometimes eyed with suspicion. Amherst's Hezekiah Wright Strong, for example, was accused of letting people read and mix up other people's newspapers, before he left the position in 1842. But it was John Jameson whose conduct enraged so many that a petition was circulated to have him fired. Amherst split over the controversy, with the Amherst Record favoring removal, and Vinnie and Emily Dickinson supporting their dear friend, John Jameson.

The Jamesons came to Amherst from Boston in 1875, and settled into a house on the corner of Main and Seelye Streets. Living across from the Dickinson Homestead, the Jamesons became close friends. Vinnie Dickinson sent sweet peas and quinces to them, and Harriet Jameson visited Emily when she was ill.

Early on, Emily had sent a message to Mrs. Jameson: "Many and sweet Birthdays to our thoughtful neighbor, whom we have learned to cherish, though ourselves unknown —"

John Jameson was appointed postmaster by the Hayes administration on December 20, 1876, but in just over a year he was in serious trouble. A petition circulated and extensively signed in April, 1878, accused him of "incompetency, neglect of duty, refusing to deliver mail matter to the party addressed, and sending matter through the mails contrary to postal laws." The Amherst Record reported that Jameson had never been popular and that frequent complaints had been made. One letter, containing money, had somehow ended up as waste paper at a North Amherst paper mill.

A federal investigator was sent the following September, but Jameson retained his post. Nevertheless, opposition to Jameson swelled. A year later, dentist Joseph J. Vincent was tried for assaulting Jameson and throwing bricks at his house. When Vincent was acquitted, a celebration was thrown in his honor, complete with a band.

Interestingly, the Dickinsons remained great supporters of neighbor Jameson, choosing to find humor in his bungling. In December, 1881, Emily Dickinson was amused to find that a letter written to her and her sister, addressed to "Misses Dickinson," arrived late because it was misread by the "rustic eyes" of Postmaster Jameson. He sent the letter to all the "Mrs." Dickinsons he could find before sending it to Misses Emily and Vinnie. When Jameson's son Frank went to Washington in 1885 to plead on his father's behalf, both Emily and Vinnie expressed hope that Jameson could keep his job.

In March, 1885, John Jameson learned he had lost the position of Amherst Postmaster. He wrote to his son that "Vinnie (Dickinson) was in this evening and was very indignant, consolatory & also very diverting." Mrs. Jameson wrote that Vinnie said "she considered civil service reform 'a damned lie.' She had no use for that nor belief in it —or the present administration — She is always intense you know —"

Jameson stayed in Amherst and practiced law on Phoenix Row for a few years, and by 1891 was in practice in Boston. Throughout their troubles the Jameson family remained close friends of the Dickinsons. One of Emily Dickinson's last notes before her death was sent to Mrs. Jameson (who was one of the few invited to see Dickinson in her coffin), and John Jameson was one of the honorary pallbearers at Emily Dickinson's funeral.

The Nest-Hiding Scandal of Henry Ward Beecher

Henry Ward Beecher, a much admired minister whose life was plagued by scandal.

Gazing down over the Amherst Common is the imposing bronze statue of Henry Ward Beecher. An 1834 graduate of Amherst College, and brother of Harriet Beecher Stowe, he was the greatest preacher of his day. Whether measured by influence, wealth, or number of passionate followers, Beecher is among the most noted religious leaders in American history.

Seen from a slightly different angle, however, the Beecher statue begins to resemble a brooding Rev. Jim Bakker, or possibly a swaggering Jimmy Swaggart, with a little Gary Hart thrown in. Emily Dickinson's time and place may sometimes seem to be the definition of New England piety. The 1870 Beecher scandal adds an unexpected patina of 20th century spiritual disgrace to the poet's era.

Henry Ward Beecher arrived in Amherst in 1827 to attend Mount Pleasant Classical Institution. In 1829, he underwent a religious conversion when Christ appeared to him rising over the Amherst horizon. The young man began preaching in many of the surrounding towns while an Amherst College student. Beecher's early interest was phrenology (the study of bumps on one's head), but he later became known for his stand against slavery, support of women's rights, and his acceptance of the theory of evolution.

Beecher's fame as the first religious spokesman for the nation came after he moved to Brooklyn's Plymouth Congregational Church in 1847. As preacher to the largest congregation in the country, he was paid an astonishing $20,000 a year, and earned an additional $15,000 writing and speaking. Beecher acquired a taste for precious jewels, while his church grew into a major industry. It took in $60,000 a year from pew rentals and $40,000 from collections. The church itself was quite sumptuous, complete with a fountain in the Sunday school room.

At the center of this empire, Beecher was a supreme showman. He swept up audiences by acting out his sermons, sweating, crying, laughing, and strutting. His powerful charisma became difficult to control, and it was said he received 100 love letters a day.

In the fall of 1868, Elizabeth Tilton went to Beecher for consolation after the death of her son Paul. Their sessions together grew into what Beecher termed "nest-hiding," a kind of "divine" love, supposedly as proper as a handshake or a kiss. The devout Mrs. Tilton believed him, thinking God wouldn't allow their relationship if it were wrong.

When Mrs. Tilton confessed to the affair in 1870, other women came forward to accuse Beecher of seduction. The greatest scandal of the era was born. Every newspaper in the country covered the story — which dragged on for years as lurid accusations, rumors, leaks of love letters and poems, and lawsuits kept the presses rolling.

The New York Sun called Beecher "an adulterer, a perjurer, and a fraud." But even as letters between Beecher and his paramours were published, many refused to believe he was guilty. A servant of the Tiltons, Bessie Turner, accused Mr. Tilton of propositioning her, leading some to claim Beecher was merely being framed by the immoral Tilton. When Mrs. Tilton suffered a miscarriage at the end of 1870, rumor spread that she had actually aborted Beecher's baby. The Hartford Times said, "It is a disgusting mess, all of it." The Mercury Mail decried "this vial of scandal whose odors the world is snuffing up its nostrils."

Tilton's charge of adultery against Beecher finally came to trial on January 11, 1875. Thousands descended on Brooklyn, including hordes of press people. Ticket scalpers worked the crowds outside the courtroom, where sometimes 3,000 a day were turned away. Those inside were unruly and refused to leave for lunch. Vendors sold them sandwiches and opera glasses. Lawyers for both sides clothed their accusations in grand oratorial style during the six-month ordeal.

The jury could not agree on a verdict and Beecher was acquitted. The New York Times said the evidence was clearly against Beecher, the Louisville Courier Journal labelled Beecher "a dunghill covered with flowers," and Beecher called Mrs. Tilton an "unbalanced clairvoyant." Meanwhile, the crowds at Plymouth Church grew even larger.

The bronze monument of Beecher was erected at Amherst College in 1914, 27 years after his death. It is identical to the one that stands in Brooklyn. Theologically, Henry Ward Beecher far surpasses the likes of Bakker and Swaggart. But sometimes one wonders who Beecher really was and what he symbolizes as he gazes over the Amherst Common.

Chapter Fifteen

HEALTH: THE BENEFITS OF OPIUM AND WET SHEETS

The Common, Amherst, Massachusetts

*I like a look of Agony,
Because I know it's true -
Men do not sham Convulsion, -
Nor simulate, a Throe -
#241*

298

Opium, Tape Worms, and Water Cures

In September of 1856, Emily Dickinson's mother was suffering from chronic depression. Emily Norcross Dickinson was the mother of the then virtually unknown Emily. What did the sophisticated, well-educated Dickinsons do about the health of Mrs. Dickinson? She was sent to the Round Hill Water Cure Establishment in Northampton for an unusual, scientifically dubious treatment. The

Round Hill in Northampton, where Emily Dickinson's mother underwent dubious water cure for depression.

budding medical profession scoffed at this kind of remedy, but water cures flourished, along with other questionable treatments.

In the first century of the Massachusetts Bay Colony, the Calvinist settlers believed that the first cause of all was divine. Therefore, most regarded illness as a judgment of God. Illness and death were to be borne humbly and submissively. But the colonists also believed that God gave them intelligence that could be used to lessen the suffering of earthly ills.

Prayer was the first of the healing arts. We shouldn't be surprised then that ministers were among the first to practice medicine. Prayers and potions, blessings and bloodlettings complemented each other. The few doctors were self-taught or slightly trained, and all were expensive. The use of midwifes or self-treatment flourished throughout the 19th century.

By the mid-19th century, there was a battle for patients fought between untrained, quack practitioners and the new, certified doctors from medical schools. Newspapers were filled with ads for quack remedies for all diseases. Lydia Pinkham's vegetable compound swept the country, yet this medication proved to be 19 percent alcohol, in other words, 40 proof.

Health and nutrition movements came and went in the 19th century, just as they do today. One way we can get an idea of what people suffered, and what treatments there were, is to look at home health books of the day. Two such books that were used in the Connecticut River Valley are *Health at Home, or Hall's Family Doctor: Showing How to Invigorate and Preserve Health, Prolong Life, Cure Diseases, etc., etc.* (1874); and *The Guide-Book to Health, Peace and Competence: or the Road to Happy Old Age* (1869), both by Dr. W.W. Hall.

These books were written to educate people away from quack remedies. Dr. Hall's philosophy was basically sound and optimistic. In his words, "The fundamental principles of successful medical practice are few and simple. When the body is weary, rest it. When burning up, cool it. When racked with pain, soothe it. When pressed to death's door by morbid and excessive accumulations, put no more into it, empty it — all to be done by going to bed, abstaining from food, and purgation; then to build up, not by tonics, not by spirits, not by bitters, but by out-door air, by moderate activities, and a nutritious diet of coarse bread, ripe fruits, lean meats, and garden vegetables." (*Health and Home*, p.299)

Hall recommended three levels of medical treatments for people to use at home. For external use on cut, bruised, or inflamed skin, he had poultices, ointments, and washes. These included whiskey, rum, brandy, or gin, which were applied to the parts where it hurt. The problem with these is they had to be reapplied often.

Hall's prefered treatment was the poultice. He said, "A great ado is often made about the particular sort of poultice to be used; one advises to take the entrails of a live chicken and apply at once, but the entrails of a dead dog, if just killed would be just as efficacious, for both are moist and warm, and would remain moist and warm for several hours."

If the pain was too acute for poultices and lotions, the doctor suggested a second level of treatment, the stronger mustard plasters. These were made from ground mustard mixed with vinegar and some flour. The plaster was spread on linen or cotton cloth and placed on a muslin cloth over the skin (the muslin kept the skin from blistering). "This mustard plaster relieves by drawing the blood to the surface, thus relieving the ailing part from the excess of blood which causes the pain."

For the most severe pain, there was a third level of treatment. This included chloroform, opium, and morphine. Externally, chloroform was used as a liniment, combined with sweet oil and camphor. It was applied to the skin for no more than 15 to 30 seconds because it caused the skin to blister. Opium and morphine were of course addictive and deadly.

Sadly, worms were a constant problem in the 19th century. According to Dr. Hall, about 30 kinds in all were to be found in the human body. Internal worms were usually pinworms, fishworms, and tapeworms. Fishworms resembled earthworms that were used for fishing. They were mostly found in the small intestines, but sometimes made their way into the large intestines and into the stomach, even coming up into the throat and out of the mouth. Dr. Hall wrote, "Sometimes it has been half a foot to half a yard long, and as large round as a gold guinea. These worms get into the body by drinking water from shallow wells or muddy streams."

Pinworms, though very small and slender, infested the body in incredible numbers. They caused terrible itching and were treated by enemas of camphor water, or sometimes limewater.

Tapeworms were said to form in links within the body, with sometimes 300 to 400 links, making a worm some 30 feet long. Hall: "Eating largely of pumpkin seeds has the credit of having cured several serious cases of tapeworm. Gourd seeds peeled and made into a paste with honey ... have been efficient in a number of cases. These remedies are more efficient if nothing has been eaten for twenty or twenty-four hours; this causes the worm to be ravenously hungry, and thus to take into its stomach what its instincts would otherwise forbid. The next morning a strong cathartic will bring away the entire worm, dead or alive. In one case this brought a worm away, twenty-five feet long."

Hall's *Guide-Board to Health, Peace and Competence* ... talks a great deal about healthy diet. His fruit diet is an excellent one for us to follow today. And similar to today's emphasis on all kinds of bran to keep regular, Hall has good recipes for corn bread and corn meal waffles to cure constipation. But then he does a very odd thing. In a very sardonic way he claims that doing away with constipation will only give one a healthy appetite. With tongue in cheek, he asks whether it's a good idea to have a strong appetite when "beef is thirty cents a pound, green apples two dollars a bushel, and flour twelve dollars a barrel. The most direct and prompt cure for the present hard times is to become costive (constipated), and then you can snap your finger and thumb triumphantly at butchers, hucksters, green-grocers

—all that fraternity."

He follows this with his "Receipt For Becoming Costive":

"For yourself, take a little opium, or a few drops of laudanum, which is opium in a liquid form, two or three times a day.

"If you want to begin at the beginning, and economize from the baby upward, and make a pint of milk last as long as a quart, give it a little paregoric (diluted laudanum) every time it cries, or Godfrey's Cordial.

"If you want next to attack your wife, and anorexiate her, and yet would rather do it on the sly, find out if she has got a little dryness in the throat, or a slight hack, or hem ... get her one of those nice little boxes filled with any sweetish lozenge ... it has the two essential requisites — sugar and opium. Opium causes want of appetite ... it causes constipation, and that causes loss of appetite.

"As for the baby ... they will take the lozenge or the syrup from the father's or the mother's hand, with such loving, smiling confidence ... in a few weeks, an unusual brightness of the eye, succeeded by water on the brain on the first attack of sickness; and its little body dwindles, and its eyes stare out with a maniacal frenzy or an idiotic blankness, closing soon in death; but then you have saved a pint of milk a day for a good while."

This brings us to addiction in general, which was extremely serious but little understood. By 1830, alcohol and drugs had become so pervasive in the Valley and elsewhere, that Amherst College professor Edward Hitchcock was prompted to publish "An Essay on Alcoholic & Narcotic Substances, As Articles of Common Use. Addressed Particularly to Students." The essay, which won an award from the American Temperance Society, is a fascinating look at a deadly problem.

Hitchcock stated that there were "few genuine opium eaters among us; but the laudanum and paregoric phial are considered almost indispensable in every family." The unconscious irony of this is that laudanum was actually opium mixed with liquor or wine, and paregoric was opium laced with aromatics. The drug was in such common use that it was apparently given freely to children. In Hitchcock's words, "Nor does the mother hesitate, night after night, to quell the cries of her infant child, by administering increasing doses of these poisons, and thus almost infallibly to ruin its constitution."

It became fashionable for adults to calm themselves with drops of laudanum or opium pills after returning late at night from dances, lectures or tea parties. This led to one's destruction "as surely as if he were swallowing arsenic, or had the pistol applied to his head."

On October 10, 1854, the Dickinsons would have read the following article on the front page of their copy of the Hampshire and Franklin Express:

"A Family of Opium Lovers.—Some six months ago a person visited our town (Elmira, Illinois), asking for money to purchase medicine for his mother who was sick. Recently the same solicitor has been around on the same errand for other members of the family. What success has attended his solicitations we know not; but the object to which the funds are applied is of so objectionable a nature that all should withhold their names, out of regard for the family, who are the slaves of a habit to which drunkenness is a comparative blessing. The entire family, it is said, subsist for the most part on opium or its exhilarating and soporific influence, and this fearful habit has been so long indulged as to have grown into second life.

"The example of Coleridge before the world, acknowledged it the basest and most destructive of vices and at the same time most absolute of tyrants, should, we think, be a sufficient warning to all after-comers to avoid the drug. But here is an example of a whole family addicted to the same habit; and it has brought upon them all its certain results, apathy, indolence, poverty, misery, and will eventually end in the most wretched death."

At the same time, alcohol was widely thought of as a medicine, essential in the treatment of many illnesses. Even Hitchcock, who advocated abstinence, felt alcohol was beneficial medicine when prescribed by a doctor who was not himself an alcoholic. Doctors were accustomed to giving brandy and water, or wine, for dyspepsia (indigestion). Liquor and wine were thought to help one resist disease, give one energy, relieve depression, and to act as a sedative. Under these circumstances, no one, according to Hitchcock, was safe from the road to drunkenness. He pointed to literary people and the clergy as being perhaps the worst abusers of alcohol's medicinal properties.

Hitchcock believed that narcotics and liquor would destroy the individual, the family, then the country. They lead to a "grossness of manners," which "induces the dram drinker, the wine bibber, the smoker, the chewer, and snuff taker, to avoid the society of refined and virtuous females," and seek out "grosser public amusements, such as theatrical exhibitions, circus-sports, horse-racing, cock-fighting, bull-baiting, boxing matches, and gladiatorial contests."

In the mid-1800s, temperance societies abounded in and around the Valley. Lectures and conventions were held as the movement grew, yet alcohol was still to be used as a medication for many decades. In 1883, the medical dictionary used by Amherst doctor Orvis F. Bigelow — the doctor who cared for Emily Dickinson at the end of her life — recommended administering "cognac,

Champagne, old Gin or Whiskey, and the heavier Southern wines" for patients. The author of the dictionary, Richard Quain, stated that for children, a "really good and pure wine or brandy can be advantageously employed, even for infants."

By the 1880s, opium abuse was all too obvious, and many infants died from overdoses. Dr. Bigelow's medical dictionary offered much advice for the treatment of opium addiction, including this: "Alcoholic stimulants should be freely given."

Nineteenth century physicians had no scientific knowledge of germs and viruses, consequently they had some fanciful ideas about the air we breathe. Illness was thought to be transmitted by foul air, and one way to avoid it was for people not to sleep together. Dr. Hall: "One sleeper corrupts the atmosphere of the room by his own breathing, but when two persons are breathing at the same time, twelve or fourteen times in each minute, in each minute extracting all the nutriment from a gallon of air, the deterioration must be rapid indeed. Many infants are found dead in bed, and it is attributed to having been overlaid by the parents; but the idea that any person could lay still for a moment on a baby is absurd. Death was caused by the want of pure air.

"The most destructive typhoid and putrid fevers are known to arise directly from a number of persons living in the same small room. Healthy, robust infants and larger children have dwindled away, and died in a few months from sleeping with grandparents, or other old persons.

"It would be a constitutional and moral good for married persons to sleep in adjoining rooms, as a general habit. It would be a certain means of physical invigoration, and of advantages in other directions, which will readily occur to the reflective reader."

Another area that wasn't well understood until late in the century was cleanliness. In *The Guide-Board to Health,* Dr. Hall stated, "It is my opinion, founded on observation, that a daily bath, to one in good health, is not only not beneficial, but is injurious. A daily bath, shower, or otherwise, is a modern invention, devised to sell bath-tubs. I personally have known but two men who acknowledged to a daily shower bath, literally a shower bath, every day. One of them died years ago of chronic diarrhea, ... the other was ... a great, stout raw-boned six footer ... he was always bathing, and was always sick ... When a man is not well, bathing of some kind is advisable under certain circumstances, but it should not be continued too long. Once or twice a week persons may advantageously perform the following for the sake of personal cleanliness: dip a coarse cloth in cold water; squeeze it so that the water shall not dribble about ... on getting out of bed in the morning ... rub fast and hard, gradually extending it all over the body. This operation should be performed within ten minutes in summer, and within three or four in winter. Keep on the stockings, and when done, dress quickly, and go to the fire, if in cold weather, or take some exercise, active enough to make you feel comfortably warm."

Now, at the same time that Hall was warning against using too much water, there was a fanatical rush to a new treatment that called for just the opposite. This was the water cure, which, as noted, Emily Dickinson's mother had undergone. Water cures were introduced in this country in the 1840s from Europe. Also known as hydropathy, these cures deemphasized doctors and drugs, and were considered by physicians to be quackery.

Cold water cures sought to rid the body of "sickly matter" and to replace it with healthy matter. Water was either taken internally or used in soaks, wraps, plunges; and head, arm and eye baths, etc. This supposedly restored the body's balanced state.

Western and Central Massachusetts were primary centers for water cures. There were five of them in these regions: one each in Athol, Easthampton, and Westboro, and two in Northampton. The Round Hill Water Cure where Emily Dickinson's mother was treated, was one of the larger, more prosperous establishments, and was really much like a resort.

In 1847, it had over 100 rooms, a dining hall, saloon, several reception rooms, an office, kitchen, and bathing facilities. By 1855, it expanded to 150 rooms, with several bathing, dressing and packing rooms, piazzas, walkways, exercise and amusement facilities.

An example of a day at a water cure went something like this: "First thing in the morning dripping sheet; pack at 10 o'clock for forty-five minutes, come out of that, take a shower followed by a sitz bath, with a pail of water at 75 degrees poured over the shoulders, after which a dry sheet, then brisk exercises." This program was repeated four times daily.

This movement slowly died out between 1860 and 1900, as indoor plumbing made the benefits of cleanliness more easily available, and diseases began to be reduced.

Now, if all the above treatments had no effect, and a person had the misfortune to pass on, there was still another worry in the 19th century. How did one verify that someone was actually dead? Quoting Dr. Hall again, "A deep cut across the arm with a lancet or other sharp instrument would be very apt to wake to life again, if not really dead ... . If a lighted candle is held to the skin there will be a blister; if on sticking a needle into it, a fluid escapes, there is life; if only air, death is there certainly ... ."

The Wild Raid
on the Orient House, 1875

In 1875, an angry mob of Amherst men stormed the Orient House in Pelham in an attempt to take by force property they claimed they owned. The Orient Springs Health Institute had been in decline, and its proprietor, Dr. G.W. Rhodes, had just filed for bankruptcy.

The health spa had begun attracting visitors in 1853, later becoming quite popular with its large Orient House hotel, bowling alley and other amenities in West Pelham. G.W. Rhode purchased the property in 1872, but according to the Amherst Record, "this famous hostelry, medical institute, or whatever name it may be called, was under a cloud." Rhodes filed for bankruptcy in March, 1875. The newspaper printed a list of 43 creditors, most from Amherst, several from Boston, and others from as far away as Cincinnati. In the paper's opinion, they had all been swindled by the slick Dr. Rhodes.

Orient Springs, a health resort, was raided in 1875.

On March 22, "quite a lively skedaddle occurred," as the Record reported it, when "some dozen of Amherst's men of valor" raided the Orient House. They were ordered to disperse by Dr. Rhodes and when they hesitated, one of the doctor's larger employees, named Wellin, appeared on the scene waving a pistol. "This decided the matter at once, and such a getting out of the place was never seen before. The crowd tumbled themselves downstairs without waiting for one another. The coal merchant jostled the aristocratic grocer, while the truckman jostled both; the parson didn't wait for the benediction ... . The affrighted host fled in dismay declaring that was the most unhealthy 'Health Institute' they ever visited."

Wellin was arrested for pointing the pistol and fined $3.00 plus costs, which Rhodes paid. Within a month Mrs. Rhodes, described as "partially insane," threw herself in front of a local train.

Some of the creditors returned to the Orient House on April 12 and were surprised to have their demands met by a polite Dr. Rhodes. The newspaper reported that "this staggered them nearly as badly as the pistol did a short time since, and they left, somewhat demoralized in their minds, but in good order."

The final proprietor of the Orient Springs Health Institute was Dr. Herman Heed, who had the misfortune of seeing the place accidentally burned to the ground on February 23, 1881.

A Young Woman
Horsewhips a Quack

More than 100 people gathered to watch when a quack doctor was horsewhipped on the streets of Westfield. "Doctor" Levy, who had been preying on the people of the Connecticut Valley with phony remedies, had moved on to Westfield where former victims were waiting for him. It was the summer of 1880 when, to the delight of onlookers, a cracking whip was wielded by a young woman who had been scorned and insulted by the quack.

Levy came to the area from New York where he received his training — not as a physician but as a cigar maker. In August of 1880, the Amherst Record reported that Levy had "bulldozed people in this vicinity of late, administering cure-for-all-ills."

Medicine was barely a science at the time and people were faced with an overwhelming confusion of questionable cures sold by questionable people. The Amherst Record was filled with ads for such medications:

> Collins's Voltaic Plaster for local pains,
> lameness, soreness, weakness, numbness, and
> inflammation of the lungs, liver, kidneys,
> spleen, bowels, bladder, heart and muscles, is
> equal to an army of doctors and acres of
> plants and shrubs. Price 25 cents.

> Gray's Specific Medicine. The great English
> remedy. An unfailing cure for Seminal
> Weakness, Spermatorrhea, Impotence, and all
> diseases that follow, as a sequence of Self-
> Abuse; as Loss of Memory, Universal Lassitude,
> Pain in the Back, Dimness of Vision, Premature
> Old Age and many other Diseases that lead to
> Insanity or Consumption and a Premature Grave.

> D.I.C. is an absolute and irresistible cure
> for Drunkenness, Intemperance and the use of
> Opium, Tobacco, Narcotics, and Stimulants,
> removing all taste, desire and habit of using
> any of them, rendering them perfectly odious
> and disgusting.

> Feeble Wives, Mothers, and every weakly,

sickly person can surely strengthen and build
up the broken-down system by taking Richard's
Teetotal Tonic.

The phony Doctor Levy was staying in Westfield on August 9, 1880, when he was confronted by two women: the wife and daughter of blacksmith Charles Simmons. In addition to swindling his patients, Levy had apparently been circulating derogatory rumors about the Simmons daughter. Mother and daughter, whip in hand, sought out Levy at his boarding house. Failing to find him, they walked down Elm Street and saw him at the corner of Franklin. After a brief "interchange of compliments in which the doctor applied one or two vile epithets to the young woman, she struck him with a whip." Levy threw her on the sidewalk, turned and also threw her mother down. "Then both women mounted him simultaneously and the 'Dr.' came near being annihilated, to the intense delight of the spectators."

Levy was grabbed by two officers as he tried to run off, looking a mess, with one eye badly blackened, his silk hat crushed and his coat partially torn off. The newspaper reported that he "indulged in wild ejaculations about his God and reputation."

Apparently no one questioned this form of punishment. The Amherst Record said it was "richly deserved," and the young woman said she would administer a similar treatment to any man who meddled with her reputation. Horsewhipping was an oddly appropriate form of punishment in Westfield, known as Whip City for its huge production of buggy whips.

The Unsteady Mind
of Tailor Cowles

It was a classic case with some odd twists. When Erastus Cowles died in 1884, a fierce courtroom battle erupted over his estate. Cowles had died leaving his large house on North Prospect Street in Amherst to his housekeeper, instead of his children, as was expected. The children sued, claiming Cowles was "of a demented mind and physically feeble, and that he did many things in the last year of his life which a man of sound mind would not have done."

Erastus Cowles was born in Amherst in 1813, the year Emily's grandfather built the Dickinson home. He learned the druggists' trade in Iowa, and returned to Amherst to marry Eliza Ward in 1846. He then built his house on North Prospect and worked as a druggist for several years. The gradual breakdown of Cowles's senses was dated from his arrest for illegal sales of liquor by state and federal authorities. He was heavily fined and soon exhibited "spells when he appeared very singular," according to the Amherst Record. Cowles became a tailor and was known locally as Tailor Cowles.

After his wife's death in 1861, the two children, Henry and Frances, lived elsewhere. Cowles hired the widow Marietta Merchants as his housekeeper, paying her $1.50, and later $2.00, each week. Toward the end of his life, Mrs. Merchants apparently nursed him as well. Upon Cowles's death, it was revealed that on August 28, 1884, he had signed a deed transferring his house and goods to Mrs. Merchants.

Cowles's son Henry, a Boston jeweller, and daughter Frances, who had married Greenfield machinist Fred Wells, sued for the property. The newspapers reported the bitter testimony, which included statements by many prominent people about the soundness of Cowles's mind when he signed the deed.

Mrs. Merchants claimed the children seldom visited their father, had no feelings for him, and hadn't even seen each other for several years. The children said Cowles was of "unsound mind when he signed the deed," and had been manipulated by Mrs. Merchants.

Levi Stockbridge testified that Cowles sometimes appeared confused, others told of him getting lost on the local trains. A woman who had boarded in his home was astonished that he burned lights at night, once even burning two to a room. Dr. Thompson, an expert on "mental diseases," labeled Cowles's problem as "senile dementia."

The jury found in favor of Mrs. Merchants, which set off angry letters by Frances Cowles's husband Fred to the editor of the Amherst Record. He claimed the press had entirely misrepresented the trial and had affected its outcome.

Meanwhile, an auction of some of Erastus Cowles's goods was held, which included "every kind of tool that Yankee genius has ever invented, except burglers' tools." This antique tool collection numbered over 1,000, and Cowles had painted each one with thick layers of bright stripes, mainly in reds and blues. The newspaper commented that this reflected the workings of "a very eccentric mind."

The Liveliest
Dead Man Ever

Dr. D.N.B. Fish, who it was rumored examined the frozen Bub Jucket.

In January of 1887, everyone in and around Amherst seemed to be asking "Where is Bub Jucket?" The Springfield Republican declared he was found dead on South East Street in Amherst, and the Northampton Herald repeated the story. Yet, rumor had it that the mysterious man was still alive.

The first reports claimed that Amherst milkman James P. Smith rose at his usual early hour on Saturday, January 15, 1887, and found Bub Jucket dead on or near Smith's South East Street farm. But Smith himself denied seeing Jucket that day.

It was also reported that Jucket had been found frozen to death and that Medical Examiner D.N.B. Fish viewed the body, examined his feet and toes and decided that he could save one of Jucket's feet, but the other had to go. When Fish was questioned, he said he hadn't been called to see Bub Jucket dead or alive, "and made no examination of his feet or any part of him."

Just who was Bub Jucket and why was it so hard to keep track of him? He was Leonard J. Jucket of the Dwight section of Belchertown. Born in 1842, he lived for a time in Amherst, served in the Civil War, and farmed in Belchertown. Jucket married Emma Gibbs and the couple had seven children, including Louis, a railroad laborer, and Grace, a hat sewer. Jucket's demon, sadly, was the bottle, and he had been known to go "on the bat" when his pension checks arrived.

The Amherst Record attempted to clear up the mystery with the following report of Bub Jucket's whereabouts: "He dined in this village a few days ago, and the morning he was reported dead, passed through East Street with a jug of hard cider, and appeared to persons at the meat market that evening, and to others since, the liveliest 'dead' man ever seen in Amherst. He is neither frozen nor dead. He may be dead, — dead drunk — many times, but no doubt will resurrect as often and appear long before the flowers will bloom in the spring."

The Ballad of
Munyan's Raid

Deuel's Drugstore on South Pleasant Street was raided for illegally selling liquor in 1884.

In 1884 when Amherst was a dry town, and the temperance activists were fighting to keep it that way, a dramatic liquor raid embarrassed two of the town's leading businessmen. The raid stirred such emotion that the Amherst Record published a sardonic 186-line ballad called "Munyan's Raid." With color and wit, the anonymous poem described the night whiskey and rum were seized at the Amherst Common.

It had all started months before when a professional liquor spotter named George Wood was sent from Boston to expose illegal liquor sales. He worked for a temperance group called the Citizen's Law and Order League, and for 14 dollars a week he visited places "suspected of retailing ardent spirits illegally." Wood's prime targets in Amherst were the drugstores of Henry Adams, on the corner of Main and North Pleasant Streets, and Charles Deuel, on South Pleasant Street.

Certain drugstores had licenses to dispense alcohol for medicinal purposes only. But Wood supposedly observed Deuel's son Fred selling rum from a bottle in the back of the store.

Wood went to the authorities in Northampton with his evidence and a full-scale raid on the town of Amherst was planned for the night of March 12, 1884. The raid was mounted by State Detective Munyan, Sheriff Wright and his son, two other Northampton officers, and from Amherst Sheriff George Gallond and Constable William Smith. They went to wrestle with King Alcohol on a quiet Amherst night, accompanied by the "chords and dischords of the choral assembly rehearsing in Palmer's Hall."

Adding to the drama was Amherst's own Paul Revere — an anonymous man who raced to Amherst on the Old Hadley Road in advance of the police to warn his friends that Amherst was about to be raided. The ballad states,

> Forth from the West at the close of day,
> Bringing to Amherst sore dismay,
> A man from Hamp with a message came,
> An Amherst man, never mind his name,
> But he said that Munyan had started out
> And 'twas plain his squad was on a liquor rout.
>
> The officers searched the forewarned Wood's Hotel from
> top to bottom by kerosene lamp. They
> Peeped up the chimney and down the well,
> But found of whiskey not even the smell.

The simultaneous raids made around the Common also included Sumner Polley's Saloon on Main Street, of whom they asked,

> Have you any liquor, such as we seek?
> Where's your bourbon, and where your rye,
> Where's your Scotch and old 'red eye?'
> Let us see your soda and all your stock,
> Of ales and porter and Old Shamrock.

But they found only what Polley could legally sell: soda, spruce beer, ginger-pop, and so forth. However, at both the Adams and Deuel drugstores they had better luck:

Say, Mr. Druggist, we're feeling sick;
Give us Jamaica ginger, quick,
Put in a little good eau de vie,
Haven't got any? Well, now we'll see.

In the basements of both drugstores they found kegs, casks,and barrels of ales, porters, wines, rum and whiskey.

The editors of the Amherst Record made it very clear that they considered all involved in the raid troublemakers. The Record hoped the druggists would be voted licenses and be left to sell liquor "medicinally," without the interference of the temperance crowd. After all, said the Record, it was only because so many lazy people didn't have jobs that they had time to "import a professional sneak" and harass the town's most respected businessmen.

A Family Devastated
by Diphtheria in 1864

It's sad to see the headstones of the Smith family lined up in Amherst's South Cemetery. In the space of 12 days most of the family was wiped out, leaving only Susan Pettengill Smith and one daughter to carry on. On February 10, 1864, Charles M. Smith died at the age of 12; the following day his 13 year-old brother Chester died; six days later their father Chileab died at 57; and four days later, seven year-old George Dwight Smith died. All were stricken by the then mysterious disease of diphtheria.

Diphtheria is a highly contagious disease that attacks the throat and nose. An epidemic swept France and England in the late 1850s. It next appeared in California, then in 1860 the eastern U.S. was engulfed by the epidemic. Unfortunately, medical wisdom of the day believed that diphtheria was not contagious, and that it was caused by "Filth and over-eating," bad air, or simply the effects of wet and cold on a weak system. Dr. Hall's book *Health and Home...* describes the "nausea or vomiting or dizziness, palpitations, faintness ..., very foul breath ... patches all about the mouth, tongue, inner cheeks and throat ... ." The suffering became even worse as the disease progressed, but it's enough to state that death often came by slow strangulation.

South Amherst, where families were destroyed by diptheria in the 1860s.

Dr. Hall's treatments included eggs mixed with brandy, milk and sugar; wine or champagne; hot baths followed by cold wet towels; and a number of herbs and chemicals. None of this did much good and even into the 20th century, diphtheria was one of the leading causes of death among children.

Susan Smith had gone through the grief of death even before her terrible losses of 1864. Her first marriage, to Elihu Eastman Dickinson, ended when he died in 1841. Two of their three children died — their son Elihu died in 1857 at 16. After second husband Chileab Smith and the three children died, Susan's daughter from her first marriage, Mary Ann, died in 1866. She married her third husband, Fortune Graves, a South Amherst farmer, in 1867. Susan became a widow for the third time when Graves died in 1876.

By the time the 73 year-old Susan died in 1887, she had suffered through the deaths of three husbands and six children. She was survived by only one child, Rufus T. Dickinson.

Today, the bacteria that causes diphtheria has been identified. It lodges on the tonsils and can be treated with antitoxin and antibiotics. Moreover, the disease is preventable by routine immunization. But because cases of diphtheria are now relatively rare, some are neglecting to have children innoculated, and there is some fear that the disease can again become widespread.

A Jug of Cider
Was Their Joy

A Pelham couple making cider, a cheap but dangerous form of alcohol.

By the end of the 1800s, many people in the the Dickinsons' prosperous Connecticut River Valley were surprised to hear of the desperate lives of some families in their midst. In the fertile meadows along the river, families could achieve wealth. Poverty among whites, so they thought, was concentrated in the mountains of the Southern states. But in the isolated hilltowns, families sometimes scratched out lives as sad as the southern poor.

Just seven miles east of Amherst, south of Pelham's Mount Lincoln, elderly Reuben Allen and his second wife lived. By the end of the 19th century, she was feeble and her son from a previous marriage, William O'Brien, had run away. The son, it was said, met his wife in the Northampton jail, then the couple moved in with the elderly pair. After a binge in which the old man, the son and his wife reportedly drank 23 gallons of cider, the delirious William O'Brien disappeared out of the west window wearing only his night shirt.

For days, 75 people scoured the woods, and the ponds were dragged, but it would be three years before his body was found. The Reuben Allen family lived its own sour life surrounded by the ironic views of Mount Lincoln, Sugar Loaf, Mount Toby and the Holyoke Range. The old couple owned nothing, having deeded their property to the town of Pelham. In exchange the town supported them.

William G. O'Brien was 39 years-old when he died. He made a very precarious living as a woodchopper. Eventually everyone, including Northampton's Detective McKay and Amherst's Sheriff David Tillson, gave up the search for O'Brien and all but forgot him.

On September 20, 1904, Peter Pierre and his son made their unnerving discovery of O'Brien's skeleton. The Belchertown pair had been cutting wood on Pelham's Mount Lincoln for about three weeks when they came upon the remains in the undergrowth. The skeleton lay on its back with its arms beneath it and roots growing up between the bones. Without disturbing the remains, the Pierres hurried to Belchertown, marking trees along the way so that their steps could be retraced. In Belchertown they first notified Sheriff Barton, then Detective McKay, medical examiner Dr. C.F. Branch, and Sheriff Tillson were informed.

By means of an unusual fracture of the left leg, certain characteristics of the facial bones, and a bit of shirt, the remains were identified. The body had been found within three-quarters of a mile of O'Brien's parents' house.

While rumors of foul play had surrounded the mysterious disappearance of William O'Brien, it appeared most likely that he died of exposure after passing out from the effects of alcohol.

Fragments of other similar lives provide grim contrast to the towns in the valleys below. North of the Allen family, on the edge of Leverett, the combination of a white couple, black couple, and a jug of cider startled the community. Some "disgraceful actions" took place, which the newspapers refused to name. Soon after in the same area two men drinking cider argued over the cutting of grass on a back lot. One shot the other with a pistol. Not far off from that spot a young man, not seeing a future worth living, walked into the woods and shot himself. Other stories of the poor surface — a house mysteriously burns down, further south among the hills a family of children was rescued from starvation.

The more prosperous towns were stunned by such news of the poverty "within cannon shot of the colleges and churches of Amherst," but they could offer few solutions. One newspaper described the plight of the hill people like this: "They live in tumble-down houses. They are poor. In Winter they are snowed in. Taxes are high, frequently $25 on the thousand. They have few if any schools or church privileges. The roads are poor. Their nearest neighbor is distant and difficult to reach. The soil is sterile. They have no literature to read. Their pleasures are few. A jug of cider is their joy. The blackest shadow lies just beyond the electric light. In all these towns are many excellent people, as good as the world produces; these must not be confounded with the others. These do their best to ameliorate the condition of the others, but the burden has been too heavy; the task too difficult."

Careful Mothering
at the Pratt Health Cottage

When Amherst College built its Pratt Health Cottage in 1897, it was the culmination of decades of concern for student health care. Professor Edward Hitchcock, Jr., had begun delivering popular health lectures in 1830, in which he recommended eating simple foods in minimal quantities, during a time when students tended to overindulge in food and alcohol. Hitchcock also warned against wet feet, against a too early change of winter underwear, the dangers of night air, and "the mighty and dangerous influence of love."

Hitchcock's health lectures were in such demand that he published them as "Dyspepsy, Forestalled and Resisted." Moral issues color the section on exercise, particularly when the discussion turned to whether exercise should be allowed on the Sabbath. Hitchcock found no Biblical reason not to exercise on Sunday, but suggested taking it indoors, as not to offend neighbors. He particularly recommended walking about the room for an hour or two, or swinging a heavy chair over one's head a few hundred times.

Early on, Amherst College had a full time physician with an office in the gymnasium. By the 1890s, it became clear that a complete infirmary was needed where, in the words of Dr. Hitchcock, a student "may go at any time of day or night and find a welcome and receive careful mothering and, if needful, medical treatment."

In 1896, the Pratt brothers of New York, recent graduates of Amherst, donated funds for the Pratt Health Cottage. The infirmary was designed by William B. Tubby of New York, and built by the Allen Brothers of Amherst. This remarkable building contained nursing and operating rooms, a dining room, laundry, sitting room, a matron's room, offices, and bathrooms finished in oak, porcelain and ivory. Galleries, decks and skylights made the upper story bright and airy. This floor was reserved for contagious diseases and had no entrance from within the building, only a separate stairway in the rear.

The interior was plastered and finished with wainscoting and trim of quartered oak and Michigan ash. Perhaps most notable was the design for the shape of the rooms. In order to facilitate cleanliness, no corners existed anywhere. The plans called for curves to replace all angles where floors, walls and ceilings met.

The Health Cottage charged Amherst College students one dollar a day, and Massachusetts Agricultural College students $1.50. In 17 beds, the infirmary treated the usual sprains and colds, plus cases of typhoid, diphtheria, and scarlet fever. It was the influenza epidemic of 1918 that most clearly demonstrated the limits of the building, which had become crowded by 1907.

In 1938, a new infirmary was built, complete with private rooms, solaria, waiting rooms and a guest suite. In 1939, Pratt Health Cottage was sold to the Town of Amherst, which had the building taken down and the acreage turned into a community playground.

Amherst College students were mothered in Pratt's Health Cottage.

The Horror
of Yellow Fever

As summer came to a close in 1878, Amherst was shocked out of its pleasant torpor by news of a dreadful yellow fever epidemic in the South. That summer in Amherst had been one of blooming masses of geraniums and phlox. Families picnicked on Mount Toby in Sunderland, and The Pacific Lodge of Masons even brought the Hopkins Orchestra to the top of the mountain for their annual outing.

Oyster time had arrived, with fresh seafood available at Henry Paige's Fish and Oyster Market every Saturday. It was said that the oyster stews and fries at Wood's Restaurant were the best ever. Amherst schools were about to open on August 26th, and the newspaper reported that only one drunk had been arrested during the previous week.

But in the South an epidemic of yellow fever was killing hundreds daily. One doctor who went to the aid of New Orleans described what he found: "The city is a vast charnal-house, and the stench of the fever fills the air. The streets are empty, save when a death-cart passes. The stores are closed; neither medicines nor provisions are to be had; the poor sufferers, many of them starving, crawl into their tenements or lie down under fences of the parks to die unattended. Such ghastly scenes make the blood run cold."

Yellow fever was little understood in the 19th century. Sometimes known as "yellow jack" from the yellow flags flown over quarantined ships, the disease seemed to arrive from the tropics and would leave only when winter came. Treatment was primitive at best, and the outcome was often death within a week.

Doctors covered their patients with blankets, closed the windows, and gave them tea — all to produce a tremendous sweat. As days went by sometimes only barley water and chicken broth were given. If the fever broke the patient became ravenous, but it was insisted that allowing food or drink would cause sure death. Medical dictionaries suggested swallowing ice to stop vomiting, and to use opium only with great caution. Alcohol could be very beneficial, "champagne appearing to be the best form."

News of the epidemic was reported every week in the Amherst Record, and collections were taken up at the Post Office and in the churches. College Church raised $60 and First Church sent $97. The outpouring of aid from the North to the South was seen as proof that the union so recently won in the Civil War was firm.

It wasn't until 1900 that Walter Reed, a U.S. Army surgeon stationed in Cuba, proved that yellow fever was transmitted by the vector mosquito. Immediately, attempts were made to eradicate the mosquito from Havana and other tropical cities, with encouraging results. The vector mosquito is now gone from many countries and there is a vaccination, yet even today no complete cure exists.

When a Broken Leg
Was Almost as Bad as Bubonic Plague

On January 26, 1866, Charles D. Dickinson's leg was amputated. It was an agonizing ordeal for the 24 year-old and he wasn't expected to survive. When he finally died six months later, the actions of the Amherst and Northampton doctors were questioned. Did Dickinson die because of the primitive state of surgery, or was it malpractice?

Charles Dickinson lived in South Amherst with his father and mother, Oliver and Clarissa Billings Dickinson. While living on the family farm, Charles probably worked at Hayward's factory, which made children's carriages. On October 16, 1865, Charles fell while running and broke his right leg six inches above the ankle. It was a compound fracture, with the bone coming through the skin, the most difficult break to treat. Dickinson was carried to Charles Hayward's house and Dr. A.W. Barrows was called.

In the mid-19th century, medicine was just on the verge of major breakthroughs in pain-killing and in antiseptic surgery. Dickinson's accident happened too soon, however, for as one medical historian phrased it, "A compound fracture in 1866 was nearly as dangerous as the bubonic plague." Without an understanding of antiseptics, a compound fracture often lead to an amputation, which often led to death. In one study, between 1864 and 1866, 45 percent of amputees died.

There weren't many good choices for easing Charles Dickinson's pain. Morphine was perhaps the most popular. During the amputation itself he might have been given ether or chloroform. In later years nitrous oxide (laughing gas), and opium became available. It wasn't until a year after Dickinson's accident that Joseph Lister of the University of Glasgow published his major work, "On the Antiseptic Principle in the Practice of Surgery."

Lister realized that doctors should wash their hands and instruments before an operation, not just after. Moreover, infections could be prevented by treating wounds and incisions with carbolic acid. Doctors were reluctant to believe this.

Dickinson's ordeal became apparent when, after his death, the doctors had to quell rumors of malpractice by publishing their side of what happened. Amherst's Dr. A.W. Barrows was the first doctor to reach Dickinson. Without antiseptics, and without gloves or a mask, he set the leg, dressed it and left Dickinson for the night. Barrows was worried and notified Dr. R. Beldon. After leaving the leg in a fracture box for 28 days, Barrows reported, "the union was so perfect that he could raise the limb and move the ankle joint and the limb healed as kindly as any I ever attended or in fact ever saw, until about the 48th day I observed a slight swelling and redness near the point of fracture ... . At a subsequent visit I made an incision from which oozed a dark grumous blood, which indicated a malignant disease."

Dr. Beldon was called in and he advised calling Northampton's Dr. Daniel Thompson. In a few weeks the ankle became inflamed and Thompson and Beldon pronounced the limb hopeless.

Another exam was done by Doctors Beldon, Taylor, Daniels and Barrows. All agreed amputation was necessary, only to disagree on whether the cut should be below or above the knee. On January 26, Dr. Daniel Thompson amputated Dickinson's leg, with four other physicians attending. Barrows, who had originally set the bones, reported in his defense that all the doctors agreed the fracture had set beautifully.

Dr. Barrows was cleared of wrongdoing, but unfortunately on August 9, 1866, the Amherst Record reported that Charles Dickinson had died because his "system was so prostrated ... that he could not rally."

The state of medicine and general health care in the 19th century seems primitive and chaotic. It's easy to ignore the reality of the terrible diseases and death rates of those days, and to focus on sleighrides and cozy fires. Looking bluntly at the horror of it, one comes away with great respect for the stoicism of the ordinary person, and, at the same time, great relief at having been born in the 20th century.

Chapter Sixteen

THE FINAL FRACTURING OF THE DICKINSON CIRCLE

The Emily Dickinson House, Amherst, Massachusetts

*A Shade upon the mind there passes
As when on Noon
A Cloud the mighty Sun encloses
Remembering*

*That some there be too numb to notice
Oh God
Why give if Thou must take away
The Loved?*
#882

The Death of Edward Dickinson: "And where was Aunt Emily"

Emily's father, Edward Dickinson, was struck with "a fit of apoplexy" on June 16, 1874.

Edward Dickinson, the much discussed, much misunderstood father of Emily, was "taken with a fit of apoplexy" on June 16, 1874, while serving in the State Legislature in Boston. At dinner time, news reached Amherst that he was ill. As Austin harnassed the horses to go to Boston, word arrived that Edward Dickinson was dead.

The funeral was held at the Dickinson Homestead on Friday afternoon, the 19th, and, like the funeral held later in 1886 for Emily, it was brief and simple. The rooms of the Homestead were filled with people. Many others had to sit outdoors, listening through open windows and sitting on benches brought from the church. The service consisted of singing, the reading of Scripture, and prayers by Rev. J.L. Jenkins of First Church. The family requested that no eulogy be given, in accordance with Edward's own wishes.

The only flowers allowed were white daisies in the form of a simple wreath on the coffin. Again as with Emily's later funeral, no hearse was hired, and instead the coffin was carried to West Cemetery by the Dickinsons' neighbors — 18 of them. Among them were several dignitaries of Amherst College, where Edward had been treasurer from 1835 to 1873, and also the local photographer John L. Lovell.

At the grave, a brief passage from the Bible was read, and the Lord's Prayer recited. All Amherst businesses were closed during the funeral. As the Amherst Record reported, the village was shocked by the death, word of which was received with "a profound feeling of sorrow" for "our distinguished townsman ... our loss and bereavement is an almost irreparable one."

Born in 1803, Dickinson was a lawyer, a representative to the General Court of Massachusetts (1838-39 and 1873-74), and a state senator (1842 and 1843). He was a member of the State Council under Governor Briggs, and he represented the Tenth Massachusetts District in the U.S. Congress from 1852 to 1855. It was during the latter stint that Emily and her sister Lavinia travelled to Washington with their father and toured the city monuments.

The outpouring for this man of "sterling worth and unimpeachable integrity" was overwhelming, some claiming that the success of Amherst College was largely due to his efforts. One modern critic, however, has examined Edward's personal finances and asserts he "played fast and loose" with his brother-in-law's estate for his own gain.

Dickinson's great passion had been the railroad, particularly the Amherst and Belchertown Railroad, and at the end of his life, the Hoosac Tunnel, which he hoped would allow Amherst access to upstate New York. The Amherst Record went so far as to claim that "the cause of his death was undoubtedly owing to overexertion in speaking in the House (on the morning of his death) on the Hoosac Tunnel bill."

Edward's outwardly stern personality has often been cited for the effect it might have had on Emily's psyche. Among the testimonials after his death, however, Ithamar Conkey stated that it wasn't true that Dickinson was "austere, aristocratical, perhaps coldhearted." Behind his public, dignified presence "lay a kind warm heart."

Edward Dickinson was a rare man whose life has since been overshadowed by his brilliant daughter. About the funeral, his granddaughter Martha wrote, "The world seemed coming to an end. And where was Aunt Emily? She stayed upstairs in her own room with the door open just a crack, where she could hear without being seen."

Emily's Captain Cuttle:
"Like the death of College Tower"

Emily Dickinson's private drama was peopled by several minor players who, for the semi-recluse, sometimes became larger than life. One of the great local characters of 19th century Amherst was Horace Church, gardener for Emily Dickinson's family, groundskeeper of Amherst College, and sexton of the First Congregational Church. While Church didn't actually have a hook, in the poet's eyes he bore a striking resemblance to someone who did.

Dickinson called Horace Church the "Captain Cuttle" of Amherst. She had long been familiar with Cuttle, an eccentric Charles Dickens character, a man with a big heart and a hook in place of his right hand.

Horace Church is mentioned in the Dickinson family papers as early as 1854. He was born in 1825 and seems to have done some farming before moving into the Dickinsons' barn. Emily found humor in this man who was a constant presence around Amherst, at the Dickinson home, at the church on Main Street, and at the College. In an 1870 letter to her cousin Louise Norcross, Emily mentioned Church, who could often be found pruning or grafting fruit trees: "Mr. Church is not in the tree, because the rooks wont let him, but I ate a pear as pink as a plum that he made last spring, when he was ogling you. Mother has on the petticoat you so gallantly gathered while he sighed and grafted."

Emily's father, who had to deal with Horace in all three places of the man's employment, found him less than amusing. A letter to his son Austin in 1874 reflects some friction between the men: "I hope that everything will go right, at home. I hope, too, that you will ask Horace to bring his bill against you, that we may judge better what I ought to pay him. I should like to finish up with him, as soon as I can."

Captain Cuttle appears in Dickens' *Dombey and Son* as a retired skipper. Cuttle was a great friend of Solomon Gills, a ship's instrument maker, and his description of Gills is given with characteristic rhetoric: "'... he's chockfull of science,' he observed, waving his hook towards the stock-in-trade. 'Look'ye here! Here's a collection of 'em. Earth, air, or water. It's all one. Only say where you'll have it. Up in a balloon? There you are. Down in a bell? There you are. D'ye want to put the North Star in a pair of scales and weigh it? He'll do it for you.'"

Captain Cuttle's favorite saying was, "May we never want a friend, or a bottle to give him!"

After Horace Church died in 1881, Emily Dickinson wrote of him in a letter to Elizabeth Holland: "Did you know that Father's 'Horace' died — the 'Cap'n Cuttle' of Amherst? He had lived with us always, though was not congenial — so his loss is a pang to Tradition, rather than Affection — I am sure you remember him — He is the one who spoke patronizingly of the Years, of Trees he sowed in '26,' or Frosts he met in '20,' and was so legendary that it seems like the death of the College Tower, our first Antiquity — I remember he was at one time disinclined to gather the Winter Vegetables till they had frozen, and when Father demurred, he replied 'Squire, ef the Frost is the Lord's Will, I dont popose to stan in the way of it' — I hope a nearer inspection of that 'Will' has left him with as ardent a bias in its favor —"

"The Mother That Could Not Walk, Has Flown"

The poet's mother, Emily Norcross Dickinson, had a unique place in the family. Her death in 1882 was a mixed blessing.

When the chill of November arrived in 1882, Emily Dickinson's mother caught a violent cold and never recovered. Unlike the death of the poet's father, Edward, in 1874, and her brother Austin's death in 1895, Amherst businesses did not close.

No lengthy obituaries appeared, no proclamations were made. After years of illness, Mrs. Dickinson passed on without interrupting the flow of life around her. Yet, hardly more beautiful prose has been written about a mother's death in Victorian times.

In the Dickinson family legend, Emily Norcross Dickinson appears as a ghostly image. She raised three children with little help from their father, and received high praise from many, including Joseph Lyman who, as a boy, was often at the house: "Vinnie's mother was a rare and delicate cook in such matters as crullers and custards and she taught the girls all those housewifely accomplishments ... . Em is an excellent housekeeper — Vinnie is sometimes afraid of soiling her little fat hands but can do very well when she chooses."

Mrs. Dickinson was also known for her gardening skills, and would surprise neighbors with fresh figs she learned to grow in this cold climate. Unfortunately, the early onset of debilitating illnesses led to a reversal of roles — the children eventually mothered the mother. She suffered from depression and the almost cruel treatments for it. In 1843, one visitor wrote of her, "She was as usual full of plaintive talk."

While raising three remarkable children, Mrs. Dickinson moved the household three times, and after the last move, suffered a breakdown in 1856. By May of 1858 she hadn't recovered and Emily wrote, "Mother is much as usual — I know not what to hope of her." After her husband Edward's death in 1874, her physical and mental health declined rapidly. In 1875, she became paralyzed and completely reliant on her daughters.

Emily's relationship with her mother was complex, and she admitted that affection came only as the end neared: "We were never intimate Mother and Children while she was our Mother — but Mines in the same Ground meet by tunneling and when she became our Child, the Affection came — When we were children and she journeyed, she always brought us something. Now would she bring us but herself, what an only Gift — Memory is a strange Bell — Jubilee, and Knell."

After the death on November 14, 1882, Emily wrote movingly of her mother: "She seemed entirely better the last Day of her Life and took Lemonade — Beef Tea and Custard with a pretty ravenousness that delighted us... After a restless Night, complaining of great weariness, she was lifted earlier than usual from her Bed to her Chair, when a few quick breaths and a 'Dont leave me, Vinnie' and her sweet being closed."

Her obituary read, simply, "In this town, Nov. 14, Mrs. Emily Norcross Dickinson, widow of the late Hon. Edward Dickinson, aged 78 years." A stark letter by a neighbor, Mrs. Jameson, said,

"Old lady Dickinson is dead — I went right over. She died Tues A M at 8 o'clock in her chair. She has been suffering a good deal this fall from rheumatism and the poor body has at last found rest."

One sure sign that life would go on in the Dickinson house, was a letter Emily wrote to Otis Lord, four days after her mother's death: "The celestial Vacation of writing you after an interminable Term of four Days, I can scarcely express ... . Emily 'Jumbo' (Lord's nickname for her)! Sweetest name, but I know a sweeter — Emily Jumbo Lord. Have I your approval?"

Emily's most eloquent words about her mother were written at about the same time, to her close friend, Elizabeth Holland: "The dear Mother that could not walk, has *flown* — It never occurred to us that though she had not Limbs, she had *Wings* — and she soared from us unexpectedly as a summoned Bird ... . That the one we have cherished so softly so long, should be in that great Eternity without our simple counsels, seems frightened and foreign, but we hope that our Sparrow has ceased to fall, though at first we believe nothing —"

The Loss of Gib:
"The dyings have been too deep for me"

On October 17, 1883, a remarkable obituary appeared in the Amherst Record titled "Death of a Promising Boy." Thomas Gilbert Dickinson died of typhoid fever at the age of eight, shocking a town that had been captivated by his brightness and warmth. He was remembered for stopping adults on the street for serious talk, or for having pictures of friends turned to the wall when they were away and missed.

The significance of Gilbert's death went beyond the grief of the town, for at his bedside in his illness was his aunt, Emily Dickinson. The death was a turning point in the Dickinson family, marking irrevocable changes in his aunt Emily and in Austin, his father.

Emily Dickinson had been torn by death many times throughout her life — close friends, her mother and father. Her closeness to her nephew Gilbert and, in fact, her affinity for children in general, made the boy's death especially devastating. She wrote, "The Dyings have been too deep for me, and before I could raise my Heart from one, another has come —." It had been 15 years since Emily had set foot in her brother's house. After watching Gilbert die, Emily became ill for weeks with a "Nervous prostration." She never fully recovered her health and died a year and a half later.

For Austin Dickinson, Emily's brother, the death was unbearable. His other sister, Lavinia, wrote to friends that "Of course you knew little Gilbert has disappeared & Emily & I have had hard work to keep Austin from following him —." Like Emily, Austin too was changed by the death, but in a surprising way. Mabel Loomis Todd, with whom Austin had been having a controversial affair, later quoted Austin as saying she kept him alive through "the dreadful period of Gilbert's sickness and death. He could not bear the atmosphere of his own house ... . He recovered from the blow enough to wish to live for me ... ." At that point the rift in the Dickinson family deepened radically.

Shortly afterwards, on December 13, 1883, Austin's affair with Todd was consummated in the dining room of the Dickinson Homestead (acccording to Mabel's diaries). The ramifications were extensive, later affecting the course of the publication of Emily Dickinson's poems.

Emily's description of Gilbert's last moments is significant, reflecting the family's intense feelings, and Emily's defiant brilliance:

"'Open the Door, open the Door, they are waiting for me,' was Gilbert's sweet command in delirium. Who were waiting for him,

The death of Emily's eight year old nephew, Gilbert Dickinson, in 1883, had a profound effect on the Dickinson family. Gilbert's death brought his mother, Susan Dickinson, and Emily together for the first time in 15 years.

all we possess we would give to know — Anguish at last opened it, and he ran to the little Grave at his Grandparents' feet — All this and more, though *is* there more? More than Love and Death? Then tell me its name!"

Waltzing With
the Dickinsons' Cow

Dennis Scanlon was a complex man. As a workman for the Dickinsons, he did everything from gardening to helping carry Emily Dickinson's casket. Unfortunately, Scanlon drank too much, but his sorrow may have driven him to it. Considered by some to be a fine father, Springfield officials refused to return his runaway son Jeremiah. Scanlon's long ignored obituary — written by Emily's sister-in-law Susan — reflects the unusual relationship between a Victorian family and one of its servants.

Timothy and Catherine Scannell (the family name appears with no fewer than five spellings) came from Ireland in the 1840s. Their son Dennis worked for the Dickinsons in the 1870s, as did Tim (another son?), who became the Dickinson's stableman in 1868.

In Dickinson family letters we glimpse the family's affection for and distance from the people who worked for them. In a letter from Emily to her nephew Ned she wrote of Dennis's drinking, not with concern for his health, but with amusement: "Dennis was happy yesterday, and it made him graceful — I saw him waltzing with the Cow — and suspected his status, but he afterward started for your House in a frame that was unmistakable — You told me he had'nt tasted Liquor since his Wife's decease — then she must have been living at six o'clock last Evening—"

Scanlon's wife died in 1876, leaving him to raise six children. In December of 1880, the local newspapers reported one of Scanlon's sons as missing: "Jerry Scanlan, a lad of 14 summers, who has suddenly disappeared from home once or twice and then returned several days after, wandered away a few days ago and his father, Dennis, was summoned to Springfield yesterday." The boy's feet were frostbitten and his father was not allowed to take him home. In all probability Jeremiah was cared for by the county for a time.

In a letter to Mrs. J.G. Holland, Emily wrote, "A Little Boy ran away from Amherst a few Days ago, and when asked where he was going, replied, 'Vermont or Asia.' Many of us go farther. My pathetic Crusoe—"

Dennis Scanlon was among the workmen who, at Emily's request, carried the poet's casket through the fields to her grave in 1886. In April of 1894, Scanlon died. Susan Dickinson, wife of Emily's brother Austin, wrote this touching portrait of Scanlon for the Amherst Record: "I have no fulsome praise for a dead man because he is dead. I will not speak of a tender personal regret for an old friend. I would like to pay public tribute of admiration to his unusual talent as a skilled laborer. Coming to Amherst when a young man, untrained in any wise use of tools, left by the death of his wife, with six young children from a baby up, he not only fought his hourly battle with care, pinching poverty, incessant toil, but raised his little brood in such a way that all are capable, wholesome and good as men and women and left a neat little home and money in the savings bank as proof of an industrious life.

"It is of interest to know and remember that old Dennis somehow had his ideals and always worked toward them whether his employer was near or afar. His work was perfectly done and his hours never cut short. No rough streaks on a lawn of his mowing, not a weed left in the garden borders he weeded, and as for his lines and curves one could only find them equalled in geometric pages, although compass and quadrant were unknown to him."

The Strange Hair
of Austin Dickinson

Austin Dickinson, the poet's brother and close friend, died in 1895.

Rumors get started in very strange ways, and one of the oddest of Dickinson rumors was not about Emily, but about her brother, Austin. Nineteen ninety-five marked the 100th anniversary of the death of Emily's brother Austin. When this "most influential citizen of Amherst" died, thousands of words were printed praising his achievements. Years later, however, one bit of information about Austin's remarkable appearance became a problem. Could it be true that Austin, a century before florescent hair color became popular, wore a green wig?

Hardly anyone in Emily Dickinson's life was as close to the poet as Austin. Their letters to each other are filled with great warmth and humor. In later years, Emily missed the intimacy they had when young and wrote to Austin, "I wish we were children now. I wish we were always children, how to grow up I dont know." Austin's public side attracted a different kind of language. After his death on August 16, 1895, every local paper, and several businesses and institutions, wrote editorials or passed resolutions:

"Rarely is a community called upon to mourn the death of a man who has been so prominent in its affairs, so thoroughly representative of what is best in its citizenship, so honored in public and beloved in private life ... ."

"The announcement of the death of the beloved and honored Treasurer of Amherst College was both a surprise and a sorrow to every friend of Amherst."

"While his associates need no reminder of his constant activities in the Parish, future parishioners need but to learn that the beauty and condition of the First Church property, its handsome building and exceptional grounds are evidence of his taste, skill, and labor."

"He was ever kind to the poor and the suffering, and was the friend of any man of whatever station whom he knew to be in need of sympathy."

More than 30 years later, his daughter Martha remembered him "in a certain light tan-colored driving-coat and a wide-brimmed felt hat of the same shade, such as Southern gentlemen used to wear, turned up smartly in front. ... we liked the mood that went with his orangewood cane when he stepped jauntily over to church on Sunday morning, while other people dragged along with intentionally depressing gait."

She said nothing of his unruly hair hidden under that hat. Her aunt Emily referred to it several times and actually urged him to cut it off: "I hope the hair is off — you must tell me about it as soon as you write again." Then a few days later, on June 13, 1853, she wrote, "You dont tell us about your hair — wont you next time, Austin, for your peace is our's." Even sister Vinnie couldn't help but comment on Austin's problem: "Be cheerful & happy & dont mind the hair. Have it done now & then you'll feel relieved."

Then in July, Vinnie was elated by the news that Austin had, apparently, shaved his head and acquired a wig: "I'm rejoiced that your hair is gone. Dont ever worry about it."

But long after Austin's death, the color of that wig was put in doubt by the president of Amherst College. In describing Austin's work as treasurer of college, President Stanley King wrote "... he permitted himself more personal eccentricities than is usual with a college treasurer, from the yellow hunting coat he wore as a young man, to the green wig he affected in his later years."

This rather bizarre biographical point was finally settled in 1955. Unlike King, Millicent Todd Bingham actually knew Austin when she was a child. She wrote, "In recent years there has been a rumor that Austin Dickinson's wig was green. As to that, I can only say that the person who started such a rumor must have been color blind. With Mr. Dickinson's appearance up to his last illness in August, 1895, I was intimately familiar ... . For some reason or other the ladies of the family seem to have been worried about Austin's hair. Of a reddish color, it was thick and unruly; he had difficulty making it stay in place ... . I do remember wondering why his hair was so long. And I vividly recall the coppery glint of it and the shining highlights. I remember other peculiarities of his countenance, too, such as the exact location of two strange warts which fascinated me. But in spite of daily opportunity, I never saw him wear anything at all resembling a green, or greenish wig."

"Sisters are brittle things"

Lavinia Dickinson, with one of her many cats. Trapped in a legal tangle, her lawsuit against Mabel Loomis Todd resulted in a fracture that would never heal.

Through every tragic death Emily suffered, she turned to her sister, Lavinia. After the deaths of both parents, only Emily and Lavinia were left living in the Homestead that was suddenly too large. Lavinia, the tough, practical sister who could confront the world Emily couldn't, became, as she said, the man of the household.

Lavinia lived to attend, not only the funerals of both parents, but also those of her young nephews Gib and Ned, and her sister and brother. Her last years in the Homestead, as the last survivor of the Dickinson nucleus of five, were focused on two critical events. Vinnie triumphantly managed Emily's poetry into print, and she precipitated a bitter lawsuit that forever split the Dickinson circle.

It was, of course, Lavinia who found Emily's poems, hundreds of them, within the poet's bureau after her death. Emily had never kept secret the fact that she wrote poetry, yet the sheer volume of poems sewn neatly into fascicles, came as an utter surprise to Vinnie. Recognizing the imperative of opening that desk to the world, she also realized she wasn't up to the task.

Lavinia first approached sister-in-law Sue about preparing the manuscripts for publication. Though Sue was intimately familiar with the poetry, and an extremely perceptive reader of it, she was unable to take on the daunting responsibility. Two years went by before Vinnie retrieved the manuscripts from Sue. She then risked her relationship with her by asking Mabel Loomis Todd —lecturer, writer, *and* the lover of Sue's husband, Austin Dickinson — to take on the project.

Thomas Wentworth Higginson, editor and correspondent of Emily, was also approached, but both he and Todd were reluctant. Lavinia gained the gratitude of future generations by her dogged insistance that Todd and Higginson take the poetry seriously. With her urging, Todd slowly began transcribing and editing the poems. With the advice of Higginson, the first book of Emily's poems began to take shape. Along the way, both Todd and Higginson were overtaken by the power of Dickinson's genius, and what Lavinia set in motion took on a fierce momentum.

Lavinia was the least complex of the Dickinson siblings. Vivacious when young, a witty conversationalist, she, like her sister, chose not to marry. Lacking Emily's genius for language, and the professional goals of Amherst women like Mabel Todd or Helen Hunt Jackson, her world became the Dickinson circle itself. Her parents gone, her brother's marriage destroyed, and those closest to her dying one-by-one, it was her occupation to hold what was left of the Homestead together.

Austin's death in 1895 left Lavinia with the most difficult

dilemma of her life. Austin had promised Mabel Loomis Todd that he would leave his share of Edward Dickinson's estate to her. However, he couldn't write his mistress into his will without causing great scandal. Instead, he left his father's meadow, stocks, and bonds to Lavinia, with the understanding that she would transfer all of it to Mabel. This would make Lavinia an overt and active participant in his relationship with Mabel.

Awkward in the extreme, she would have to either ignore her brother's last wish, or make a complete break with his wife, Susan, by fulfilling it. Lavinia, to her credit, struggled to find a compromise. She chose to partially fulfill Austin's wishes by deeding a 53-foot-wide strip of the Dickinson meadow to Mabel Todd. This, presumably, would satisfy Mabel, since it was a part of the meadow that abutted, and thus extended, her own property. Lavinia had the deed secretly drawn up, and she avoided registering it as long as possible, hoping to keep Susan in the dark.

When the deed was recorded, on April 1, 1896, it became public. Susan and others in Amherst were outraged to learn that Austin Dickinson's lover was to have a share of the Dickinson estate. Then Lavinia made a critical mistake: She panicked and claimed she *hadn't* signed the deed. In a lawsuit that was very public and very ugly, Lavinia accused Mabel of obtaining her signature by fraud.

In April of 1898, the verdict was read. Judge Hopkins found in favor of Lavinia and Sue; Mabel was not to receive the land. But the Dickinson circle suffered an ugly fracture, from which it has never recovered.

One day after the verdict, Ned, Susan and Austin's son, suffered an attack of angina. He died two and a half weeks later. Within a year and a half, Vinnie died.

Living out her last months in the Homestead, Vinnie became a local legend. She tolerated the long series of visitors, the friends, former servants, and admirers of Emily. But her passion was her garden, and it was there that she was entirely herself. When approached there, she would offer a "Glad to see you! Glad to see you!" After one such interruption, she confessed to her niece, Martha, "Mattie, I had on my most bog-mire clothes — my worst hat, the ends of my shawl tied around my waist Gypsy-fashion, — only my white gauntlets were reputable; but I offered him a seat in James' wheel barrow, hoping he would prefer it to the parlor!"

On the last day of March in 1899, she took to her bed, a tiny figure in a huge mahogany four-poster, with a failing heart. Some time after mid-summer, she decided to defy doctor's orders and leave the bed for one more walk through the rooms of the Homestead. She crept downstairs in the moonlight and explored

Susan Gilbert Dickinson. Lavinia risked her relationship with Susan by asking Mabel Loomis Todd to edit Emily's poems.

room after room. Vinnie saw her sleeping cats in the kitchen, her own chair drawn up to the east window in the dining room, her books on the library table, and the cinnamon roses in the parlor.

Lavinia died at the end of August, and the last member of the Dickinson household was carried out to West Cemetery to be buried beside her sister, Emily. Mabel Todd's acid comment was, "I have no feeling about it, one way or the other. Only I am glad it is she and not I who has to face God with perjury to report." In a final blow to the Dickinson legacy, Mabel closed the lid on the chest of Dickinson manuscripts in her possession, and the publication of Emily's poems was stalled for many years.

Edwin Marsh and the
Funeral of Emily Dickinson

When Edwin Dwight Marsh died in December, 1913, his passing, like Emily's father's, was front page news. He was described as "warm-hearted" and the "best-liked man" in Amherst. A gregarious and sensitive man, he was well suited to his double life as a furniture dealer, and as Amherst's most prominent undertaker. Marsh's most famous funeral was that of Emily Dickinson.

The "E.D. Marsh Furniture and Carpet Rooms" faced the Amherst Common on Main Street, not far from the Dickinson Homestead. The business was the largest of its kind in western Massachusetts, outside of Springfield.

Marsh's ads read, "Headquarters for furniture of all kinds. Parlor suits, easy chairs, lounges, chamber sets, sideboards, dining

This bird's-eye-view from the year Emily died shows the Dickinson Home on Main St., the barn, and the cemetery where Emily was buried.

tables and chairs. Spring beds, mattresses, pillows, window shades, draperies. Brussels tapestry and ingrain carpets, mattings, rugs, oil cloths, etc., at lowest prices." One could purchase a solid mahogany Martha Washington sewing table for $15, or a brass bed for $11.75.

Edwin Marsh's outgoing nature led to multiple involvements in the community. He was president of the Street Sprinkling Association in 1891 (dirt roads were sprinkled to keep dust down in summer), he was one of the first directors of the Amherst Board of Trade, president of the nascent Amherst Gas Company, one of the original directors of Wildwood Cemetery in 1887, and the cemetery's treasurer and superintendent for 20 years. The latter activity takes on added significance when one notices the discreet mention in Marsh's ads that he was the town's "Funeral Director and Furnisher."

In searching for the identity of the man who buried Emily Dickinson, it makes sense to look among the local furniture makers. They sometimes made the leap from hammering together coffins in the back room, to accompanying them to the cemetery, and making arrangements for flowers and services.

Emily's niece, Martha, recalled the description of the funeral given by Marsh's assistant, Ellery Strickland. He was surprised to find the poet so young looking, "her reddish, bronze hair without a silver thread." In a letter to Martha, he wrote, "How well I remember her passing to join the others, your mother and Mrs. Powell planning the robe... . Then the cortege across the lawn, through the hedge, across the fields, a special bier borne by faithful workmen of her father's grounds, Dennis Scanlon, Pat Ward, Steven Sullivan, Dennis Cashman, Dan Moynihan, Tom Kelly."

The old Marsh account books contain the stark, business-like description of the funeral of one of the world's great poets. To this day, the date of Dickinson's funeral is marked by a procession and poetry readings at the grave site.

Marsh's account states the cause of Emily's death as Bright's disease, an illness of the kidneys. Dr. Orvis Bigelow is listed as the certifying physician, and the date of Emily's burial May 19, 1886. Perhaps the most significant fact revealed is that Emily's casket measured 5'6", a significant figure for those eager for any clue to her appearance. According to Robert Studley, regional manager of the Boston funeral corporation, Doane, Beal & Ames, Inc., the poet's height would therefore be 5'2" or 5'3".

Dickinson is legendary for dressing only in white in the latter part of her life. To this she was true even at the end, for her casket was white, it was furnished with white flannel, and had white textile handles. Though simple, the cost was an expensive $85, at a time when the average casket was bought for between $12 and $35.

Before burial, Emily's casket was placed in a $5 pine box. The cost of a flannel wrap with ribbons was $9.25, and the making of the bier on which the casket was carried cost $2.50. No carriages were hired, no chairs rented or flowers bought. Yet the total cost of Emily Dickinson's funeral was $121.75, one of the most expensive that spring.

In Amherst in the late 1800s, a pauper could be buried for $12.50 or, as in the case of Samuel Boltwood in November of 1886, funeral costs could mount to $423. Boltwood's casket had satin pillows, purple plush, and was fully lined in satin. There were seven bouquets of flowers, and no fewer than 13 rented carriages. The average cost of most Amherst funerals, however, was between $25 and $80.

Contemporary accounts by mourners include descriptions of the funeral by Mabel Loomis Todd, who wrote of the "dainty, white casket ... lifted by six Irish workmen ... . They carried her through the fields, full of buttercups, while the friends ... followed on irregularly through the ferny footpaths to the little cemetery."

Thomas Wentworth Higginson wrote that "E.D.'s face (was) a wondrous restoration of youth — she is (55) and looked 30, not a gray hair or wrinkle, and perfect peace on the beautiful brow. There was a little bunch of violets at the neck ... the sister Vinnie put in two heliotropes by her hand 'to take to Judge Lord.' I read a poem by Emily Bronte. How large a portion of the people who have interested me have passed away."

The Dickinson family grave site in West Cemetery.

Behind Me — dips Eternity —
Before Me — Immortality —
Myself — the Term between —
Death but the Drift of Eastern Gray,
Dissolving into Dawn away,
Before the West begin —

'Tis Kingdoms — afterward — they say —
In perfect — pauseless Monarchy —
Whose Prince — is Son of None —
Himself — His Dateless Dynasty —
Himself — Himself diversify —
In Duplicate divine —

'Tis Miracle before Me — then —
'Tis Miracle behind — between —
A Crescent in the Sea —
With Midnight to the North of Her —
And Midnight to the South of Her —
And Maelstrom — in the Sky —

Emily Dickinson

Poem #721

AFTERWARD

Dickinson friend and editor, Thomas Wentworth Higginson,
shown with his daughter Margaret, the year before Emily died.

A Computer Critique
of Emily Dickinson

This book opened with obtuse remarks on Dickinson's poetry by critics of her day. While writing the chapters that followed, I accidently exposed the poetry to one of today's most stringent critics — my personal computer. It is equipped with Grammatik, a grammar-checking program which calls itself "a complete electronic writing analyst."

This program has the remarkable ability to interrupt a sentence like, "There were three charcoal kilns on Coke Kiln Road" to tell me that "Coke" is a copyrighted trademark, and I should, in its words, "Try cola or soft drink." My computer continued to find plenty to carp about in my writing, then it began to pick on Emily's.

I had quoted this line from one of Emily's letters: "I found abundance of candy in my stocking, which I do not think had the anticipated effect upon my disposition, in case it was to sweeten it ... ."

Grammatik winced at the use of "in case." It flashed "Hackneyed, Cliche, or Trite" on the screen. Then Grammatik arrogantly told Emily to "Avoid cliches, they distract the reader and weaken your message. Cliches are a symptom of lazy writing."

After 30 years of studying the poetry, the great critic Thomas Wentworth Higginson was still bewildered by Emily's writing. Grammatik got right to the point in a microsecond. She was lazy.

If Grammatik could so handily polish Emily's prose, what improvements could it make in her poetry? Grammatik quietly read Emily's beautiful poem about a hummingbird:

> *A Route of Evanescence*
> *With a revolving Wheel —*
> *A Resonance of Emerald —*
> *A Rush of Cochineal —*
>
> *And every Blossom on the Bush*
> *Adjusts its tumbled Head —*
> *The mail from Tunis, probably,*
> *An easy Morning's Ride —*

This is a poem in deep grammatical trouble. Grammatik discovered that the poem contained no verb whatsoever. It concluded, "This may be an incomplete sentence." Grammatik also thought this one-sentence poem was a bit too long. It advised Emily that "Long sentences can be difficult to understand. Consider revising so that no more than one complete thought is expressed in each sentence." As an added insult, it commented that one would need 17 years of education to comprehend the poem as it was.

If only Mabel Loomis Todd had had Grammatik in the 1890s when she and Higginson edited Emily's poems ... . We could have avoided decades of arguing about who Emily's "Master" was. Or why she felt a funeral in her brain.

I was tempted to subject "Emily E. Dickinson" to the scrutiny of Grammatik for comment. But I was afraid it would say "Obtuse, difficult poet. Try Ogden Nash."

Index

Photographs indexed in bold type.

About The Author

Daniel Lombardo is the Curator of Special Collections at the Jones Library in Amherst, Massachusetts, where he is responsible for historical  and literary collections, including those of Emily Dickinson and Robert Frost. He writes a history column for the Amherst Bulletin, and a column reviewing art books for Library Journal. Lombardo is the author of TALES OF AMHERST: A LOOK BACK (Jones Library, Inc., Amherst, MA, 1986), A DIRECTORY OF CRAFTSMEN IN THE CONNECTICUT VALLEY OF MASSACHUSETTS BEFORE 1850 (Opus Publishing, 1987), and IMAGES OF AMERICA: AMHERST AND HADLEY (Arcadia Publishing, Dover, NH, 1997).